HIStory

From Event to Event The Bible is One Story—

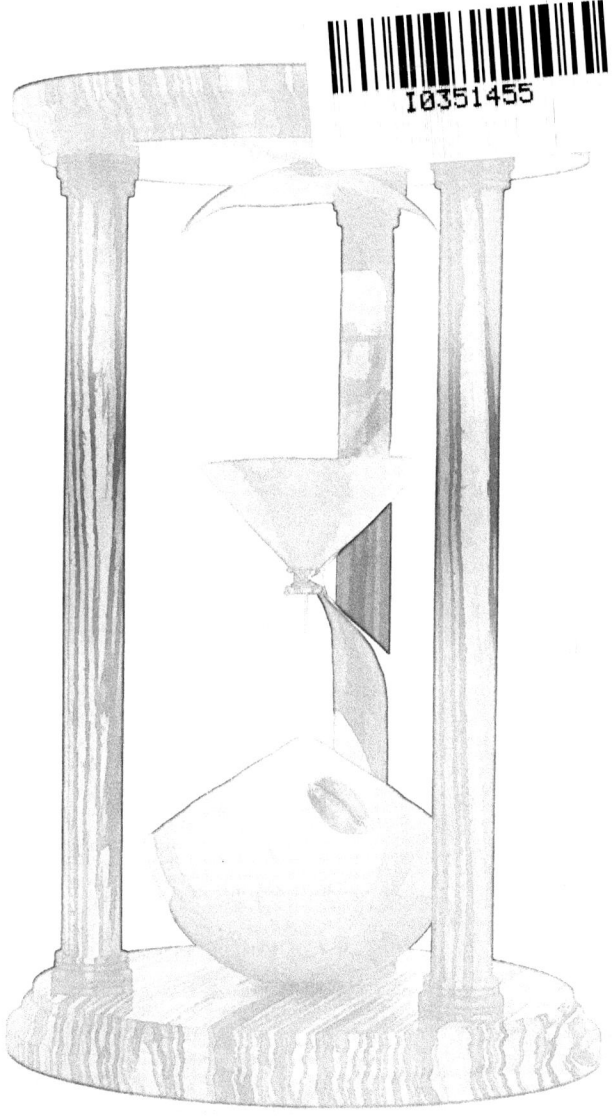

Cover Art Concept:

When Adam sinned, he died spiritually and all of his descendants inherited the result of his sin. So God promised to send a SEED into the world to bring Spiritual Life. From that time forward, the world waited for God's Promised SEED.

Jesus said that "unless a grain of wheat falls into the earth and dies, it remains alone; but if it dies, it bears much fruit." John 12:24
Jesus was speaking of Himself.

The world did not recognize Jesus as the Promised SEED from God. They killed and buried Him, but God brought His SEED back to life to produce a harvest—a harvest of Glory for Himself. That harvest is Spiritual Life—His very Own Life in those who believe in His Promised SEED— His very Own Son.

HIStory

From Event to Event
The Bible is One Story—HIStory

Copyright © 2000, 2003, 2013 Sharon Jensen

All rights reserved.
No part of this publication may be reproduced in any form
without written permission from Sharon Jensen.
WORD Center Ministries, 22250 Pioneer Trail, Council Bluffs, IA 51503
info@WORDCenterMinistries.org

Scripture taken from the New American Standard Bible®
Copyright © 1960, 1962, 1968, 1971, 1972, 1973, 1975, 1977, 1995
by the Lockman Foundation. Used by permission.

WORDCenterMinistries.org

HIStory

From Event to Event
The Bible is One Story—

Thank you for deciding to study **HIStory**. It is my desire, as author, that you would come to know God and His ways more intimately through studying His written Word. I pray that you would take the time to search for Him through diligent study. He promises to reward those who do so… and the reward is Himself!

The Bible is not a hundred (or a thousand!) different stories, all saying different things that have been compiled into one book. It is one book, with one message. The Bible does not have a hundred (or a thousand) *different* things to say. It does, however, say the *same* things over and over a hundred (or a thousand) different ways!

My goal is to help you to see the main things in the Bible all at once. I want to help you see God's message to you "put on the table all at once." What are the main things? Quite simply, they are the plain things! What are the plain things? Quite simply, they are the main things! **HIStory** materials will help you to understand the main things! Once you have the main things mastered, you will find that we have materials to help you see the "not so plain" things. (You can find them at *WORDCenterMinistries.org*.) But always, the "not so plain" things will be explained by the main things!!! Never the other way around.

Let me explain the idea to you by using an illustration. Let's say you wanted to purchase sixty-six acres on which to build a home. (The Bible is composed of sixty-six books.)

You go to the property and drive up the lane. After you park your car, the real estate agent tells you to walk around and see everything. Great! You can't wait! The hilly land is sprawled out before you. There are timbered woods ahead in several different directions. You cannot see all the land at once—just a small portion of it at a time. You randomly decide which direction to begin walking. However, before ten minutes are up, you are beginning to realize that this piece of land is quite extensive!

You keep hiking along and are excited when you come to a small pond somewhere in the woods. Next to it you notice a creek and decide to follow the water up to its source where you discover a natural spring. When you look back toward the direction you came from, you realize you have walked a long way, but you are no longer able to see the starting point where you left the real estate agent. You wonder if you will be able to find your car when you are done hiking.

You leave the creek and walk in a new direction and before long you come to an open meadow. It's beautiful. You see several deer running off into the woods ahead of you. You want to keep exploring, so you walk into the woods at a different point than where you entered the meadow. You sit down on an inviting rock and find yourself lost in the life of the woods around you.

The rest of the day involves finding fox and badger holes, a ten foot ravine that cuts jaggedly into the side of one of the bluffs, several clearings in the thicket, some old out-buildings that have deteriorated to the point of looking dangerous (but still interesting enough to enter), along with numerous other meadows, bluffs, and trails.

You realize your day of exploration has to end because the sky begins to darken. You need to head back, but you recognize that you have no way to determine which direction leads to your car. You have seen plenty of the property, but you don't know where those places are in relationship to each other or to your car. You, my friend, are lost!

That's how many, many people are today when it comes to the "Land" of God's Word. They know it's a sizable book; they have tried to navigate it for themselves and come up lost! They have seen plenty of good "stories" to apply to their lives, but they have little to no understanding of how they all fit together. They have gone from one Bible story or teaching to the next without seeing the connection between them!

Think with me—if, when you wanted to purchase those sixty-six acres, instead of walking the land without a plan, you flew in a plane over the land and looked down on it, you would have seen an overview of the entire piece of property; you would have seen the hills, the major trails, the pond, the creek and the other "main" and "plain" parts of the property; you would have a general outline of the lay of the land in your mind. Then, when you decided to walk the land, you would have been able to go from one area to the next and still know where you were in the context of the whole piece of property; you would not have become lost; you would have known where you were at all times!

That's what **HISTORY** can do for you. It's like you are going up in a plane over the entire "Land of the Bible" so that you can view everything in it from above. You will be able to see the whole Bible all at once. Then, when you decide you want to "walk the property" of God's Word, you will not get lost. You will know where you are at all times and be able to relate Scripture to Scripture. That's when knowledge starts to become understanding and later yields the fruit of wisdom!

So what are some of the main things in the Word of God?

- God exists in His Glorious Glory and always has.

- God created the universe and mankind to bring Glory to Himself.

- Mankind disobeyed his Creator and died spiritually as a result, becoming God's enemy and incapable of bringing Him Glory.

- As God's unrighteous enemy, man needed to be reconciled to God in order to be saved from His wrath. Once saved from God's wrath, man then needed the ability to obey his Creator as a way of life.

- God promised to send THE SEED to reconcile individuals to Himself—thereby saving a person from God's wrath and giving him a new life—thereby making him *able* to obey his Creator.

- Mankind waited for THE SEED.

- God sent THE SEED from heaven to earth.

- Most of mankind rejected THE SEED and killed Him.

- God accepted THE SEED's death as full payment for the sins of anyone who would believe in THE SEED, and therefore brought THE SEED back to life.

- THE SEED returned to God where God highly exalted Him and gave Him what God had promised—His Holy Spirit.

- THE SEED poured forth His Holy Spirit on anyone who would believe.

- Those individuals who believe in THE SEED are baptized by the Holy Spirit into the body of THE SEED. They are saved from God's wrath, reconciled to God, and receive the very life of THE SEED which brings forth fruit. While believers are waiting for THE SEED to return to earth from heaven, that fruit brings Glory to God!

- THE SEED will return to earth and judge all of His creation.

- THE SEED will rule all of His creation forever!

- Those who don't believe the truth of THE SEED before the end, refusing to repent, will be judged and then punished forever.

- Those who believe the truth of THE SEED and repent of sin will live with Him forever.

How to use the HIStory Study Guide

POINT OF PERSONAL STUDY

Where does all Bible Study begin? Asking God to teach you from His Word—One on one. The **POINTS OF PERSONAL STUDY** will simply accompany you as you walk through the Word of God, pointing out the obvious. You, however, must do the walking and observing yourself! Start your study with the "**READ AND OBSERVE**" section for each event, follow with the "**READ AND ANSWER**" section, and finish your study with the "**READ AND REASON**" material.

> **READ AND OBSERVE**
> Read through the stated text slowly and thoughtfully just to get the main idea of the passage. Feel free to take a pen in hand and mark the text when you notice something interesting. For example, you might want to mark God with a red triangle every time He is mentioned, or you might want to mark the idea of God's Glory when you see it with a yellow box filled in with purple. You might want to mark terms of conclusion with a pink capital "T" or outline time phrases with a blue box.
>
> **READ AND ANSWER**
> Read the Scriptures through a second time and answer the questions directly from the text. Don't try to change the words. Use the ones that God chose! Most answers will be easy to find because we will be sticking to the main and plain things in the text. The answers will begin to build upon one another as you move through the events in **HIStory**. As you are doing your personal study, write down any verses or thoughts the Holy Spirit may put in your mind. Write down any questions you may have as well.
>
> **READ AND REASON**
> Make sure you do not read this section until *after* you have completed both the **READ AND OBSERVE** and **READ AND ANSWER** sections answering all the questions from the text of your Bible. Then, and *only* then, read through the **READ AND REASON** material, looking up each and every Scripture reference. Slow down and meditate on the Scripture. Don't put your interpretation on it, but listen to God's Word and let it speak to you. What is written is to help you reason through and see the connections in God's Word.

If you feel that you want to dig deeper, I have written **POINT OF CONNECTION** and **POINT OF DEPTH** study materials to help you. (It's a little like going from "exploring the main deer trails" down to "exploring the more numerous and intricate bunny trails.") You will be able to see how the main things help to explain the "not so plain things." Scripture is the best—actually Scripture is the *only* interpreter of Scripture. If you will just let Scripture speak for itself, you will be amazed at what God is saying! Remember, let your beliefs come from the Bible alone. Don't believe something just because it's in a book.

POINT OF CONNECTION
The further you study in the Bible, the more you realize one verse connects to another—one chapter connects to another—one book connects to another. I will try to help you see a few choice connection points!

POINT OF DEPTH
As a Bible teacher, I couldn't help giving you a few extra verses here and there to chew on. The Holy Spirit is your resident Teacher if you are a believer; if you are not a believer, the Holy Spirit wants to speak to you through God's Word! God has placed the power of salvation in the Gospel itself. The whole Bible declares and proclaims salvation in Jesus Christ! And the whole Bible explains why each and every person alive is in desperate need of salvation! Believer or not, it is the Holy Spirit Who will lead you and guide you into all Truth.

Other HIStory Resources

HIStory Bible Timeline (Point of View)

I have tried to make the format of **HIStory Bible Timeline** (Personal size—38"X4.75" pictorial Timeline) easy enough to understand with nothing more than an attentive glance. However, you may want to note some of the particulars below.

Books of the Bible are designated with a scroll on the bottom of the Timeline.
Bible books are listed on the Timeline in the general order that they happened or were written. For example, although we are accustomed to the gospels in this order: Matthew, Mark, Luke, and John, it is generally accepted that they were written in this order: Mark, Luke, Matthew, and John.

Certain themes are designated by color. Simply follow one of the themes by color and you will find an independent study on that particular subject.
   THE SEED → Green
   COVENANT → Red
   GLORY → Purple

The Timeline itself will split on two occasions to show two separate groups at once.
   - **When the nation of Israel is divided** → The Timeline will follow both the Northern and Southern Kingdoms until the Bible stops following the story of the Northern Kingdom and follows exclusively the Southern Kingdom of Judah.

   - **When the Church is birthed** → Both the events in the life of Israel and the events in the life of the Church will be followed (Jews first) until their stories unite in the coming of our Messiah, Jesus Christ!

Although we will look at what the Bible tells us about the Rapture of the Church, its exact timing is a mystery.
There can be speculation, even hope, concerning when the Rapture will happen, but the Bible doesn't really tell us for absolute sure! And where God doesn't give us information, we would do well to keep silent!

The back of the Timeline contains summary information concerning each event.
The titles for each event are listed across the top. All the Scriptures used in **HIStory** are placed below each event title. A pictorial "miniature" Timeline is provided at the bottom in order to help you remember the events in their biblical order.

Plus, you will find an additional Timeline called the "**Temple Line**" with symbols of the places where the Glory of the LORD has, is, or will be manifested with man. The final **POINT OF CONNECTION** in **HIStory Event 17** will teach you more about this awesome subject!

HIStory Flash Cards (Point of Memory)

HIStory materials also include **POINT OF MEMORY FLASH CARDS** (COMPANION FULL COLOR FLASH CARDS FOR EACH EVENT IN **HIStory**). Children and adults alike will find the **HIStory FLASH CARDS** a perfect tool to help memorize the main events of the Bible.

Each Flash Card displays the picture representing the HIStory BIBLE TIMELINE event on the front and the event number and title on the back.
Using the cards will familiarize you with the main events in the Bible, helping you to understand His Word even more.

Before You Begin

You might be wondering how to start using HISTORY, so let me give you a few important instructions before you begin:

You must take time to pray and begin by asking God, through His Holy Spirit, to open your eyes so that you may behold wonderful things from His Word. Ask God to be your Teacher, before you begin to study. Psalm 119:18.
Always start with prayer. God is the One Who reveals Truth! He is the Author, after all, and He knows how to explain what He is saying better than anyone else. Ask the Holy Spirit to be your Teacher. It is God's will that you know what He has said. He will help you! Ask Him to open your eyes, unstop your ears, and give understanding to your mind!

You must be willing to "empty your cup" of pre-conceived ideas or beliefs.
Your cup is filled with everything you have heard and believed since you were young. Your cup may be filled with Truth, but chances are, like most people, though there is some Truth, mixed in with that Truth are lies from our enemy, Satan.

I am a Bible teacher and I always tell my students to empty their cups at the beginning of any course they are taking. If they come to the Bible with "lies" or "false beliefs" in their cup, then even if they pour pure, unadulterated Truth from His Word into their cup they will still have a mixture of Truth and lies—and so, consequently, have a cup full of lies! (Diluted Truth is 100% lie. A diluted lie is still 100% lie.)

However, if you are willing to empty your cup and let God alone put His Truth in your cup as you study the Bible inductively, then you will have nothing to fear. If what you previously had in your cup was a lie, then praise God you are getting rid of it! If, however, you had some Truth in your cup, you can rest assured that God will put that very same Truth right back into your cup. Only this time it won't be surrounded and diluted by other untruths! This time you will *know* it is Truth because you learned it straight from God in His Word. (No third parties!)

In case you are hesitant about emptying your cup, let me ask you something. How do you know what you know? Do you believe what you do about the Bible and God because you've heard about Him second-hand or because someone has told you what to believe? Or do you believe what you do because you have studied God's Word for yourself and He has taught you His Truth Himself? We are completely safe when we let God be our Teacher!

I heard a question asked years ago that has stuck with me. It was profound in its intent. The question asks, "Do you want to know Truth more than you want to be right?" My answer is, "Yes! Yes! A thousand times Yes! I *do* want to know Truth more than I want to be right!!!" I try to come to God's Word each and every time with a heart that wants to know Truth more than it wants to be right—I come with an empty cup and let Him fill it up for me.

You must be willing to spend time in His Word, searching for Him and His ways.
Learning is a process more similar to preparing a five-course home-cooked meal than driving through a fast food restaurant! It takes time and effort!

You must be willing to listen as He speaks to you supernaturally through His Word. He will! He promises!
God gave us His Word so that we might know Him and respond accordingly. He most certainly will speak to those who are willing to listen to Him! Trust Him!

You must determine right now to finish this course—no matter what!
Determine to walk through and carefully observe all sixty-six "acres"!

You must complete each event; you will find that the answers will build on one another as you move through HISTORY.
You will begin to see connections and understanding will come. God chose to reveal **HIS**TORY to us progressively. Be faithful and continue to work through the study. When you have completed the course, you may find that you understand things you have never even pondered before.

May you be blessed "Beyond the Horizon" as you seek God in His Word.

...Before the Beginning GOD Exists in His Glorious Glory!!!

HIStory Table of Contents

Event 1	...Before the Beginning GOD Exists in His Glorious Glory!!!
Event 2	...In the Beginning GOD Creates so His Glory will be Seen!
Event 3	...Man Sins and Dies Spiritually – GOD Promises THE SEED to Bring Spiritual Life!
Event 4	...GOD Destroys the Distorted Image of His Glory
Event 5	...GOD Creates and Scatters the Nations
Event 6	...GOD Creates the Nation of Israel
Event 7	...GOD Sends His Nation, Israel, to a Foreign Land
Event 8	...GOD Delivers Israel
Event 9	...GOD Gives His Law to Israel
Event 10	...GOD Brings the Nation of Israel into The Land
Event 11	...GOD Sends Judges to Rule Over Israel
Event 12	...Israel Rejects GOD as her King
Event 13	...GOD Splits the Kingdom of Israel in Two
Event 14	...GOD Sends Prophets to the Northern Kingdom of Israel (Israel)
Event 15	...GOD Sends Assyria to Take the Northern Kingdom into Captivity
Event 16	...GOD Sends Prophets to the Southern Kingdom of Israel (Judah)
Event 17	...GOD Sends Babylon to Take the Southern Kingdom into Captivity
Event 18	...GOD Promises a New Covenant...THE SEED!
Event 19	...GOD Brings Israel Back to The Land
Event 20	...GOD Calls Israel Back to Himself...Then He is Silent...
Event 21	...GOD Sends THE PROMISED SEED!!!
Event 22	...GOD Anoints THE SEED!
Event 23	...THE SEED Dies
Event 24	...THE SEED is Buried
Event 25	...THE SEED Lives and is Seen!
Event 26	...THE SEED Returns to GOD
Event 27A	...The Nation of Israel – Set Aside and Purified Until THE SEED Returns
Event 27B	...The Church – THE SEED Sends His HOLY SPIRIT as Promised!
Event 28	...THE SEED Returns in Glory!!!
Event 29	...THE SEED Reigns!
Event 30	...The Last Rebellion Against GOD
Event 31	...GOD's Great White Throne Judgment and the Lake of Fire
Event 32	...Beyond the Horizon of Eternity GOD Exists Forever in His Glorious Glory!!!

HIStory Event 1
...Before the Beginning
GOD Exists in His Glorious Glory!!!

Genesis

Genesis is the book of beginnings. We see God existing before all else. In Genesis, God creates and establishes things that are familiar to us today—our universe, our world, mankind, marriage, civilizations, languages, promises, etc. Most importantly, God creates the nation of Israel, which will carry the bloodline of His Son.

God owns His Creation; He has all rights over it— and He expects it to respond rightly to Him! Man, however, does not respond rightly to his Creator and through man's rebellion, we see the birth of sin, idolatry, adultery, rebellion, and false worship.

READ AND OBSERVE

Read through the following text slowly and thoughtfully just to get the main idea of the passage. Feel free to take a pen in hand and mark the text when you notice something interesting. For example, you might want to mark God with a red triangle every time He is mentioned, or you might want to mark the idea of God's Glory when you see it with a yellow box filled in with purple. You might want to mark terms of conclusion with a pink capital "T" or outline time phrases with a blue box. (Follow these instructions for each and every "READ AND OBSERVE" section.)

1. Genesis 1:1; Deuteronomy 33:27; Romans 16:26; Isaiah 41:4; 43:10; 48:12; Revelation 21:6; 22:13
2. John 1:1-2; Micah 5:2; Hebrews 1:8
3. Hebrews 9:14
4. Job 36:26; Isaiah 40:28; 46:4; Habakkuk 3:6; Romans 1:18-21

READ AND ANSWER

Read through the Scriptures a second time, then answer the questions directly from the text. Do not try to change any words. Use the ones God chose. We're not trying to interpret or translate right now—just continue observing. Most answers will be easy to find because we are only looking for the main and plain things! (Follow these instructions for each and every "READ AND ANSWER" section.)

1. Genesis 1:1
Did anything or anyone exist before the heavens and the earth were created? (Get your answer from the text.)

Who or what?

Deuteronomy 33:27; Romans 16:26
How is God described? What kind of a God is He?

Isaiah 41:4
Who existed before everyone and everything else?

Isaiah 43:10; Isaiah 48:12
Did any other God exist before God?

Will there ever be another God?

Revelation 21:6; Revelation 22:13
Who is the Alpha?

Who is the Beginning?

Who is the First?

Who is the Omega?

Who is the End?

Who is the Last?

2. John 1:1-2
What or Who existed in the beginning?

    1.

    2.

Does this passage in any way show that the Word was distinct from God?

Does this passage in any way show that the Word was the same as God?

Micah 5:2
From where will a future ruler come?

Where will He rule?

Do you remember Who was born in Bethlehem Ephrathah?

Was He alive before He was born in Bethlehem?

For how long?

Hebrews 1:8
What does God call the Son?

How long will His Son sit on His throne?

What kind of a Ruler is He?

3. **Hebrews 9:14**
Who else is eternal besides God, the Father and God, the Son?

4. **Job 36:26**
Just how old is the Eternal God?

Isaiah 40:28; 46:4; Habakkuk 3:6
Do you ever get tired?

Does God ever get tired?

Will you ever change? How?

Will God ever change?

Will His ways ever change?

Romans 1:18-21
How does a person know that God is eternal without even reading the Bible?

    1.

    2.

Who made sure every living person would know about God?

How long has this information been understood by humans?

List the three things of which every person is aware about God:

    1.

2.

3.

Once someone is aware that God exists, what should be that person's response?

1.

2.

What do some people do instead?

What happens to them?

1.

2.

READ AND REASON

Once you have read and observed all the Scriptures and answered all the questions in the previous sections, read the text for a third time. Then read the additional information provided below. (Follow these instructions for each and every "READ AND REASON" section.)

1. **Genesis 1:1; Deuteronomy 33:27; Romans 16:26; Isaiah 41:4; 43:10; 48:12; Revelation 21:6; 22:13**

Oh! The wonder of those four words... "In the Beginning GOD." In other words, He existed before the beginning. In a sense, that is all we really need to know—that God exists and always has. It most definitely is the first thing we need to know. Neither you nor I have existed since the beginning, but God has existed before all else. He is eternal.

2. John 1:1-2

A glorious parallel Scripture with **Genesis 1:1** is **John 1:1-2**. The Word existed before all else. The Word has been in existence with God since before time began. The Word is God. The Word is Jesus. Jesus is God.

Micah 5:2

When Bethlehem is mentioned most people's thoughts go to a baby born in Bethlehem, Israel almost 2,000 years ago named Jesus. The Bible tells us that this "baby" had been in existence long before He was born on the earth. In fact, it says He has been around from the days of eternity. He wasn't a baby—He *is*, always *has*, and always *will* be GOD!

Hebrew 1:8

God calls Jesus His Son and states that He is a Righteous Ruler Whose throne is forever and ever. But God also calls Him GOD!

3. Hebrews 9:14

Not only are God, the Father and God, the Son eternal, but so is God, the Spirit. Jesus is GOD! The Holy Spirit is GOD!

Don't worry if you are not sure at this point Who Jesus is, or Who the Holy Spirit is. We will simply let Scripture tell us as we move along in our study.

4. Job 36:26

So just how old is eternal? It's beyond our ability to compute and even more than that! The Bible calls it "beyond the horizon" because you can only see to the horizon, but there is much more beyond that you cannot even see! God's existence is beyond the horizon for us! It's not just that you can search for an answer without obtaining it—you can't even comprehendingly search for the answer because the whole concept is just too great!

Isaiah 40:28; 46:4; Habakkuk 3:6

We see change in ourselves and others each year—a little taller (or a little shorter), a little bigger (or a little smaller), more patient, less patient, nicer, kinder, meaner, crankier and so on and so forth… What a great truth to know that God does not change—ever! He stays the same! He does not get old or tired! And if we belong to Him He will always carry us and deliver us. He will always be GOD!

Romans 1:18-21
I know of a bumper sticker that says, "God doesn't believe in atheists." That's right! The reason is because they don't exist! Every person who has ever lived *knows* there is a God, that He is invisible, and that He is eternally powerful. Why can I say that? Because God made Himself known *through* His creation and *in* His creation; He made it evident *within* each man and *without* each man in the creation itself! He didn't hide it from anybody—it's seen by all, and it's seen clearly!

So what if you know someone who is an atheist? Will you believe God or will you believe the "atheist"? Every self-proclaimed atheist knows for certain there is a God and even knows certain facts about Him. He is lying to you when he calls himself an atheist. He is lying to himself and has deceived himself if he actually believes himself!

In other words, God gives light or truth to every single human being. If he responds to that light, God will give him more light/truth. If a person rejects that light, he will go into further darkness and not be able to understand anymore. The good news is that if you quit suppressing the truth and start receiving and believing the light God will give you *more* light! The process can be reversed!

It all starts out with recognizing (acknowledging) that God is Who He says He is and honoring Him and giving Him thanks! He's given all mankind an easy place to start. Just believe what you already know and understand—God is GOD! Why don't you start right now?

So the first event in **HISTORY** is simply this: God exists. GOD alone exists.

POINT OF DEPTH

In the second book of the Bible God will give His personal memorial Name for all generations to a man named Moses. In biblical times a name meant much more than it does today. It spoke of that person's nature, character, or attributes. It was often prophetic of what that person would someday do or represent.

God says in Exodus 3:14 that His Name is Jehovah, the transliterated form of Yahweh, which in turn came from the Tetragrammaton YHWH. God's personal Name was so awesome to Moses' people that they would not even say it aloud. Consequently, we cannot be sure of how to pronounce God's Name even today. In some Bibles, if you see the word "lord" in all small caps like this "LORD," you can know that the word being translated is the Hebrew word YHWH.

Jehovah means I AM WHO I AM. The Great I AM is the Self-Existent One, the God Who exists totally separate and apart from anything else. Yahweh needs no one and nothing else to exist. That cannot be said of anything else in existence, especially mankind. We are

dependent on virtually everything around us. Without air, water, gravity, blood, food, etc., we would cease to exist. We are totally and completely dependent upon the One Who needs no one—Jehovah! Our next breath is His decision because our next breath is in His hand! We need Him! Job 12:10

HIStory Event 2
...In the Beginning GOD Creates so His Glory will be Seen!!!

Sometimes we don't look at familiar passages in the Bible as closely as we should. We think we already know what they say. The problem is, many times what we have become familiar with is only what we have been taught the Bible says; we have never really studied it for ourselves.

In order for you to see that this may even apply to you, I want you to take a quick and easy quiz before you start reading and observing the following passages about Creation. If you are just guessing, put a question mark beside your answer. If you know the answer for sure, put a check mark beside it. I give this quiz to my students before I teach on Creation. It's always very humbling. And that is the best place for each of us to start studying the Word of God—humbled before Him, willing to listen to *every word* He speaks!

After you finish **Event 2**, check out the answers in the appendix to see how well you did. Make sure you even check out the answers that you "know for sure" are right. You just might be surprised.

A. For how many days did God create?

B. On what day did God make man?

C. On what day did God make light?

D. Out of what did God make the earth?

E. Who did God tell to not eat from the Tree of the Knowledge of Good and Evil?

F. What was it that God named "night"?

G. On what day did God create the waters?

H. What did God do to the waters?

I. What was it that God named "earth"?

J. From where did the trees and the vegetation on the earth come?

K. What did God call the expanse?

L. What was the expanse for? What did it do?

M. What did God tell the sea monsters to do?

N. What is the key repeated word in **Genesis 1-2**?

O. Name five things man was to rule over (or as many as you can).

    1.

    2.

    3.

    4.

    5.

P. What did God say was "very good"?

Q. What did God give man to eat?

    1.

    2.

R. Did God create the heavens and the earth or did He make them? Was it a process?

S. Which did God make first—Adam or the Garden of Eden?

T. Why did God make Eve?

U. Did God create the animals or make them?

V. Who named all the fish?

*(The answers to these next few questions come from **Genesis 3**, which will be covered in **Event 3**.)*

W. Why are there weeds?

X. How did Adam become like God when he sinned?

Y. Why did God send Adam out from the Garden of Eden?

Read and Observe

1. Genesis 1-2; Revelation 10:6; 14:7; John 1:1-3; Hebrews 1:1-5, 8-12; Psalm 102:25-27; Colossians 1:16; Genesis 1:26
2. Genesis 1:28
3. Isaiah 45:18

Read and Answer

1. Genesis 1-2
What was God's assessment of what He had made?

Revelation 10:6
What all has been created?

    1. _____ and

    2. _____ and

    3. _____ and

Revelation 14:7
Who made the heaven, earth, sea, and springs of water?

What does He deserve?

    1.

    2.

    3.

John 1:1-3
How did all things come into being?

Has anything—anything at all—ever come into being without Him?

Hebrews 1:1-5
Through Whom did God make the world?

Hebrews 1:8-12; Psalm 102:25-27
Who is to rule forever and ever?

What type of rule will He have?

What specifically did Jesus do in the Creation?

    1.

    2.

What will happen to the works of Jesus' hands?

    1.

    2.

    3.

    4.

Who will cause them to perish?

Colossians 1:16
Who created all things?

How are "all things" described?

    1.

    2.

    3.

4.

5.

6.

7.

8.

How have all things been created?

Why have all things been created?

Genesis 1:26
In Whose image was man made? According to Whose likeness was man made?

What was man's position to be?

What was man to rule over?

1.

2.

3.

4.

5.

2. Genesis 1:28
What was the first instruction God gave to man? List His instruction step by step.

1.

2.

3.

4.

5.

6.

7.

3. Isaiah 45:18
What was God's purpose in creating the earth?

READ AND REASON

1. Genesis 1-2; Revelation 10:6; 14:7; John 1:1-3; Hebrews 1:1-5, 8-12; Psalm 102:25-27; Colossians 1:16; Genesis 1:26

In the beginning, God created the world. It seems obvious, but let me say it anyway—God created our entire universe. At the beginning of a fixed period of time, when nothing existed except God, God created.

God, the Father, God, the Son, and God, the Holy Spirit were all three involved in creating what now exists. The Holy Spirit hovered over the waters and said, "Let Us make man in Our image." Jesus very clearly had an enormous part in creation. All things came into being by or through Him. He laid the foundation of the earth. The heavens are the work of His hands. Nothing that has come into being has come into being apart from Jesus. All things have been created *for* Jesus! Through Him, God made the world. And yet, at the very same time it is true that all things have been created through God. All things have been created *for* God! He founded the earth. The heavens are the work of His hands.

I had a student one year who had been in church for most of her life. While we were studying what the Bible has to say on the subject of covenant, God turned on a "light bulb" for her. She went home and joyously told her husband, *"I know why I was created! I was created for God!! I was created for His pleasure and His Glory!!!"* **Revelation 4:11** Wow!!! What a change has happened in my friend's life. She has grown and grown and grown in her walk with Jesus. She knows the purpose of her existence and lives her life seeking to bring pleasure to her Creator!

2. **Genesis 1:28**
The first instruction God gave man was to *"Be fruitful and multiply, and fill the earth, and subdue it and rule over the fish of the sea and over the birds of the sky, and over every living thing that moves on the earth."*

3. **Isaiah 45:18**
God formed the earth with a purpose → for it to be inhabited!

POINT OF DEPTH

Why did God instruct man to have lots of children and scatter over the face of the earth? **Because God created man for His Own Glory. Isaiah 43:7 Glory is a great word! The Hebrew word for glory is "kabowd" and refers to the substance of something, its weight, splendor, or reputation. The Greek word is "doxa," which means to give a correct opinion of something or to show an accurate estimate of something. God created man in His Own image. He wanted to fill the earth with men, women, and children who were a picture of Himself. It brings God pleasure to receive Glory. Revelation 4:11**

To truly bring God Glory, we must live in the light of Who He really is. Our walk and our talk show the world what we truly believe about God. What does your life say to others? Do you show the world that He is God, Most High, Ruler of all that is? Do you show the world that He is Ruler of you? Are you fulfilling His purpose in creating you? Romans 11:36

HIStory Event 3
...Man Sins and Dies Spiritually – GOD Promises THE SEED to Bring Spiritual Life!

Read and Observe

1. Genesis 2:7-9, 15-17
2. Genesis 3:1-6; Revelation 12:9; 20:2
3. Romans 5:12
4. Genesis 3:7-24; 5:1-3
5. Genesis 3:15

Read and Answer

1. Genesis 2:7-9
Who made man?

Out of what did He make man?

Who made the dust?

From where did man's life come?

Genesis 2:15-17
How did man end up in the Garden of Eden? (Who put him there?)

What did God expect man to do in the Garden of Eden?

    1.

    2.

What did God allow man to do in the Garden of Eden?

What did God forbid man to do in the Garden of Eden?

What would happen to man if he disobeyed his Creator and Master?

2. Genesis 3:1-6
The serpent asks Eve a question. Does he really want to know the answer or is he just trying to cause her to disobey God?

When Eve responds to the serpent, he goes one step further and actually calls God a liar. Who *really* was the liar?

Revelation 12:9
Who was the serpent that was in the Garden of Eden? How else is he identified?

Revelation 20:2
Give three other titles for Satan. (These are titles of identification, not of honor.)

    1.

    2.

    3.

3. Romans 5:12
How did sin enter into the world? (Sin was not in the earth when God created it; remember, He said the earth was good!)

How did death enter into the world?

4. Genesis 3:7-24
What happened immediately after man disobeyed God?

    1.

2.

3.

4.

In **verse 14**, what did God tell the serpent would happen to him?

1.

2.

3.

4.

In **verse 15**, what did God tell the serpent would happen?

1.

2.

3.

4.

In **verse 16**, what did God tell the woman would happen?

1.

2.

3.

In **verses 17-19**, what did God tell the man would happen?

1.

2.

3.

4.

5.

God made clothing for Adam and Eve. Out of what did He make their clothing?

Do you think the animal would have been alive or dead?

Why did God send man out from the Garden of Eden never to return?

What did God do to make sure man did not come back into the Garden of Eden?

Why do you think God was so careful to make sure man did not eat from the Tree of Life?

Why would God not want man to live forever? What condition was man in now—sinful or sinless?

When God created man, male and female, in Whose likeness were they made?

Genesis 5:1-3
When Adam and Eve bore children, of whose likeness were they? In whose image were they?

Why were they born in Adam's image? What had changed?

5. Genesis 3:15
Take time to go over this verse carefully. Then try and draw out what this verse is saying using stick figures. This will help you to see it more clearly and possibly understand it more. It will also serve to write it on your mind more deeply. When you have finished your sketch, look in the appendix for my version and compare the two. Remember—do yours first!

Read and Reason

1. Genesis 2:7-9, 15-17
God created man, placed him in a garden, and as man's Creator and Master, gave him very clear instructions: "Do not eat from that tree! If you do, you will die!"

2. Genesis 3:1-6; Revelation 12:9; 20:2
The serpent, Satan, said to man, "Oh, come on! God didn't really say that, did He?" Satan is still doing this today. He's saying to us, "Did God really say that?" One of the devil's greatest tools is simply → deception!

Point of Depth

Who is this serpent called Satan?

When God created the heavens and the earth, He created beings as well—mankind and animals, birds and creeping things. Before He created the earth and the things on it, He created heavenly creatures, like angels, etc.—beings who would serve Him. Nehemiah 9:6; John 1:3; Colossians 1:16 Satan was one of those angelic beings. God created him as the most beautiful of all the angels. But Satan wasn't content serving his Creator. He became puffed up because of his beauty. His pride turned to rebellion. He wanted to be "God"!

Most scholars believe Ezekiel 28:11-19 and Isaiah 14:3-15 refer to Satan. However, it is most definitely not clear, nor is it repeated doctrine concerning him; therefore, we must hold the teaching we have from these two passages with a loose hand whenever we apply it to Satan.

3. Romans 5:12
Sin came into the world through one man → Adam; through sin something else came into the world → death.

I like to think of it this way: Adam is standing in a room with a door that is closed. Adam hears a knock at the door. Adam opens the door and finds a package sitting on the stoop outside the door. He picks up the package and brings it inside. Although his first mistake was opening the door (listening to Eve), he steps into real trouble by bringing the package (sin) inside of his room (the world). Little did he know that inside of this package of sin was another enemy called "death" which would compound his troubles! By bringing the package inside, he brought the contents inside as well. Death came into our world inside the package of sin. The package was unwrapped way back during the lifetime of Adam, but sin and death are still at large on our planet today!

4. Genesis 3:7-24; Genesis 5:1-3

Things happened as a result of sin!
1. Adam and Eve's eyes were opened. They knew that they were naked.
2. They heard God coming to talk with them in the garden and hid from Him. Before that time they had a wonderfully open relationship with God; now they were ashamed and guilty before Him.
3. When God cornered them, Adam and Eve blamed everyone and everything except the tree itself!
4. God was true to His Word. They died spiritually that day. God, Who had been with them, now departed.
5. God cursed the serpent and the ground itself. (It is amazing to me to think what my garden and lawn would look like if the ground hadn't been cursed. Can you imagine a world without weeds?)
6. From this time until the end of the earth, creation would groan under a curse!
7. Because Adam and Eve both disobeyed God, man would now have to "sweat" to get his bread and a woman would go through much more pain in childbirth. A woman's desire would be for her husband, but he would rule over her.
8. God sent Adam and Eve out of the Garden of Eden to cultivate the ground of the earth.
9. God stationed the cherubim and the flaming sword, which turned in every direction, to guard the way to the Tree of Life to make sure no one would eat from it. We will see the Tree of Life once more, but not until the last chapter of the Bible in **Revelation 22:2**.
10. Now the world would be filled with sinners from the loins of Adam rather than men, women, and children who gave a true estimate of God. God made Adam in His likeness, but Adam begot sons in his own likeness and now all mankind's blood would be tainted with sin.

Adam and Eve tried to cover their nakedness with fig leaves—not the best of ideas. God, instead, made garments of skin and clothed them. Obviously God killed an animal to make the clothing for Adam and Eve. We see here the first mention of the shedding of blood in the Bible. He was painting us a picture of what was now needed for all mankind—a substitute sacrifice!

Point of Depth

When Adam and Eve sinned, they owed God something—their lives! The wages of sin is death! Romans 6:23 When you sin, you have to pay with your own death!

You see, man tried to cover his sin himself (with fig leaves) but to no avail. The only thing that could cover sin was blood. God sacrificed an animal on Adam and Eve's behalf to cover their sin because without the shedding of blood there is no forgiveness of sin. Leviticus 17:10-11; Hebrews 9:22 However, the substituted blood of an animal could never take away their sins. Hebrews 10:4 They needed a Savior, so God promised He would provide One—The Seed!

5. Genesis 3:15

God is talking to the serpent. God tells him He will put enmity between the serpent and the woman and between the serpent's seed and the woman's seed. He, the woman's seed (Jesus), would bruise or crush the serpent (Satan) on the head. The serpent would bruise the woman's seed on the heel.

This is the beginning of the Promise of the Gospel of the Blood of the Eternal Covenant!

(Remember to check out the version in the appendix!)

30

HIStory Event 4
...GOD Destroys the Distorted Image of His Glory

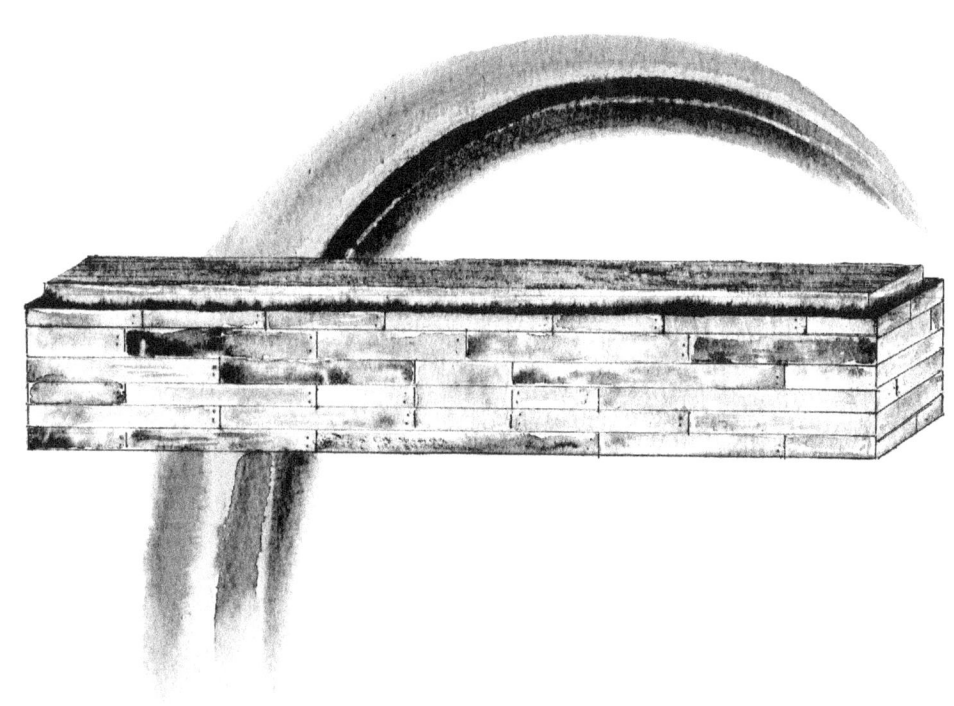

Read and Observe

1. Genesis 6:5-8
2. Genesis 6-8
3. Genesis 6:17-18; 9:8-17
4. Genesis 9:1, 7; Isaiah 45:18; 43:7

Read and Answer

1. Genesis 6:5-8
Whereas once God looked at His creation and declared that it was good, now when He looked He saw something very different. What did He see?

    1.

    2.

How did the LORD feel?

    1.

    2.

What did God say He was going to do?

Why didn't God blot out Noah from the face of the earth?

2. Genesis 6-8
Try to read the account of the flood like it is the first time you are hearing it, or try reading it out loud to someone else.

3. Genesis 6:17-18
What did God say He was going to do to the earth and everything on it?

Did you notice the "but" that starts out **verse 18**? How is God going to deal differently with Noah, Noah's wife, his sons, and their wives than He is with the rest of the world?

    1.

    2.

Genesis 9:8-17
What did God establish?

With whom did God establish it?

    1.

    2.

    3.

What was God's Covenant that He established with Noah?

    1.

    2.

After a flood like that one, what do you think Noah and his descendants would remember every time it started to storm?

God wanted to remind Noah and his descendants of the promise He had made and that He would never break that promise, so what did He do?

4. Genesis 9:1, 7
God gave Noah and his sons a task to accomplish when He put them back on dry land. What was it?

   1.

   2.

   3.

Does this command sound familiar? Where have you heard this before?

Isaiah 45:18
Why did God form the earth in the first place?

Isaiah 43:7
Why did God want the earth to be inhabited?

READ AND REASON

1. Genesis 6:5-8
God saw that mankind was continually evil. God's heart was continually grieved. God decided to wipe out mankind, but He put His favor (grace) on one man → Noah. Noah *found* favor in the eyes of the LORD. Grace is never, ever earned! Grace is never, ever a reward!

2. Genesis 6-8
God sent a flood and destroyed the earth except for Noah and his family.

3. Genesis 6:17-18; 9:8-17
God makes a Covenant with Noah and his descendants after him, and with every living creature with Noah. Covenant is the most solemn, binding agreement ever known to mankind. God is a Covenant-keeping God! God promised that the water of the flood would never destroy all flesh again. God promised He would never again destroy the earth by a flood. God went so far as to give Noah (and us, his descendants) a sign of His Covenant → a rainbow in the cloud.

This Covenant that God made with Noah, and us, and every living creature is an everlasting Covenant. It will always be in effect! When you see a rainbow → know for certain that the hand of God put it there! He is speaking to you!

4. Genesis 9:1, 7; Isaiah 45:18; 43:7
After the flood, God gave Noah the same instruction He had given Adam years earlier, "Be fruitful and multiply, and fill the earth." He told Noah and his family to populate the earth again by having lots of children and scattering over the face of the earth.

You see, God was still planning to fill the earth with men, women, and children who would bring Him Glory. That's what He still planned on having → Glory for Himself! He wanted there to be plenty of people on the earth, so that when the Savior came—The Seed Who would bring Life—God would receive an abundance of Glory from the sheer number of people who walked in His ways.

Point of Depth

Before the flood, all the animals were only supposed to eat "greens," but due to sin and the corruption of all flesh, some became carnivorous in contradiction to God's command. Genesis 1:30 After the flood, God put the fear of man in the animals. Genesis 9:2 Do you realize that animals are more afraid of us than we are of them?

Before the flood, God never opened up the heavens to send rain. A fine mist or springs watered the earth. Mankind had never seen rain. But they would when the flood came! Genesis 2:5-6

Point of Depth

This POD is worth repeating here. *Why did God instruct man to have lots of children and scatter over the face of the earth?* **Because God created man for His Own Glory. Isaiah 43:7 Glory is a great word! The Hebrew word for glory is "kabowd" and refers to the substance of something, its weight, splendor, or reputation. The Greek word is "doxa", which means to give a correct opinion of something or to show an accurate estimate of something. God created man in His Own image. He wanted to fill the earth with men, women, and children who were a picture of Himself. It brings God pleasure to receive His true Glory. Revelation 4:11**

To truly bring God Glory, we must live in the light of Who He really is. Our walk and our talk show the world what we truly believe about God. What does your life say to others? Do you show the world that He is God, Most High, Ruler of all that is? Do you show the world that He is Ruler over you? Are you fulfilling His purpose in creating you? Romans 11:36

HIStory Event 5
...GOD Creates and Scatters the Nations

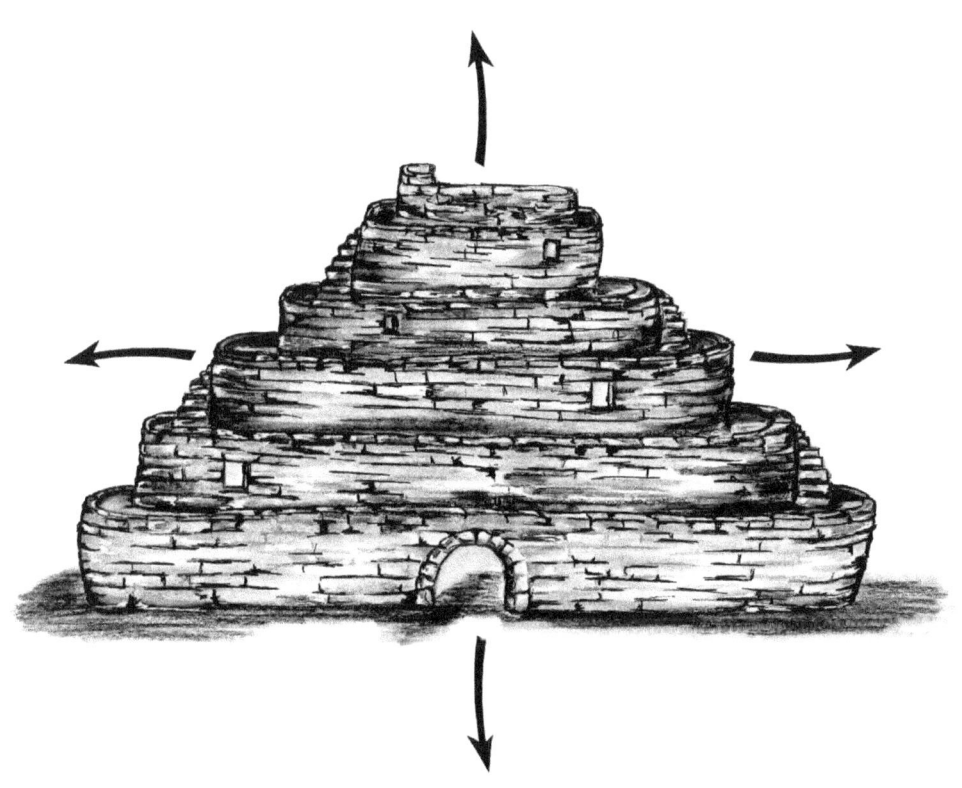

Read and Observe

1. Genesis 11:1-9; Isaiah 43:7; 45:18
2. Genesis 10:1-10
3. Genesis 11:7-9

Read and Answer

1. Genesis 11:1-9
After the flood, how many different peoples were there? (How many different languages were in the world?)

As mankind grew in population, they journeyed east from where God had parked the ark. What did they decide to do that was in direct rebellion to God's command to Noah and his sons, as well as the command God gave to Adam and Eve?

Why did God confuse mankind's language? Was it so they would stop building the tower? Or was there another, more important reason?

What had God commanded Noah and his sons to do?

Isaiah 43:7
Why did God create man?

Isaiah 45:18
Why did God create the earth?

Reason together with me. If God created the earth for it to be inhabited, and He created man for His Glory, do you see why God commanded man to swarm the earth, to be fruitful and multiply, and fill the earth? What would that bring to God?

2. Genesis 10:1-10
Who was Nimrod's father?

Who was Cush's father?

Who was Ham's father?

How was Nimrod related to Noah?

What famous city was the beginning of Nimrod's kingdom?

3. Genesis 11:7-9
According to **verse 8**, what caused the people to stop building the city?

According to **verse 9**, what was the result of God confusing the language of the people?

Would this have been the beginning of nations on the earth?

READ AND REASON

1. Genesis 11:1-9; Isaiah: 43:7; 45:18
After the flood, when God gave Noah instructions to multiply and scatter over the face of the earth, everyone spoke one language. At first the people were traveling east – that was fine, they were scattering as God had commanded, but they made a terrible decision! They found a nice place to live and decided that this was as far as they were going to go! It was the plain of Shinar. They sent God a message, *"NO! We won't obey You! We don't want to make a Name for You or bring Glory to You! We want to make a name for ourselves and bring glory to ourselves!"*

They even went so far as to admit that they were directly and defiantly disobeying God! They actually said, *"Let's stay here and make a name for ourselves so that we won't be scattered abroad over the face of the whole earth!"*

Do you see that what they were doing was trying to rob God of His Glory? God wanted His Name to be known throughout His creation! Man, the creation, wanted to make a name for himself! (Are you robbing God of His Glory—the Glory that is due Him?)

God still had the same program in place that He established when He created mankind and told Adam and Eve to multiply and fill the earth. He wanted to bring Glory to Himself through their obedience to Him. He wanted all of mankind to bring Glory to Himself. His purpose hadn't changed when He brought Noah and his family through the flood. The command He gave them upon leaving the ark to begin living on the earth again was the same → Be fruitful and multiply and fill the earth! Since He could receive Glory through men when they obeyed, He wanted *lots* of men and *lots* of obedience so there would be *lots* of Glory!

POINT OF DEPTH

Lest you might be hearing Satan lying at this point and saying *"That is mighty prideful of God,"* let me assure you *"That IS mighty prideful of God!"* Are you surprised to hear me say that? Let me explain. The reason it is wrong and sinful for humans to feel prideful is because we don't deserve to boast in ourselves. We are just the creation. It is not wrong at all for God, the Creator, to feel prideful or to want praise because He is worthy of *all praise!* Isaiah 43:7

God will not give His Glory to another! Isaiah 42:8 Man is to bring Glory to Him → not rob Him of it! As much as man would like to forget it, he needs to remember that the world does not rotate around him. Rather, the creation, the universe, and the world are all rotating around the LORD God Almighty, Who was, Who is, and Who is to come!!!

2. Genesis 10:1-10
Follow the line of Noah through the man named "Nimrod." Nimrod's father was Cush. Cush's father was Ham. Ham's father was Noah. Noah → Ham → Cush → Nimrod. Nimrod was Noah's great-grandson.

Nimrod's name meant *"let us rebel."* Nimrod is described as a mighty one before (against) God, or more literally, a mighty tyrant in the face of Jehovah. He was a mighty hunter all right; he persuaded men to obey *his* will rather than God's! He had a kingdom that began in the plain of Shinar.

God was not going to stand for man defiantly disregarding His command to scatter over the face of the earth! He watched what they were doing and then did something about it! Man had declared, *"No! We won't scatter!"* God responded with, *"Oh, yes, you will scatter!"*

3. Genesis 11:7-9
God divides the people to create the nations of the earth. Before this time there was only one people and they all spoke the same language. He confused their language adding various languages so they couldn't understand each other's speech. That, **verse 8** tells us, is what caused

them to scatter over the face of the earth! It is only a secondary result that they stopped building the city and the tower!

POINT OF DEPTH

Isn't it interesting? We may have been taught that God was angry about the tower the people were building for one reason or another, and that was why He confused their language. I thought God was mad because it was so tall! I never understood it, but that's what I was taught so that's what I believed! *Sigh*... But that wasn't it at all. God was simply exercising His sovereign will over mankind.

God said to scatter → so they would be scattered! If they wouldn't do it of their own free will, then God would superintend His divine will upon man. Man was going to obey whether he wanted to or not!!! God's purposes can *not* be thwarted by anyone or anything! Job 42:2

By the way, in the Hebrew language, verse 4 of Genesis 11 reads *"Let us build a tower whose top is unto heaven."* Many believe that this tower was a ziggurat, a tower built to worship the sun, moon, and stars. Many even believe that the zodiac system had its beginnings right here on the plain of Shinar, or Babylon, as its name is more commonly called.

In Babylon, we can observe the beginning of idolatry, false religion, false worship, and the beginning of the city that still exists in Iraq today. Revelation 17 calls Babylon the "Mother of harlots." It stands to reason that when God scattered the peoples living in Babylon, they would have taken their pagan and idolatrous ways with them!

Did you know that Saddam Hussein, for decades,
was literally rebuilding the city of Babylon?[1]

Did you know that the work of rebuilding Babylon continues even today?

Did you know that Babylon, the city, *must* be in existence in the last days?
Isaiah 13-14; Jeremiah 50-51; Revelation 17-18

Did you know that a temple will be built in Babylon in the last days? Zechariah 5:5-11

---

[1] An excellent book to read on the subject of Babylon is *Rise of Babylon* by Charles Dyer.

42

HIStory Event 6
...GOD Creates The Nation of Israel

Read and Observe

1. Genesis 12-17; 22:17-18; 26:3-4; Galatians 3:8, 16
2. Genesis 11:27-32; 15:7; Acts 7:1-4
3. Genesis 12:1-7
4. Genesis 15
5. Genesis 16
6. Genesis 17:1-23

Read and Answer

1. Genesis 12-17
Read these chapters all in one sitting. Note who the main characters are. Note what the main events are.

Genesis 22:17-18
What promises did God make to Abram?

1.

2.

3.

4.

Genesis 26:3-4
What does God promise Isaac?

1.

2.

3.

4.

5.

6.

7.

Is this the same promise (Covenant) that God made to Abram (Abraham)?

How do you know?

Galatians 3:8
What Covenant promise is mentioned here?

When God promised Abraham that "ALL THE NATIONS WILL BE BLESSED IN YOU," what does this verse say that God was actually preaching to him?

Justify, in this case, means to legally declare someone innocent. Who would God eventually justify?

How?

Faith in what?

Galatians 3:16
To whom were the Covenant promises spoken?

   1.

   2.

2. Genesis 11:27-32
Who was Abram's father?

Who was Abram's wife?

Did Sarai have any children?

Terah moved his family. From where did they move? (Check the map in the appendix to see what this land is called today.)

To where did they move?

Why did they move?

Genesis 15:7
Who took Abram's family out of Ur?

Why?

Acts 7:1-4
Did Abram know why he was leaving Ur?

3. Genesis 12:1-7

What does the LORD tell Abram to do?

    1.

    2.

    3.

    4.

What does the LORD tell Abram He will do?

    1.

    2.

    3.

    4.

    5.

    6.

    7.

    8.

What will happen to those who bless Israel (Abram's descendants)?

Who will bless them?

What will happen to those who curse Israel (Abram's descendants)?

Who will curse them?

Does this promise still apply today?

Would you say America has blessed Israel in the past?

Would you say God has blessed America in the past?

Would you say America is continuing to bless Israel?

What should you pray for your government leaders to do in regard to Israel?

If America does not bless Israel, what will God have to do?

4. Genesis 15
God had made a promise to Abram, but he thought God was a little slow in delivering; so what does Abram suggest to God?

What is God's reply?

God took Abram outside and showed him the sky and told him his descendants would be as great in number as the stars of the heavens. Did Abram believe God?

What did God do for Abram when he believed Him?

Mark this in your Bible as the day of Abram's salvation!

What are the three *main* things that God promises to Abram?

    1.

    2.

    3.

When Abram asks God how he can know that he will possess the land, what does God tell Abram to do?

    1.

    2.

    3.

    4.

    5.

Abram brought all these animals to God and cut them in two. He laid each half opposite the other half, but he didn't cut the birds. The sun went down and Abram fell into a deep sleep. Terror and great darkness fell on him while he was sleeping. Then God spoke to him. What did God tell Abram?

    1.

    2.

3.

4.

5.

6.

After God spoke to Abram, a smoking oven and a flaming torch passed between the pieces of the animals. **Verse 18** says that it was the LORD Who made a Covenant with Abram on that day. Who do you think it might have been Who actually passed between the pieces of the animals?

5. Genesis 16
Now Sarai takes a turn at trying to get God to hurry up with fulfilling His promise. What is her plan?

What is the result of her plan, or should I ask "who" is the result of her plan?

6. Genesis 17:1-23
God reaffirms His Covenant promises to Abram once again. So once again, list what those promises were. Repetition will help you to remember them.

1.

2.

3.

4.

5.

6.

7.

8.

How old was Abram?

God now gives Abram a new name. What is it?

God also gives Abraham a new instruction. What is it?

God now gives Sarai a new name. What is it?

God then promises to bless Sarah. He promises that she will be a mother of nations and that kings of peoples will come from her. What is Abraham's response?

How old is Sarah?

Can you understand his response?

As is seemingly becoming a habit, Abraham decides to help God out in fulfilling His promise to him. What does Abraham suggest?

What is God's response to Abraham's new plan?

What does God promise concerning Ishmael?

Now God gives Abraham a date for the birth of his son from whom The Seed will come! When will Isaac be born?

What does Abraham do next?

READ AND REASON

1. Genesis 12-17; 22:17-18; 26:3-4; Galatians 3:8, 16
God made one special new nation out of all the nations He had just created in **Genesis 11**. He chose Abram to be the father of this new nation. He called Abram out of Ur of the Chaldeans to Haran and on to Canaan (Israel.) This new nation of people would eventually be called Israel. Abram, his son Isaac, and his grandson Jacob would be referred to as the "Fathers" of the nation of Israel.

2. Genesis 11:27-32; 15:7; Acts 7:1-4
God calls Abram from Ur of the Chaldeans. It is fascinating that God chose Abram to be the father of His new nation since Abram came from the area of the Chaldeans. The Chaldeans were the astrologers of Abram's time. Ur and Babylon are both in the region of the Chaldeans. **Joshua 24:2-3** informs us that Abram's father worshiped other gods.

Abram's father came as far as Haran and died there. God tells Abram to come aside from his family to the land which God would show him—the land of Canaan.

God tells Abram that He will make him into a great nation (Israel) and that He will bless him. Today, almost 4,000 years later, Israel is *still* a great nation. What other nation has been dispersed from its land for so many hundreds of years and still remains a nation? None!

God tells Abram that He will make Abram's name great and that he will be a blessing.

God promises Abram that in him all the families of the earth shall be blessed. How does God bless *all* the families of the earth in Abram? The promise of the New Covenant, Jesus Christ, comes through this Abrahamic Covenant. When a person enters into the New Covenant, by receiving Jesus as Lord and Savior (embracing all that He is), that person is blessed through the Abrahamic Covenant. That person literally becomes a child of Abraham! **(Galatians 3:29; Romans 2:28-29) Galatians 3:8** tells us that God was actually preaching the Gospel to Abraham when He said, *"All the nations shall be blessed in you."* People from all different nations will be blessed in Abraham. How? Only as they follow his example of faith and believe in The Seed. Then they are placed *in* The Seed (Christ) through faith and are blessed!

3. **Genesis 12:1-7**

What we have here is another promise of The Seed Who would bring redemption, this time showing us how God would use a nation to fulfill His promise. God is promising to save mankind through a nation. A nation from which would come The Seed, the Savior, that was promised earlier to Adam and Eve! The Seed of the woman (Eve) was going to come from Abram and bless all the families of the earth! (**Genesis 3:15**) **Galatians 3:16** tells us Who The Seed is → Jesus Christ of Nazareth!

God even promises to bless those who bless Abram (Israel) and curse those who curse Abram (Israel). Watch out, America! God has blessed us because we have blessed Israel. God will curse us if we curse Israel. If we don't stand on Israel's side, it will be a fatal mistake!

4. **Genesis 15**

God is making an Everlasting Covenant with Abram. He promises basically three things:

Land	**Genesis 15:7; Leviticus 25:23**
Descendants	**Genesis 15:5; 26:4**
Seed	**Genesis 15:1-4; 17:19; 22:17**

Abram believed in the LORD, and God saved him by counting his belief as righteousness! **Genesis 15:6; Galatians 3:5-9; John 8:56**

Abram wondered how God was going to fulfill His promise, so God cut a Covenant with him. **Genesis 15:8-21** A Covenant promise is the strongest promise that can be made. It is more binding than anything we know of today. Covenant can only be broken by death! Is everything that God *promised* would happen *going* to happen? *Yes!!! You can count on it!!!*

JOB

The book of Job was possibly written sometime during the time of the Patriarchs (Fathers of the nation of Israel—Abraham, Isaac, and Jacob).
Job perhaps lived sometime between the Flood and the time of the Fathers.
Job is an early book, but it is placed with other poetical books in the Bible.
The book shows the flawed search for the revelation of God's ways through circumstances. God reveals Himself at the end of the book and reproves the ones who do not respond rightly.

5. Genesis 16
Sarai wasn't willing to wait until God gave her a child to fulfill His promise. She took matters into her own hands. *Why is it we think we can come up with better ways than God's ways? Why do we think our ideas are better than God's?* So Sarai sends her husband, Abram, in to sleep with Hagar. The result was Ishmael.

6. Genesis 17:1-23
Abraham figures that Ishmael can be his heir to the promises of God. God has it planned differently. God says, *"No! Sarah will bear you a son and you shall call his name Isaac and I will establish My Covenant with him for an everlasting covenant for his descendants after him."* God promises to renew the Covenant with Isaac, Abraham's son.

It is at this time that God establishes the sign of the Covenant—circumcision. I think it is interesting to think about how specific the sign is in relation to the promise. In the promise God made to Noah, He gave the sign of the rainbow which would appear in the cloud. The promise had to do with rain and the sign had to do with rain. Here the promise has to do with the "Seed" and the sign, the Covenant cut of circumcision, is made on the body site closest to where The Seed would come from.

Later, God renews the Abrahamic Covenant with Isaac, Sarah and Abraham's son. Isaac has two sons, Esau and Jacob. God chooses Jacob to be the heir of Abraham's promises, not Esau, the eldest. **Romans 9:11-13** God changes Jacob's name to Israel and gives him a nation with land, descendants, and The Seed. God gives Jacob 12 sons. These are the 12 tribes of Jacob/Israel. The 12 tribes of Israel/12 sons of Jacob are the nation, Israel, which God made out of Abraham.

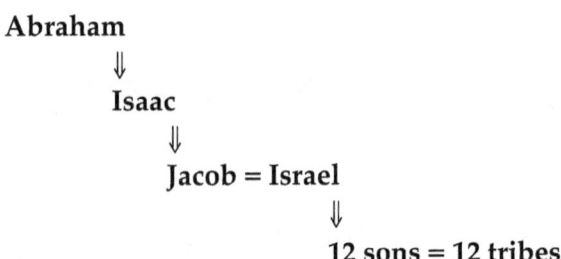

POINT OF DEPTH

In Genesis 17 God changes Abram's name to Abraham. Abram means "exalted father." Abraham means "father of a multitude." Abram was exalted to be the father of the line of The Seed, but Abraham would also be the father of a multitude of nations. Eventually people from every nation would believe in The Seed so as to be saved. This would make them the children of Abraham! **Romans 4:16; Galatians 3:7-9**

It is also significant to note that the Hebrew syllable that God added was a syllable out of God's Own personal Name, Jehovah. In Covenant, two people become one person. God is showing, by putting His Name into Abram's name, that the two of them are irrevocably joined. We still use this same ritual of Covenant when a man and woman are married. The woman takes the name of the husband.

POINT OF DEPTH

Did you know the Arabs come from Ishmael (Hagar and Abraham's son)? Arabs claim Abraham as their father too. You can see why they do, can't you?

Israel is in the news constantly. Israel is literally the most important nation on the face of the earth. It has been since the time of Abraham. It still is. It always will be. It is the most important because God has made it so! It is the land where God chose to put His Name! II Chronicles 6:5-7; Psalm 102:12-21

POINT OF DEPTH

Jacob's brother, Esau, was not chosen to be part of the ancestry of Jesus, The Seed. Esau's descendants became the Edomites. Edom is in the present day land of Jordan just southeast of Israel.

POINT OF DEPTH

Chapter 22 of Genesis is a prophetic picture of Jesus, The Seed.

God asks Abraham to make a burnt offering. Burnt offerings were voluntary. They were offerings of love. God asks Abraham to take his son, his only son whom he loves, and offer him on one of the mountains in the land of Moriah. Love is used for the first time in the Bible in this chapter. Genesis 22:2

- God took His Son, His only Son, whom He loved and offered Him on one of the mountains in the land of Moriah. John 3:16

From the time Abraham took his son and traveled to the place of the burnt offering, three days went by. Genesis 22:4

Lambs were held for three days before sacrificing them on the Passover.

- Jesus was held for three days before He was sacrificed as the Passover Lamb.
- Today the kind of sacrifice God wants from us is for us to offer our bodies as a living and holy sacrifice, pleasing to Him. Romans 12:1-2

Abraham told the young men with him that he and Isaac, his son, would go and worship on the mountain, and they both would return. Genesis 22:5 Worship is also used for the first time here. God was "worth" the offering that He asked for. Abraham worshiped God by acknowledging that God was worthy of the sacrifice of Abraham's son. Isaac worshiped God by acknowledging that God was worthy for him to give his own life as a sacrifice.

- God would sacrifice Jesus on the mountain, but He would raise Him again!
- Jesus Christ was worthy to be slain for the sins of all mankind.
- He is worthy for us to die to ourselves so that He may live His life through us.

Abraham told Isaac that God, Himself, would provide the lamb needed for the burnt offering. Genesis 22:7-8

- God is our Provider. He provided the Lamb Who would be slain for the sins of the world. God provided Jesus.

The word for "provide" is actually "see". Its meaning infers that if one sees a need, he will also make a provision to take care of that need. Abraham was reassuring Isaac that God saw that they would need a lamb, and of course, He would provide it for them.

- God saw all along that man needed a Savior. He made provision for that need before the foundation of the world!

Abraham named that place "Jehovah Jireh"—"the LORD will provide"; "in the mount of the LORD it will be provided." Genesis 22:14

- On that very mount, the LORD God provided a way of salvation for all mankind. God provided a Savior, His Own Son, Jesus the Christ!

God promised that in Abraham's seed all the nations of the earth would be blessed. Genesis 22:17-18

- God was promising Abraham that *in* THE SEED → JESUS all the nations of the earth would be blessed!

God also promised Abraham that his seed would possess the gate of their enemies.

- In the Hebrew language, however, the word for "seed" is singular and masculine, which means that the pronoun "their" should rightly be translated "his." i.e. Abraham's seed would possess the gate of HIS enemies. Hmmm…. God was promising Abraham that THE SEED → JESUS would possess the gate of all HIS enemies! The phrase "possessing the gate of your enemies" means that one has control over them.

The word "obey" is also used for the first time here in this chapter. Genesis 22:18 True worship *is* obedience. Abraham worshiped God because he obeyed God, and Abraham obeyed God because he worshiped Him!

- Once we believe in The Seed, we find ourselves able, for the first time, to obey God! Now His Spirit is inside of us, and we have a heart that wants to obey. We now have the desire and the ability!

58

HIStory Event 7
...GOD Sends His Nation, Israel, to a Foreign Land

Read and Observe

1. Genesis 15:13-14, 16
2. Genesis 3:15; 37; 39; 41:39-57; 42:1-2; 45:4-9; 49:8-12

Read and Answer

1. Genesis 15:13-14, 16
Before Abraham and his descendants would actually possess the land God was going to give to them, where must they go first?

For how long?

What would their situation be like while they were there?

What did God promise would be their situation when they would finally leave that land?

What did God promise concerning the nation that would hold Israel captive?

2. Genesis 3:15
What did God promise to mankind?

Genesis 37; 39; 41:39-57; 42:1-2
Read what God did to Joseph in order to preserve the lineage that The Seed was going to come through!

Genesis 45:4-9
Did Joseph's brothers sell him?

Were they supposed to be grieved or angry with themselves over what they did?

Why not?

Just so you won't miss it—Who was it who sent Joseph to Egypt—Joseph's brothers or God? The answer is stated three times—in three different verses! List which verses.

Why did God send Joseph to Egypt?

Do you see how Joseph's life was ordered the way it was *by God* for a purpose? Do you see God's purpose? Do you see how *everything* in the Bible is part of **HISTORY**?

Genesis 49:8-12
When Israel (Jacob) is dying, he gives a blessing to each of his sons. This passage is the blessing for his son, Judah. Judah is promised that his brothers will all bow down to him someday. God is identifying for us, and for the twelve sons of Israel, the line of The Seed! The Seed will come through the descendants of Judah.

Pay special attention to **verse 10**. "Until Shiloh comes" could be translated "until He comes to whom it belongs." This is another reference to the coming of The Seed!

Read and Reason

1. Genesis 15:13-14, 16
At that time God was making a nation out of the one man, Abraham, but God told Abraham that before he and his descendants possessed the land of Canaan forever they would be strangers in a foreign land. God told them they would be oppressed as slaves for 400 years. He also promised them, though, that after the 400 years of slavery, they would be freed and have much wealth. God also told them that He would punish the nation that had held Israel captive.

2. Genesis 3:15; 37; 39; 41:39-57; 42:1-2; 45:4-9; 49:8-12
God had promised a Seed, a Savior for all mankind, to Adam and Eve. God had chosen a very specific lineage for the Savior to come from. Abraham was part of that family line. Abraham's son was Isaac. Isaac's son was Jacob. Jacob had 12 sons. One of those sons was Judah. God chose the line of Judah to be the one to bring forth The Seed, Who would be named Jesus.

God knew He was intending to send a great famine on the land because of the iniquity of the peoples including the Amorites. **Genesis 15:16** However, God, many years earlier, made a Covenant with Abraham and He was going to keep it! God had to keep the family/nation of

Israel alive during this famine. Remember, God said in **Genesis 15:14** that they would indeed survive their 400 years of captivity.

Here's what God did. God chose Joseph, another one of Jacob's sons, to keep the family/nation of Israel alive and kicking. He sent Joseph down to Egypt ahead of time. God planned to raise Joseph up among the Egyptians so that when the time was ripe, He would bring Joseph's family on down to Egypt to be with him. There, God would provide food and sustenance for the entire 70-member family, which, by the way, would grow into a huge nation during their next 400 years.

God is Sovereign. What He said would happen *did happen* because He *made it happen*! While the rest of the world was dying of starvation, God nourished His chosen, special, precious ones → the Israelites! God used Joseph as a picture of the coming Savior. During the famine people in the known world were starving to death. Joseph wisely saved the grain so that in the time of the famine the life of Israel would be spared. People are starving spiritually and need the Bread of Life → Jesus!

Point of Depth

Did you wonder when I said that it was *God* Who sent Joseph down to Egypt? Did you think it was the ten "bad" brothers? Let's look at what God tells us in His Word. God says that it was He, Himself, Who sent Joseph to Egypt, not the ten brothers! Genesis 45:4-9 Read these verses carefully over and over, and let Truth sink deep inside of your heart. Let God carve His beautiful Word on your heart, never to be removed!

God is Sovereign! He <u>alone</u> is in control. Joseph's brothers thought they were in control, but they weren't. If it wasn't God's plan for Joseph to go to Egypt to spare the life of the nation of Israel, those ten evil brothers could not have sent him there even if they wanted to! It was God's plan all along!

God says in these six little verses that He alone was responsible for sending Joseph to Egypt! Notice, He says it not once, or twice, but three different times! Mark them in your Bible so you will notice them in the future!

And yet, were those brothers innocent in what they did? *No!!!* God held them accountable for their evil deeds.

Perhaps you are thinking, *"Well, God didn't plan it that way. He just took the evil that the brothers did and worked it out so that it brought about good!"* That's the way a lot of people like to look at things, but let's look closely at God's Word and see what He says. Read Genesis 50:18-20 Remember, we want to know Truth *more* than we want to be right! Truth is worth fighting for. It's worth dying for! If what we have believed about God is wrong, then as quickly as possible, let's lay it down and pick up Truth instead!!!

Look especially at verse 20. Joseph's brothers had a plan. They *meant evil* against Joseph. But God also had a plan. He *meant His plan* for good! The Hebrew word for "meant" means "to weave together." God didn't just take the deeds of Joseph's brothers and fix them. God had it planned His way all along!

In case you are still doubting, look at Psalm 105:16-24. Psalm 105 is an account of the history of Israel. Reading the whole chapter would be most helpful. Now look closely at verse 17. Who does it say *sent* Joseph to Egypt?

And God goes on to tell us what the purpose of His plan was. He tells us what He meant to accomplish when He *planned His plan*! It was to preserve many people alive! Who were those *"many people"*? They were God's precious chosen people, the Israelites. They were the family from which would come The Seed, the Savior, Jesus Christ of Nazareth!

God wisely reminds us of the Covenant promise He made to Abraham through Joseph in Genesis 50:24. You see, friend, the stories of the Bible are not simply a lot of different stories put together inside the cover of one book. The Bible is only one story → HIStory! He is gently and meticulously putting the pieces together for us if we will just listen to Him as He speaks to us in the Word of His Book!

POINT OF DEPTH

The Jews in Jesus' time claimed to be Abraham's children. The Jews in John 8:39 did not believe. They thought that they would receive the promises of the Abrahamic Covenant simply because they had been born into the lineage of Abraham. Galatians 3 and Romans 2 tell us otherwise! The true children of Abraham are those who are *in* Jesus Christ (having believed Him to be The Seed promised in Genesis 3:15 and having repented, bowed to Him as the LORD God!).

These Jews not only believed wrongly that they were children of Abraham, they claimed to be disciples of Moses. John 9:28 A disciple is one who adheres to what is being taught. They claimed to believe and follow what Moses taught. But what Moses taught was JESUS! And they would not believe in Jesus. Soooo... Jesus is showing them they weren't really disciples of Moses! Genesis 3:15, the first prophecy recorded about Jesus (The Seed and The Messiah), was actually written by Moses, yet they would not believe in Jesus. The reason they weren't true followers of Moses is because they weren't true believers in The Seed.

LORD, help us to be Your true disciples by truly, truly following You
—by believing Your WHOLE Bible!

We have to believe that what was written in the Old Testament is the same as what is written in the New Testament. John 5:45-47 Oh, there will be new things added, but just as certainly there will be old things repeated!

Oh, I don't want to be foolish and slow of heart! The entire Bible is needed in order for me to know what God wants me to know! Luke 24:25-27 Jesus told the men on the road to Emmaus that the Old Testament talked about Him.

You see, it's only one story → HISTORY!

LORD, help us to search the Scriptures.
Give us ears to hear.
Open our eyes that we may behold wonderful things from Your Word.
Open our minds to understand Your Story.
Explain what You have said to us!

POINT OF CONNECTION

Let's look at the words "*take care of you*" in Genesis 50:24. A literal translation could be "*visit*." I'm glad the translators of the New American Standard Bible interpreted it as "take care of you." They were right in doing so. You see, the word "visit" has lost its original import. We no longer realize the full impact of its meaning.

Let's look at a few cross-references to see what this verse is really saying.

Luke 7:16 "Fear gripped them all, and they began glorifying God, saying, 'A great prophet has arisen among us!' and 'God has *visited* (cared for) His people!'"

> Jesus raised a dead man from a coffin. He was the only son of his mother, and she was a widow. She would now have no one to take care of her. Her husband was dead. Now her son was dead. Jesus felt compassion for her because she had a great need. Jesus took care of that need by bringing her son back to life so he could take care of her. That's why the people cried out that God had visited His people. They recognized that God Himself sent Jesus to take care of them. They just didn't understand what their need really was!
>
> By the way, who was it that Jesus was sent to take care of? The lost sheep of the house of Israel! **Matthew 15:24**

James 1:27 "Pure and undefiled religion in the sight of *our* God and Father is this: to *visit* orphans and widows in their distress, and to keep oneself unstained by the world."

You can see that to "visit" is not simply to stop in and chat awhile with someone. It means "<u>to take care of the needs of someone</u>." To visit orphans and widows in their distress means to be responsible for their well being in the middle of their plight! True and undefiled religion is just that! To quickly say *"Hello!"* to someone who is in need, rather than stop whatever it is you're doing and take care of that need, is *defiled* religion!

I Peter 2:12 "Keep your behavior excellent among the Gentiles, so that in the thing in which they slander you as evildoers, they may because of your good deeds, as they observe *them,* glorify God in the <u>day of visitation</u>."

When Jesus comes again, it will be to take care of all that remains to be accomplished in God's plan to bring Glory to Himself. Sin will be abolished completely. All of God's enemies will be no more. His chosen people will be with Him forever!

Exodus 3:16 "Go and gather the elders of Israel together and say to them, 'The LORD, the God of your fathers, the God of Abraham, Isaac, and Jacob, has appeared to me, saying, "<u>I am indeed concerned</u> about you and what has been done to you in Egypt."'"

Here, the phrase "I am indeed concerned about" is the same word as "visiting" or "I have visited." To truly visit someone or to truly be concerned about someone will not leave you in neutral. You have to act! You have to do something!

By the way → You will see the phrase "The LORD, the God of your fathers, the God of Abraham, Isaac, and Jacob" throughout the Bible. Are you beginning to see what that phrase is referring to? Abraham was chosen by God to be the first person in a brand new nation that God was going to create. He gave Abraham a son called Isaac. Isaac had a son called Jacob. God changed Jacob's name to Israel. Jacob/Israel was the father of 12 sons. Those 12 sons of Jacob/Israel would produce sons. Those sons, the grandsons of Jacob/Israel, were divided into 12 different groups, according to their fathers. Each group was eventually called one of the tribes of Israel, God's chosen people!

This may seem pretty basic to some of you, but I want to point it out anyway because of my own background. I thought that there was this nation on earth called Israel just waiting for God to choose it for Himself. I didn't understand that there *was no nation* of Israel! There were only "the nations" that God had created back in **Genesis 11**. God didn't pick one of them and call them "Israel." No. Instead, God chose one man <u>out</u> of all those nations, Abram, and gave him descendants and built him into a nation → the nation of Israel! I have had student after student through the years come to me and tell me (after listening to teaching on the history of Israel or God's timeline) that a "light bulb" went off while they were listening and they realized they hadn't understood this either. They didn't know who the Israelites really were other than a group of people in the Old Testament that God talked about a lot!

Exodus 4:31 "So the people believed; and when they heard that the LORD <u>was concerned</u> about the sons of Israel and that He had seen their affliction, then they bowed low and worshiped."

By now, can you guess what word was translated "was concerned?" That's right. It's the word for "had visited"! God was truly concerned about His people. He acted. He set them free from slavery. Can you see the beautiful picture of what God does for us?

Luke 19:44 "and they will level you to the ground and your children within you, and they will not leave in you one stone upon another, <u>because you did not recognize the time of your visitation</u>."

Who is Jesus' audience here? It was the Jews. Another name for them would be the nation of Israel!

What was the time of their visitation that they didn't recognize? It was the time when The Seed, the Savior, Jesus of Nazareth, was among them. He wanted to save them, to care for them, to take care of their need → salvation! But they would not have it!

Matthew 23:37 "Jerusalem, Jerusalem, who kills the prophets and stones those who are sent to her! How often <u>*I wanted to gather your children together*</u>, the way a hen gathers her chicks under her wings, and you were unwilling."

Let's reason together here a little. What was Jesus referring to when He said He wanted to gather Israel together the way a hen gathers her chicks under her wings?

Well, let's look at the way a hen gathers her chicks. The mother hen takes those poor little chicks, helpless in and of themselves, and covers them with her own body for their protection, rest, warmth, nourishment, and well-being.

Do you see the connection? Jesus came to *"visit"* the Jews…

…to protect them… They were condemned because of their sin. They needed to be protected from the wrath of God and from themselves. But they were not willing…

…to give them rest and warmth… The Jews strove so very hard to be pleasing to God. They even added laws to make themselves more holy. What they needed was to rest from their own works and let Jesus live His life through them. He wanted to give them rest. But they were not willing…

…to nourish them… They were starving for spiritual food. He was the Bread of Life! He was the True food! He came to give them Himself. They refused to eat of Him. They were not willing…

…to take care of their well being… Oh, how they needed Him! They needed Him for direction, for protection, for salvation, for righteousness, for sanctification, for justification, for everything. But they were not willing…

The Jews have a phrase which is similar to Jesus'. The phrase is to "come under the wings of the Shekinah." If only they had not resisted the truth that Jesus Himself was the Shekinah!

POINT OF DEPTH

The word "Shekinah" comes from a root that means "to dwell." The same root is also the derivative of the word "tabernacle." It refers to the visible manifestation of God Himself over the Mercy Seat in the Tabernacle where God dwelt with His people. "Doxa," the New Testament Greek word for glory, and "kabod," the Old Testament Hebrew word for glory, both are used interchangeably with Shekinah in post-biblical times.

HIStory Event 8
...GOD Delivers Israel

Exodus

The Nation of Israel has been living in Egypt for 430 years;
the last 400 of which, the Israelites have been slaves.
Exodus means "going out" and is the record of Israel's "going out" from Egypt.
God delivers His people, Israel, by His Mighty Right Hand!

Be careful! What may seem like familiar individual stories i.e. the 10 plagues, the parting of the Red Sea, the 10 Commandments, or the golden calf...
actually are all parts of just one story—HIStory!

Read and Observe

1. Genesis 15:13-16; Exodus 1:5-14; 12:35-37, 40-41; Genesis 45:9-11; 47:27-28
2. Exodus 2:11; Acts 7:22-25
3. Exodus 12:1-14; I Corinthians 5:7; Hebrews 9:28; Mark 14:12; I Peter 1:18-19
4. Exodus 12:31; 13:17-22
5. Exodus 14

Read and Answer

1. Genesis 15:13-16
When God made His Covenant promise to Abram, what did He tell him to know for certain?

   1.

   2.

   3.

4.

5.

6.

7.

8.

Exodus 1:7
The sons of Israel were the descendants of whom? Remember who the fathers were.

Exodus 1:8-12
Did Abraham's descendants go into a land that was not theirs as promised by God in **Genesis 15:13**?

What happened to them while they were there?

Exodus 12:35-37, 40-41; Exodus 1:9, 12
Were Abraham's descendants oppressed and enslaved in a land that was not theirs for 400 years?

Did Abraham's descendants come out of a land that was not theirs with many possessions?

What about the extra 30 years? Was God's promise 30 years late?

When Joseph brought his family down to Egypt to save them from the famine, how many were in the family?

What had God's promise been to Abraham concerning the number of his descendants? Did He fulfill His promise—how does the Bible describe the number of Israelites that left Egypt?

Genesis 45:9-11; 47:27-28; Exodus 1:5-14
Can you think of a reason that would account for the extra 30 years?

2. **Exodus 2:11; Acts 7:22-25**
Joseph was a picture of The Seed Who would someday come and deliver God's chosen people. Who else was a "type" of deliverer?

Did Moses know that he was an Israelite?

Why did he strike the Egyptian?

Did he think the rest of the Israelites would know why he did it?

3. **Exodus 12:1-14**
Our yearly calendar starts in January. Did God give the Israelites the same calendar that we use? Did anyone, any nation at all, have the same calendar as the Israelites?

What were they to do during the first month?

On which day of the month were they to take a lamb?

How long were they to keep it?

What were they to do to the lamb on the fourteenth day of that first month in their yearly calendar?

What were they to do with some of the blood of the lamb?

What were they to do with the lamb itself?

If they obeyed God and did as He instructed, from what would they be spared?

What would happen to those who did not obey God?

Was this a one-time event? Would the Israelites ever be required to do this again?

Why were they to do it year after year even after they had been delivered from Egypt?

I Corinthians 5:7; Hebrews 9:28; Mark 14:12; I Peter 1:18-19
This lamb that was killed by the Israelites was the lamb required for the Passover. Just as Moses was a "type" of deliverer, the lamb was a "type" of sacrifice. (Not the real thing but a picture or shadow of the real.) Moses was a picture of The Seed Who would deliver mankind from death. Of Whom was the lamb a type?

Can you see that as the Israelites celebrated Passover each year they were reminded over and over again of The Seed that had been promised to their ancestors but was still to come? They were given a picture of that Seed and what He would do for them.

4. Exodus 12:31; 13:17-22
When God delivered His people from Egypt after 400 years of slavery, did He leave them to lead their own lives? Who led them every step of the way?

5. Exodus 14
Read this familiar story but look for the answers to these questions. You saw that God was leading the Israelites step by step as they left Egypt. But to the Egyptians it would appear that the Israelites were simply wandering aimlessly about. Why did God lead them in such a strange manner? Remember God always has a purpose!

Why did God harden Pharaoh's heart?

Do *you* know that God is the LORD?

What was the result of the Israelites seeing the great power which the LORD used against the Egyptians?

Do *you* fear the LORD?

Do *you* believe in the LORD?

READ AND REASON

1. Genesis 15:13-16; Exodus 1:5-14; 12:35-37, 40-41; Genesis 45:9-11; 47:27-28
God promised that the Israelites would go to a strange land (Egypt) and spend 400 years there. His promise to deliver them from that slavery and *bring them back* to the land was no less as sure. When the time was up (to the very day, I might add), they came out of that foreign land! Exodus means "going out." God's people were going out of bondage from Egypt.

God told Abraham that He would multiply his descendants; His descendants would become the nation of Israel. Did God ever multiply them!!! It is estimated that 1-7 million people came *out of* Egypt after their 430 years there! Remember, there were only 70 Israelites, the sons of Jacob/Israel, that came *into* Egypt. God began with just one man, Jacob's grandfather, Abraham!

2. Exodus 2:11; Acts 7:22-25
Joseph was a picture of the Deliverer because God used him to save the nation of Israel from starvation during the famine. Moses was also a type of deliverer. God used him to deliver His people, Israel, out of Egypt after God's plagues. Moses was right that he was to be the deliverer of God's people, Israel, from Egypt, but he was wrong on the timing and means. Jesus, however, being the reality and not just the type or shadow, performed the will of the Father perfectly. He delivered His people out of their sin at the exact appointed time. Oh, how wonderful He is!

POINT OF DEPTH

Joseph and Moses were both foreshadows of the Deliverer, The Seed. A foreshadow is a <u>shadow</u> that goes <u>before</u> the real thing! In other words, the real thing cannot be seen yet, only its shadow is in view.

Usually when I see a shadow, I see the real object at the same time. When light comes into my living room through our bay window and casts a shadow of one of my chairs onto the floor, I know right away what the shadow is a picture of because I can see the chair it is imitating.

But have you ever been sitting somewhere and saw a shadow approach you? If you couldn't see where that shadow was coming from you would probably pay close attention to it, either from curiosity or from fear. Finally, as it approached, it would come into view and you would see the reality, no longer just its shadow.

That is what God does—<u>His light casts shadows of The Seed for us in the Old Testament</u>. He didn't necessarily allow people to see the substance of that shadow. They saw an imperfect form of the real thing. For instance, the Tabernacle was a foreshadow of the New Covenant to come, a picture of The Seed. If His people would look intently at the shadow though, they would be able to see the Christ.

GOD'S LIGHT casts shadows of THE SEED for us in the Old Testament.

Foreshadow	Reality	GOD'S LIGHT
Shadow came first	THE SEED	ETERNAL LIFE
Old Testament	New Testament	ALL OF ETERNITY

3. Exodus 12:1-14; I Corinthians 5:7; Hebrews 9:28; Mark 14:12; I Peter 1:18-19
New life → New calendar! God was delivering the people from their bondage and giving them a new life. Here God inaugurates the Passover and a new calendar for Israel. Israel would have its very own 12 months, and Nisan, the month in which Passover would be forever celebrated, would be its first. (Nisan is its Babylonian name while Abib is the ancient Canaanite name.) Passover is one of the greatest pictures God gave us of what it is like to be redeemed. It is an actual "type" of the Gospel.

On the night that the Israelites were to be delivered from bondage, they were to kill a lamb and put its blood on the two doorposts of their homes. God was going to send His destroyer through the land of Egypt that night and strike down the firstborn of men and beast and execute judgment against all the gods of Egypt. But as God went through the land, He looked at each house—if He saw the blood of the lamb, the household inside was safe from His judgment. Everyone deserved to be destroyed—yet He spared some.

May I ask you this right now?
Is the blood of the Lamb on you? Are you safe from the wrath that is to come?
The Lamb is Jesus. His blood has been shed.

The wages of sin is death. **Romans 6:23** Sin requires, even demands, death! We have all sinned, each one of us. Jesus paid the demand of sin with His Own death rather than ours. If you will quit trying to achieve your own righteousness and accept the righteousness of Jesus Christ instead, if you will apply the blood of the Lord Jesus Christ over your life, you too, can be delivered from bondage—bondage to sin and death!

4. Exodus 12:31; 13:17-22

Well, it was time for God's people to leave. God delivered them and they left the land of Egypt. When they left, they didn't leave without direction. God would guide them with a pillar of cloud by day and a pillar of fire by night. He, as usual, had a very specific plan for them. But remember, it's not just another story. It's part of one story → **HIStory**!

5. Exodus 14

Even in the deliverance from Egypt, God made sure He received plenty of Glory. He wanted to be honored by the Egyptians so He hardened Pharaoh's heart one last time to make him chase after the Israelites. You see, God had a really big display of His Glory planned at the Red Sea and He wanted the Egyptians to see it! It was a "show" of Who God really was. He wanted the Egyptians to know that He was the Lord! God was their Owner and Master. They were *His* slaves!

Pharaoh followed the Israelites. Moses said, "*Stand back and see the salvation (deliverance) of the Lord.*" God parted the Sea. The Israelites crossed over. Pharaoh followed again and said, "*They are not leaving.*" God said, "*I have a plan for them. They are leaving!*" Before Pharaoh sank, he most certainly learned the lesson that *God* was the Lord!!!

POINT OF CONNECTION

Just a real quick reminder here. We are following the history of the Israelites for one reason only. The Israelites are the people from whom The Seed would come. The Seed was promised in Genesis 3:15 and The Seed would be the Savior of all who would believe.

Again, I am reminded of what thinking processes I experienced growing up in church. I thought that the Israelites were just a group of people whom God picked out of all the other peoples on the earth (for whatever reason) and the Old Testament was just a lot of stories about these people. Rather, the Bible is the story of how God will bring Himself His rightful Glory by saving men through His Son, The Seed. He promises The Seed in the beginning of the Bible and follows the family tree (the Israelites) of The Seed to come.

I know it seems strange that I, or anyone, could miss such a basic understanding of the Bible. But I did. And I was very involved in the church and very knowledgeable about the stories in the Bible. I missed it because Satan had blinded my eyes. God opened my eyes one glorious day, and I was saved by The Seed!

I know of many, many others who were blinded just as I was. And I know of countless others who are still blinded. It is the plain, simple story of the Gospel that opens their eyes to Truth. The power of salvation is in the Gospel itself. So please bear with me as I relate the Gospel over and over again.

Most who are blinded do not know they are blind. I pray that as they read this study material from God's Word it will pierce any darkness surrounding them.

May God Give the Faith to Believe…
May He Open the Eyes of the Blind…

HIStory Event 9
...GOD Gives His Law to Israel

79

Leviticus, Numbers and **Deuteronomy** cover the period between Israel's deliverance from Egypt under the leadership of Moses and Israel's conquest of Canaan under the leadership of Joshua.

LEVITICUS

The book of Leviticus covers only one month. The Israelites had taken one year to build the Tabernacle in which they would worship their God. Now, for the next month, the Levitical priests would learn how to serve their God and His people using His Tabernacle. God redeemed His people from Egypt back in Exodus; now He was their King and they needed to obey Him. They were to worship Him in the way He commanded and live a life that was holy unto Him.
His ways bring Him Glory!

NUMBERS

The book of Numbers begins one month after the end of the book of Exodus.
The Israelites went up to the land of Canaan,
but refused to enter it because of fear, so God gives the punishment.
Numbers then shows the record of Israel's 40 years of journeying and learning.
The road they traveled was long and hard—so were the lessons they learned.

DEUTERONOMY

The Israelites have been wandering for 40 years and are finally encamped in Moab, right across the Jordan River from their final destination, the Promised Land of Canaan (Israel). The book of Deuteronomy covers the giving of the Law one more time before the Israelites go into the land of Canaan.
In fact, it is called the second giving of the Law.

Read and Observe

1. Exodus 19:5-6; Matthew 5:13-16; Isaiah 42:6; 49:6; Acts 13:47
2. Exodus 20; Deuteronomy 4:10; 5:29; 6:24; 17:12-13; Proverbs 16:6
3. Exodus 24; 25:8; Hebrews 8:5; Revelation 21:22
4. Exodus 32
5. Numbers 13:1-3, 17-33; 14:6-10, 26-39
6. Deuteronomy 28:1-15, 58-66

Read and Answer

1. Exodus 19:5-6; Matthew 5:13-16; Isaiah 42:6; 49:6; Acts 13:47
What purpose did God have for the Israelite nation to be His Own possession among all the peoples of the earth?

    1.

    2.

By the way, Who owns the earth?

The word "priest" means "a bridge-builder to God." So what is the responsibility of being made a kingdom of priests?

Holy means "set apart to, different than, so different that it is awesome." So what is the implication of being a holy nation?

Think back to when God formed the nations. Was Israel one of those nations? Or did God form Israel by taking one man out of one of those nations and making that one solitary man into a whole new nation?

Since God wanted the Israelites to be a light to the nations, what do you think He wanted the nations to see?

If the nations saw what God wanted them to see, what would be the inevitable result?

2. Exodus 20
How was God going to accomplish His purpose for the Israelites to be a light to the rest of the nations?

What was God going to use to keep the Israelites from sinning?

Deuteronomy 4:10
What were the people supposed to remember forever?

Why were they to remember that day?

When the people remembered the terrible voice and words of God, what would be their reaction?

What would they do because they feared God all the days of their lives?

Deuteronomy 5:29
If the people would fear God and keep His commandments, what would their lives be like?

Would their lives then be what God wanted—a light to the nations?

What was the one thing they lacked in order to completely fear God and keep His commandments?

Deuteronomy 6:24
What did God command His people to do?

      1.

      2.

Why were they to fear the LORD their God?

    1.

    2.

Deuteronomy 17:12-13
What would happen to the man who disobeyed God presumptuously?

What would be the result of that man being killed?

    1.

    2

    3.

    4.

Proverbs 16:6
What keeps people away from evil?

3. Exodus 24
God told Moses to come up to Him and worship Him at a distance with Aaron, Nadab, Abihu, and 70 of the elders of Israel. Moses alone was to come near to the LORD. Moses then came and recounted to all the people what God had said to him. Basically, God had given Moses a set of rules for the people of Israel to follow and obey. This was because they were now a nation which needed to follow and obey its King and God! How did the people respond?

Then Moses wrote down all that God had said to him. What did he do the next morning?

What did the young men do on the altar that Moses built?

What did Moses do with half of the blood from the offerings?

What did Moses do with the other half?

What did Moses do next?

Did the people respond any differently this time?

What did Moses do next with the blood?

What did he say when he sprinkled it on the people?

Moses ate a Covenant meal with Aaron, Nadab, Abihu, and 70 of the elders of Israel when they saw God. This was a ritual to enforce the impact of the people's commitment to the agreement they had made with God. What did God do next?

What did God give Moses on the mountain?

How long was Moses on the mountain with God?

What covered the mountain during that time?

What was resting on the mountain during that time?

What did the appearance of the Glory of the LORD look like to the Israelites from their vantage point at the bottom of the mountain?

Exodus 25:8
What did God tell the Israelites to do for Him?

Why?

Hebrews 8:5
How did they know exactly how to build it?

4. **Exodus 32**
What happens in Israel's camp while Moses is on the mountain with God?

Who led the people out of Egypt?

Who do the people say led them out?

Who is the LORD their God?

What do the people worship as the LORD their God?

5. **Numbers 13:1-3**
What was God going to give the descendants of Abraham?

What did God tell Moses to do?

Who exactly was he to send?

Numbers 13:17-33
Did Moses obey God?

List what the spies were supposed to find out.

What did the spies find in the land?

Who did the spies find in the land?

What was their report like when they came back?

Caleb, one of the spies who had returned from the spy mission, encouraged the people to take possession of the land. What about the men who had gone up with him? What was their opinion?

Of what exactly were they afraid?

Numbers 14:6-10
Who else agreed with Caleb?

In Whom was Caleb and Joshua's faith?

Since the other men were afraid of the people in the land, in whom was their faith?

To whom did the people listen?

Numbers 14:26-39
What would be the result of the people refusing to obey God? That is, to go in and take the land He wanted to give them.

Would anyone ever be able to enter the land?

Who?

How did God choose the number of years that they would wander?

What about the ten spies who encouraged Israel to not believe God—what happened to them?

What was so important about this land? Reason with me for a moment. What had God promised to mankind when Adam and Eve sinned?

From whom would this Seed come?

After Eve, God delineated the bloodline that would bring The Seed for us to see. He showed us that Noah's descendants would produce The Seed. After Noah, who did God specifically show us would carry the line of The Seed?

What else did God promise Abraham?

Where would The Seed be born, live, grow up, and speak to God's people? Where would He suffer, die for the many, and be raised to life having an abundance of witnesses? From where would He ascend to heaven?

The Seed will eventually return and *rule the world from Jerusalem*. Do you see what is so important about this land?

6. Deuteronomy 28:1-14
Forty years pass in the wilderness and Moses rereads all the commandments of the Covenant that Israel had cut with God forty years earlier. The people are once again reminded of what God expects of them. What do the Israelites need to do in order to receive the blessings God lists here?

Deuteronomy 28:15, 58-66
If the Israelites receive the curses listed here, what can you know they most certainly have done?

Read and Reason

1. Exodus 19:5-6; Matthew 5:13-16; Isaiah 42:6; 49:6; Acts 13:47
Three months to the day that the Israelites came out of Egypt, they came into the wilderness of Sinai. There, God would give them the Law. The Law was to separate the nation of Israel from the lifestyle of all the other nations in the world. Israel's lifestyle was to be so different from the rest of the world that the world would sit up and take notice! The walk of their lives was to show Who God really was! He was a Holy God! They were to be a holy people! They were God's

people! They were to be the light that showed the Gentile nations how to approach God! They were to be God's city on a high hill shining so brightly that no one could miss seeing it!

POINT OF DEPTH

Holy is such a "churchy" word that sometimes we say it without really understanding what it means. God says we are to be holy, even as He is Holy. Leviticus 11:44-45 If we are supposed to be holy, then, by all means let's make sure we know what it means.

Holy is used in 580 verses in the Bible. The Greek word is "hagios." It means "an awful thing, consecrated, set apart, a saint." It has to do with something being totally different from everything else around it. God is Holy. He is consecrated unto Himself. He is set apart unto Himself. He is awful.

You're probably saying, "Wait a minute! God isn't awful! God is Love!!!"

I would answer you, "*God is awe-full!*" Let's look at His Word together in several passages, and then maybe you will see what I am trying to show you.

The first time we see the word "holy" is on Mt. Horeb, the mountain of God, where the angel of the LORD appeared to Moses in a blazing fire from the middle of a bush. Exodus 3:1-5 Fire consumes—the bush was definitely on fire, yet it was not being consumed. Moses saw something that just didn't make sense. He turned aside to see it more closely, but God told him not to come any nearer. God told Moses to take off his shoes because he was on holy ground.

In this first exposure to the word "holy" we see two aspects of its meaning. First of all, holy means to be *awful* or *awe-full*. It means to be full of awe! Moses was full of awe when he saw the bush. It was more than mere idle curiosity about a nonchalant event in the desert. Moses called it a *marvelous* sight!

Secondly, we see that the bush was *unique to itself*. There were lots of bushes in the desert, but none like this bush. Moses had probably seen hundreds of fires, but never one like this fire. This bush couldn't be categorized with any others. It was in a class all by itself. That made it holy!

You see, it was set apart from all others. *More importantly, it was set apart unto something! It was set apart unto God.* God was in that little corner of the desert right then, and nothing else could enter unless it, too, was holy—unless it was set apart *unto* God.

Let's look at one of the aspects of holiness: the aspect of being set apart *unto* God. Read these passages and notice the phrases "to be Mine" and "for My possession." Leviticus 20:26; 21:7-8; Deuteronomy 7:6; 14:2; Ephesians 1:4; I Peter 1:15-16

God commands His people to be holy. Why? Because He is Holy! He is set apart unto Himself, and we cannot be with Him unless we are holy. Otherwise we will make Him unholy! And that just is not going to happen!

God clearly defines holiness for us in Leviticus 20:26. To be holy is not just to be separated from the world. That alone does not make us holy. We are separated from the peoples *to be His*!

I use a simple illustration in my classes. Since I use whiteboards to teach from, I usually have a whole set of colored whiteboard markers in my desk. I take them out and lay them on the top of the desk so the whole class can see them: purple, blue, green, red, black, yellow, brown, and orange. They are a set.

Then I pick up one of them, let's say the yellow one. I give it to one of my students. Now there are seven markers in one group on the desk, and one yellow marker all by itself in the hand of a student.

Does that make the yellow one holy? Not completely. Does that make the yellow one holy unto me? No, not at all. Simply being separated *from* the other markers does not make the yellow marker holy unto me. It can be set apart from the other markers and still not be useful to me at all. It is not available for me. Rather, it has been set apart unto one of my students.

As the illustration demonstrates, separating the yellow marker from the others did not set it apart for my use, and neither does separating oneself from the ways of the world set a person apart for God's use. You see, to be holy is to be set apart unto God, for His use alone. Many people think they will give up the ways of the world and that will make them holy. Wrong! As long as they live for themselves, no matter how "good" they are, they are not holy unto God.

Let's look at a couple of verses that show us the other part of the definition of "holy." The part that means He is awful. Psalm 111:9-10; Isaiah 29:23

Let me give an illustration that might help you understand this idea. Just imagine you are the witness of a horrible car accident. You hear the screeching of tires, the blare of a horn, followed by a piercing scream from one of the passengers. You find out in moments that one of the victims is dead and the others are injured critically. You would agree with me, wouldn't you, that an accident like that would be a terrible thing to witness?

Would you, however, agree with me that an accident like that would be an awesome thing as well? Perhaps you wouldn't; but you should because terrible and awesome are cousins!

The original meaning of awe is to be "full of fear." To "be in awe" is "to stand in fear." Over the years, although the definition may have stayed the same, the connotation has changed. In the present time the connotation for something being awesome is that it is "cool!" or "great!" But when God wrote His Word that is not what it meant. Awesome meant just that—full of awe, full of fear. He is so different from anything that we know or can imagine!

God is awesome! God is to be feared! God isn't just a "really cool God!" He is to be marveled at, for sure, but not without inspiring a deep reverential fear inside of you. So when I say that God is *awful*, I mean it! He is full of awe! And Who He is should produce a fear of Him in you.

God said that in the New Covenant we will know Him. If we truly know God, then we will revere Him in respect and fear. He is awesome and terrible and fearful. We will fear disobeying Him!

If we are afraid to disobey Him, then we will do His bidding and the result will be our own holiness! We will be holy because we will be set apart to Him. The world is set apart to itself, so we will be different from the world and the world will notice our holiness!

Point of Depth

God is Holy and man needs to be holy, but can things be holy? Yes. Holy gifts are those that are dedicated to the LORD. Leviticus 22:2-3 They are set apart unto Him. They are wholly devoted to Him. Sometimes we think of holy gifts as those that are perfect and good enough for Him. And although it is true that the gifts that are given to God should indeed be worthy of Him, and of the highest quality for Him, that isn't what makes them holy. What makes them holy is the fact that they are set apart for Him. They are devoted to Him.

Someday every single thing will be holy unto God! Everything will be set apart for God's use alone. Zechariah 14:20-21

Most likely everyone who lives in your house has his own bed. Your bed is holy unto you. It is reserved for your use. Right now, although everything truly belongs to God, it is not set apart or reserved for His use. It should be, but it's not! But during the Millennial Reign of Christ *everything* will be holy to the LORD. Not just the important items like the altar in His Temple, but even the seemingly most unimportant items like pots that are used for cooking!

Every single thing will have one purpose only. That purpose is to be used *by* God and *for* God! Can you imagine? Oh, how I wish it were that way now! I wish everyone's cars were only used for God. I wish everyone's money was only used for God. I wish everyone's time was only used for God. Think of what it would be like to be in a world where every single thing existed only to be used for God! What a different (HOLY) world we would be in!

POINT OF DEPTH

A phrase that is used many times in God's Word is "under the ban." Have you ever noticed it? If something is put under the ban, it is devoted wholly to the LORD. It may not be redeemed or sold. It is devoted to destruction; whether it is actually destroyed or not, it is unavailable to man. In other words, it is most *holy* to the LORD. It is set apart for Him and for no other purpose. It is a sacrifice to Him with no strings attached. Leviticus 27:28-29; Deuteronomy 7:26; Joshua 6:17-18; 7; 22:20

Years ago our ministry had a garage sale. We needed a bathroom in our little farmhouse classroom and we needed the money to build it, so we decided to have a garage sale! That way, everyone could be involved!

God impressed upon me one night that we needed to put everything that was being donated to the garage sale under the ban. I thought, "Okay, God," but I didn't completely understand His great wisdom until later. I told my husband what I thought I heard the LORD telling me while I was reading His Word and he agreed. So we announced that all donations were to be put under the ban. In other words, none of us were allowed to buy what someone else brought. If we had money to do that, then we had money just to donate—whether it was ten dollars or ten cents!

Once we announced it, I saw what God had seen in our hearts all along. Instantly there was a small contingency of grumbling. Aughhh!!! *"What if we see something at the garage sale that we need?" "Wouldn't I be a bad steward to go and spend more for it somewhere else?" "What if no one wants to pay enough for something I bring? I only want to donate it if it brings a certain amount."* Oh, my heart was racing! I could see the dross that needed to come out of this crowd!!! And God could see the dross that needed to come out of my own heart!

You see, in the Midwest, garage sales are big business. In fact, people brag about what they get at garage sales and how cheaply they get it! I say "they," but I have done the very same thing! It somehow feeds our egos—as if we think we are so very clever in how we meet our family's needs!

Wait! Isn't God our Provider? Isn't God Jehovah-Jireh, the God Who provides? Isn't He the One Who meets our family's needs? Yes, He is! And He showed us that He didn't need any "garage sale super deals" to take care of His children!

I am so grateful God protected us from our own greed. The first night that donations started rolling in, I saw great looking baskets and wooden decorating items being hauled down to the basement for storage. That's when I felt as if God would say, *"Sharon, these are under the ban. They are all devoted to Me. If you have $3.00 to buy that basket, then you have $3.00 to give to Me without receiving anything for it."* I knew He would be right. And I was glad He had planned ahead to keep my flesh in check!

Now, I am not trying to teach anyone that all garage sales should be put under the ban. Not at all! But it sure was a great teaching lesson for our ministry. It showed us we had strings attached to our material items that shouldn't be there!

Make sure, though, that whatever you put under the ban, whatever you devote to the LORD is *truly under* the ban! Don't rashly make a vow and then back out of it! Joshua 7:11 To take back part of what you have devoted to the LORD is stealing and deceiving!

One time my boys and husband decided to give up watching sports on television for one month. They were going to limit themselves to one game per week. For them, at the time, this was quite a reduction! Their purpose was to do it for the LORD. They had been taking His time and squandering it. They wanted to give that time back to God. I reminded them of the teaching of putting something under the ban and asked them to make sure they didn't try and redeem some of that time by watching a "really important" game that might come up. They couldn't steal back from the LORD what they had given to Him even if it was a television show! (By the way, that time without a TV turned into a whole new lifestyle for our family—no TV at all! And we have never looked back!)

We must also practice putting the desires of our flesh under the ban, along with all disobedience to the prompting of the Spirit. Our hearts must be wholly devoted to God. I Kings 8:61; 11:4 If our hearts want to do things our way, rather than God's way, they are not wholly devoted to Him. That's exactly what God does for us when we are saved. He gives us a new heart, one that is wholly devoted to Him, one that desires to obey Him. Thank You, God, for putting our hearts under the ban.

2. **Exodus 20; Deuteronomy 4:10; 5:29; 6:24; 17:12-13; Proverbs 16:6**
God gave His moral laws to the people of Israel. We call them the Ten Commandments. He offered to cut Covenant with them. They would agree to enter into Covenant with Him. Sadly, they would never keep that Covenant. They couldn't—they had an evil heart that would not let them. **Deuteronomy 5:29** They would sin and He would have to curse them. God would keep His Covenant agreement with them.

However, God did something to help them keep the Covenant they would make with Him. Look at **Exodus 20:18-20**. *God terrified them!* He showed Himself awesome in their eyes. God came to them with thunder and lightning flashes, the sound of the trumpet and a smoking mountain! He frightened them in order that the *fear of Him* would remain with them. He wanted the fear of Him to remain with them because it would help keep them from sinning!

In **Deuteronomy 17:12-13**, we see that same principle at work. God said that the man who acts presumptuously by not listening to the priest or the judge who serves the LORD God must die. The immediate result would be purging the evil from Israel. The longer-term result would be that the people would finally listen and hear and be afraid. Being afraid would help keep them from sinning!

POINT OF DEPTH

Here is a chance to sneak a little peek into the wonderful difference between the Old and New Covenants! We will cover this much more in depth later, but for now, let's just enjoy this fleeting glance!

In the Old Covenant, God wrote His Law on tablets of stone. As long as the people read and understood it, they would know what to do. When the New Covenant (Jesus, The Seed) would come, God would write His Law on the hearts of those who would believe. They would know how to walk to please God.

In the Old Covenant, God scares the people into obedience. As long as they remember just how fearful God was that day, their fear of God would be a help to them. It would help them to not sin! When the New Covenant (Jesus, The Seed) would come, God would actually put the fear of Him inside of them. Jeremiah 32:38-40 They wouldn't need to remember the fearful sight they had seen. They would inherently be fearful of Him because they would *know* Him!

God said that in the New Covenant we will know Him. If we truly know God, then we will reverentially obey Him. He is awesome and terrible and fearful. We will fear disobeying Him! If we are fearful to disobey Him, then we will do His bidding and the result will be our holiness!

3. **Exodus 24; 25:8; Hebrews 8:5; Revelation 21:22**
From **Exodus 21-23**, God gives to Moses His ordinances that He expects the people to keep. Moses recounts all the words of the Lord to the people. Basically the conditions are these: If Israel obeys God, He will bless them and give them prosperity and give them life! If Israel disobeys God, He will curse them and give them adversity and give them death!

Their response is unanimous, "All that the Lord has said—we will do!" Moses mediates a Covenant contract between God and His people, Israel. After the people agree to God's conditions, Moses writes down all of God's words.

In the morning Moses builds an altar at the foot of the mountain and sets up 12 pillars, one for each of the tribes of Israel. Then he offers burnt offerings and peace offerings to the Lord. Moses takes half of the blood and puts it in basins (*we're talking about a lot of blood*!). Then he sprinkles the rest of the blood on the altar. This symbolically binds God to the Covenant agreement.

Next Moses reads aloud to the people what he had written the night before. Again they respond in agreement to God's conditions. So Moses takes the blood from the basins and sprinkles it on the people, this time symbolically binding the people into the Covenant agreement. Covenant was the most solemn, binding agreement that could be made. Only death could sever the agreement between the two parties.

Finally, Moses goes further up the mountain with Aaron, two of Aaron's sons, and 70 of the elders. They see God. Under His feet there appeared to be a pavement of sapphire, as clear as the sky itself. There they partake of a Covenant meal together. Afterward, God calls Moses to come up to the mountain.

God speaks to Moses for 40 days and 40 nights giving him instructions for the building and ceremonial use of the Tabernacle, a sanctuary where God would be able to dwell among His people. **Exodus 25:8** The word "tabernacle" means "to dwell." God wanted to tabernacle (dwell) among His people. The Tabernacle was built according to the pattern of the real Tabernacle in heaven. **Hebrews 8:5** The Tabernacle on earth gives us a picture of not only the New Covenant, but also what the end of **HIStory** is going to be. **Revelation 21:22**

Point of Depth

While the Abrahamic Covenant was a *promise* of The Coming Seed, the Mosaic Covenant or the Old Covenant was a *picture* of The Coming Seed, Jesus Christ. God gave Moses instructions and a pattern to build the Tabernacle. Exodus 25-31; 35-40 The real Tabernacle, the place where God dwells, is in Heaven. Yet, the earthly copy gave a real and true picture of Jesus Christ, the Lord, to the people here on earth. *Jesus, The Seed, would give men access to God. He would show men how to approach God → through Himself!*

God's presence dwelt in the innermost part of the Tabernacle, the Holy of Holies. Everything in the Tabernacle dealt with giving the Israelites access to God. *Everything Jesus did had a purpose—to give us access to God!*

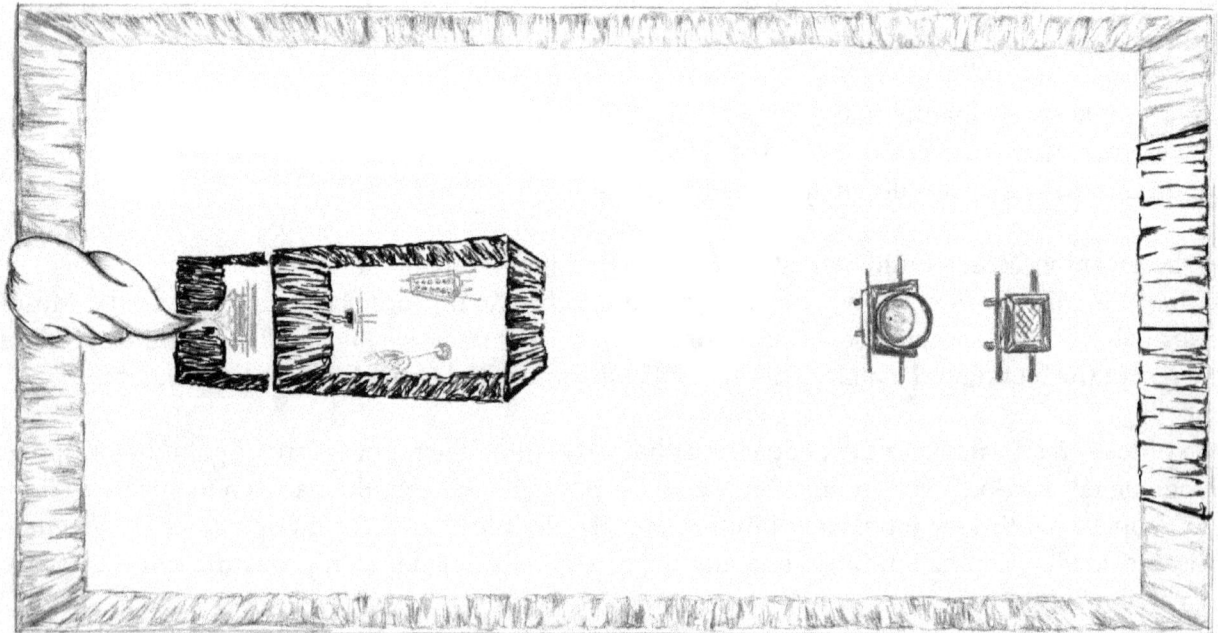

The outer walls of the Tabernacle created a rectangle that was 150 feet from east to west and 75 feet from north to south. There was a 30 foot wide by 7 ½ foot high door or opening, always on the east side. There was no other entrance to the inside of the Tabernacle. *Jesus is the Door to the Father.* **John 10:9** *Jesus is the only Way to the Father. There is no other way to the Father but through Jesus.* **John 14:6**

Inside of the outer walls there was an outer court, to which the nation of Israel had access. Then, in the middle of the outer court there was a Holy Place, where only the priests were allowed to go. And finally, inside of the Holy Place was the Holy of Holies (the Holiest of the Holy places). The high priest alone was able to enter the Holy of Holies and only one time each year on the Day of Atonement. Let's walk through that doorway and examine the outer court first as we make our way toward the Holy of Holies, where God dwelt. Exodus 29:43, 45

There were two main things in the outer court: the Altar of Sacrifice and the Brazen Laver.

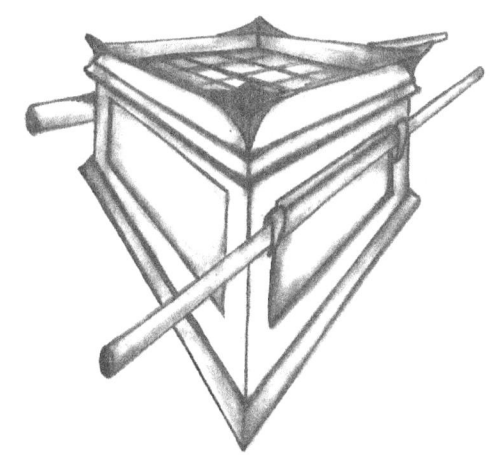

The first thing to be seen when entering the outer court would be the Altar of Sacrifice. Exodus 27:1-8; 38:1-7 It was made of brass and was 7 ½ feet square while standing 4 ½ feet off of the ground. Slain animals, or their parts, were laid on top. The idea was that because a person had sinned, he needed to die. Yet, God allowed for the animal to die instead of the person, until the supreme final sacrifice of Jesus Christ would be made that would atone for all sin. Once Jesus' sacrifice was made, there would never need to be another. His sacrifice would pay it all. *Jesus is the Lamb that was slain for the sins of the world.* **Revelation 5:12** *He was nailed to the cross because he had a baptism to undergo.* **Luke 12:49-50**

Directly behind the Altar of Sacrifice was the Brazen Laver. Bronze is a symbol of judgment. *Without the sacrifice making atonement for our sin and the daily cleansing of the water of the Word, we too, would be under the judgment of God.*

The Laver was made of finer, purer, and more transparent bronze than the Altar. It was made from the mirrors of the women who served at the doorway of the Tent of Meeting. Exodus 30:17-21; 38:8 The priests would cleanse themselves here daily before going into the Holy Place. *Jesus is the Word of God. He said that the Word He spoke cleanses us. We need to be washing daily with the water of the Word. The Word washes our minds and changes our beliefs and therefore our actions. The more we are washed, the more we are conformed into the image of Jesus Christ and reflect Him—just*

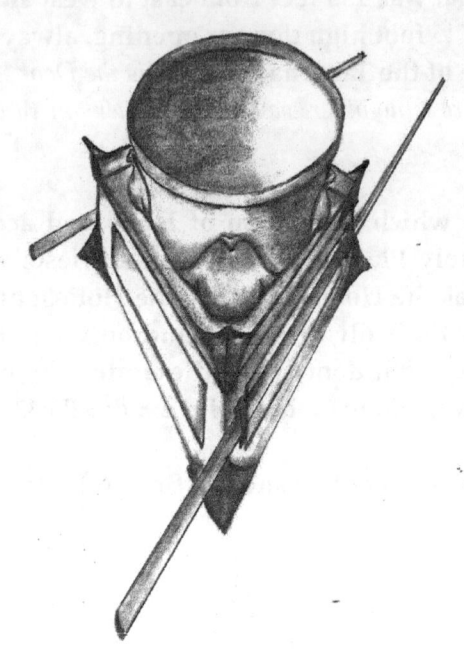

like the mirrors used in the laver would reflect the image of the priest who looked into it! **John 15:3; Hebrews 10:22; Ephesians 5:26**

Neglecting to wash one's hands and feet when entering the Tabernacle resulted in death. Think about how much more severe the consequence is if we don't wash our hearts daily in the water of the Word! **Exodus 30:20-21**

From the outer court, the priests would enter daily into the Holy Place. It was 45 feet from east to west and 15 feet from north to south and 15 feet high. The Holy of Holies (15 feet square) which sat at the western edge within this rectangle, is included in these measurements. Exodus 40:24 refers to the Holy Place as the Tent of Meeting.

If you were a priest and could have entered the Holy Place, to the right you would have seen the Table of Showbread. The table was 3 feet from east to west while only 1 ½ feet from north to south. It stood about 2 ¼ feet tall. It was made of acacia wood and overlaid with gold. On it were placed 12 loaves of bread representing the 12 tribes of Israel, God's Covenant people, the Jews. On the Sabbath, the priests would eat these loaves and replace them with new ones. Exodus 25:23-30; 37:10-16 *Jesus is the Bread of Life.* **John 6:48-51** *If we eat of Him, we will never die. The bread that He gives for the life of the world is His flesh.*

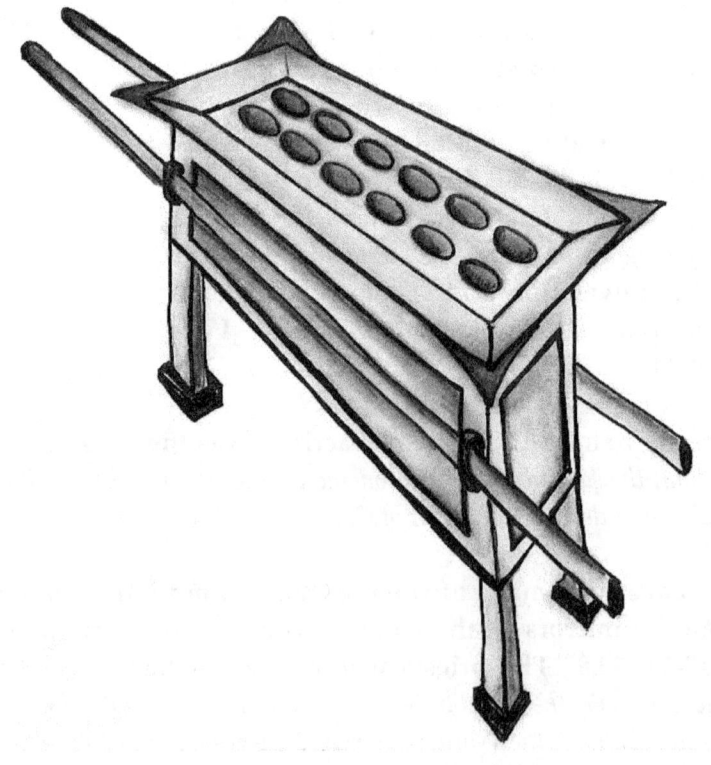

If you were a priest and could have entered the Holy Place, to the left you would have seen a Candlestick with seven branches on it. It was to burn continually, 24 hours a day! They used olive oil to keep it burning day and night. It was the only light inside the Tabernacle. It was made of pure gold. **Exodus 25:31-40; 37:17-24** *Jesus is the Light of men. If we follow Him we will not walk in darkness, but have the Light of Life! If we believe in Jesus, we won't remain in darkness!* **John 1:4, 9; 8:12; 9:5; 12:46**

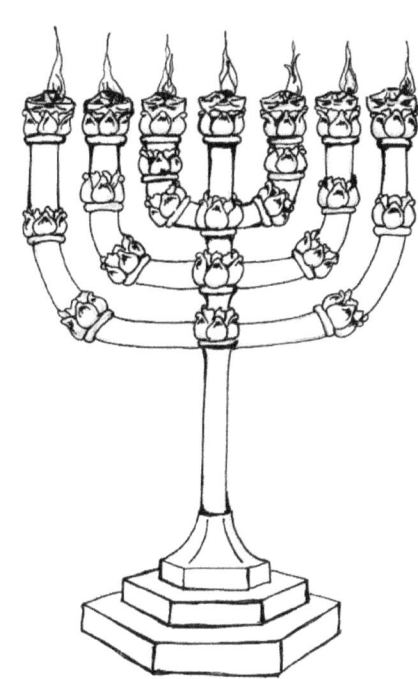

There was a Veil that separated the Holy Place from the Holy of Holies. Directly between the Table of Showbread and the Candlestick and next to the Veil was the Altar of Incense. It is possible that it was actually inside the Holy of Holies. **Hebrews 9:3-4** However, most scholars tend to believe it was in the Holy Place. **Exodus 30:6; 40:26** Either way, the Altar of Incense was made of acacia wood and gold and stood 3 feet tall,

which was ¾ foot higher than the Table of Showbread. The Altar was the place for burning pure fragrant spices in the form of incense which continually floated throughout the Holy Place. The aroma represented prayers coming before God. *Jesus prays for us continually. He is our High Priest who ever lives to make intercession for us before God.* **Hebrews 7:25**

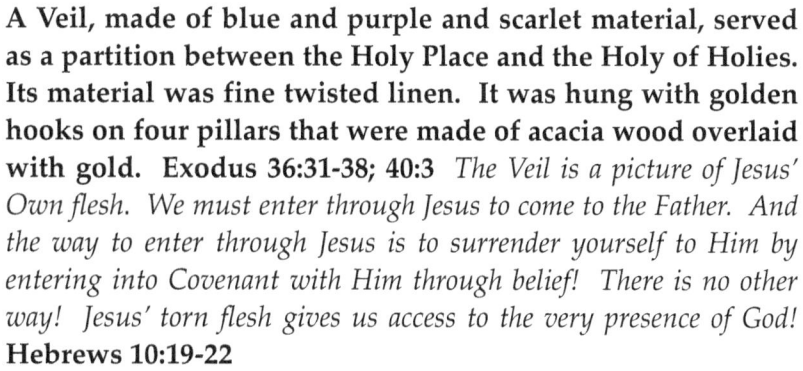

A Veil, made of blue and purple and scarlet material, served as a partition between the Holy Place and the Holy of Holies. Its material was fine twisted linen. It was hung with golden hooks on four pillars that were made of acacia wood overlaid with gold. **Exodus 36:31-38; 40:3** *The Veil is a picture of Jesus' Own flesh. We must enter through Jesus to come to the Father. And the way to enter through Jesus is to surrender yourself to Him by entering into Covenant with Him through belief! There is no other way! Jesus' torn flesh gives us access to the very presence of God!* **Hebrews 10:19-22**

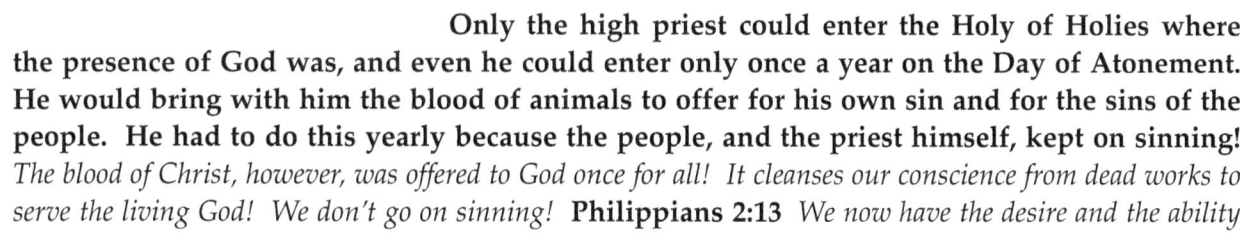

Only the high priest could enter the Holy of Holies where the presence of God was, and even he could enter only once a year on the Day of Atonement. He would bring with him the blood of animals to offer for his own sin and for the sins of the people. He had to do this yearly because the people, and the priest himself, kept on sinning! *The blood of Christ, however, was offered to God once for all! It cleanses our conscience from dead works to serve the living God! We don't go on sinning!* **Philippians 2:13** *We now have the desire and the ability*

to obey! Our High Priest, Jesus, entered the real Holy of Holies in heaven where God truly sits and offered His Own blood to pay for our sin. **Hebrews 9:11-15** God accepted the payment as final and complete! Now, through Jesus, we have access to the Father at all times! In fact, we may come boldly before the throne of God in our time of need to find mercy and grace! **Hebrews 4:16** WOW!!! What a Covenant!!!

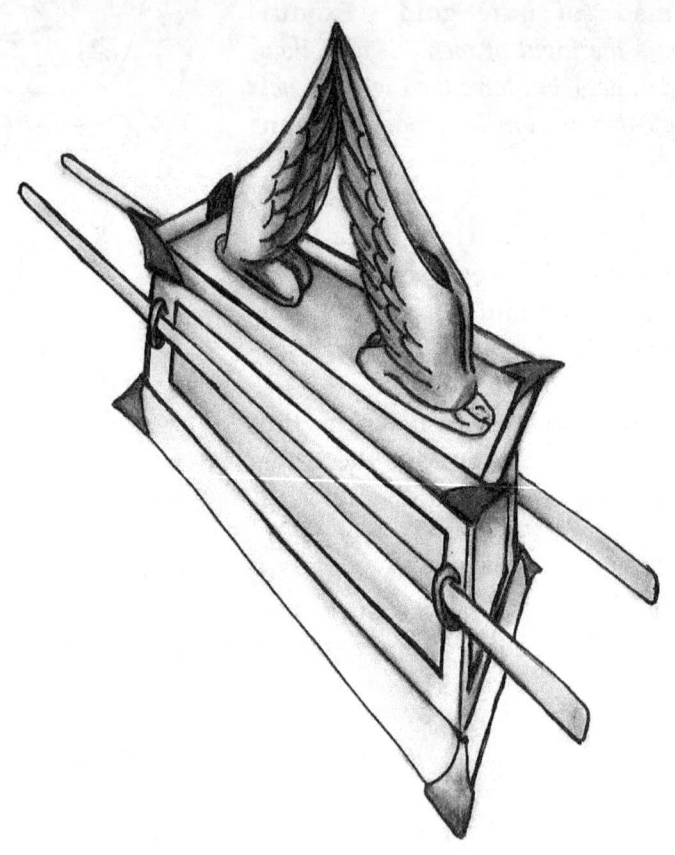

Inside the Holy of Holies was the Ark of the Covenant, the box which held the Mosaic Covenant agreement. It was made of acacia wood covered with gold and stood 2 ¼ feet high. It was 2 ¼ feet from east to west and 3 ¾ feet from north to south. The Ark held the tables of stone that God had written His Covenant commandments on, a jar of the manna from the 40 years of wilderness meals, and Aaron's rod that had budded to show that his leadership was from God. Above the Ark was the Mercy Seat of God. Two cherubim angels covered the Mercy Seat with their outstretched wings. God's presence hovered over the Mercy Seat in a great cloud called the Shekinah Glory. This is where God dwelt. *When they approached God, they were approaching Jesus. Jesus is God.* **John 8:24, 58; 10:30-33** *Jesus and God are One. What God did, Jesus did. One must believe that Jesus is God in order to be saved. Jesus is the same I AM that made the Covenant with the people of Israel!*

The Mercy Seat, which was on top of the Ark of the Covenant, was the place where the high priest would put the blood he was offering to God to cover the sins of the people. *This is where Jesus Himself, through the Eternal Spirit, offered Himself without blemish to God. God was propitiated. Because He was satisfied with the offering, He was able to extend mercy to those who would believe.* **Hebrews 9:14**

> Do you realize that the blood of Jesus was laid before God on the true Mercy Seat in heaven?
> Do you realize that blood was offered for everyone who would believe?
> God accepted the payment.
> Have you?
> Do you believe it?

POINT OF DEPTH

In addition to the pattern for building the Tabernacle, God also gave Moses instructions for its ceremonial use. He instituted offerings and feasts. Leviticus 23 There were three major feasts that were required to be celebrated: Passover, Pentecost, and Tabernacles. All three of these commemorated an actual event in the history of Israel *and at the same time gave a picture of the New Covenant in Jesus Christ.*

The *Feast of Passover* was celebrated during March or April. It consisted of three parts: 1) The Passover itself, 2) The Feast of Unleavened Bread, and 3) The Feast of First Fruits. *These three components pictured Jesus' 1) Death, 2) Burial, and 3) Resurrection.*

The *Feast of Pentecost* or *Feast of Weeks* was celebrated during May or June. Fifty days after the Israelites were delivered from Egypt, they were given the Law to show them how to live their new life of freedom. *Fifty days after Jesus was resurrected, God sent the Holy Spirit to write His Law on the hearts of people who believed that Jesus was The Seed. Under the New Covenant, instead of following the Law, they would follow the Holy Spirit's leading.*

The *Feast of Tabernacles* was celebrated during September or October. It consisted of three parts, as well: 1) The Feast of Trumpets, 2) The Day of Atonement, and 3) The Feast of Booths or Tabernacles. *The Feast was a picture of what is yet to come, the reign and rule of Jesus Christ, The Seed! 1) Christ's Second Coming, 2) Christ's Salvation of Israel in One Day, 3) Christ's Millennial Reign.*

When → Compared to our calendar

January	February	March	April	May	June	July	August	September	October	November	December
		Passover	**Passover**	**Pentecost**				**Tabernacles**	**Tabernacles**		

Fulfillment of the Feasts

Passover	Pentecost	Tabernacles
Passover Feast of Unleavened Bread Feast of First Fruits	Feast of Weeks	Trumpets Day of Atonement (Yom Kippur) Feast of Booths
Jesus' Death Jesus' Burial Jesus' Resurrection	Holy Spirit sent to start the Church	Jesus' Second Coming Israel's Salvation Millennial Reign

I. *Feast of Passover*

Let's look at the three parts of the *Feast of Passover*. All three festivals take place in the spring and commemorate events concerning Israel's exodus when she was delivered from the slavery of Egypt. **Exodus 11, 12; Leviticus 23:5, 6-8, 9-14; Numbers 9; 28:16; Deuteronomy 16:1-17**

1. *Passover* itself *(picturing Jesus' death)* happened in the land of Egypt. It occurred in connection with the last plague that God would bring upon the Egyptians before He would deliver the Israelites from their slavery. Each household was to kill a lamb and apply its blood to the outside of the lintel and two doorposts. The lamb itself, they were to eat completely. The LORD was going to pass through to kill the Egyptians, but whenever He saw the blood applied in faith by the Israelites, He would not allow His Destroyer to touch that household. If there was no blood on the doorposts and lintel, then God's Destroyer would kill the firstborn of the children in the household along with the firstborn of the cattle belonging to the household. *This entire event, although literal and real, was more importantly a foreshadow (a shadow that came before the real thing) of the very real event of the death of the Lamb of God. God instructed the Israelites to celebrate the Passover annually as a Feast to the LORD. It was to be a permanent memorial for them to remember their deliverance from slavery in the land of Egypt and a permanent promise of the future Lamb Who would take away the sin of the world.* **Exodus 12:14; Matthew 26:17-19; John 1:29; I Corinthians 5:7** *When studying, always compare the Passover to the death of Jesus, not the death of Jesus to the Passover—the death of Jesus is the real thing!*

So, for hundreds of years the Israelites would slay a lamb, offer it as a sacrifice to cover their own sins, and again have a right relationship with God. *And for hundreds of years they didn't see the picture God had drawn for them of the Lamb Who would someday come, be slain, and be offered as a perfect sacrifice, once for all, to do more than cover their sins—the sacrifice would take their sins away! God would provide that Lamb. Under the Old Covenant, when they believed that God would provide the Messiah to deliver them, that faith saved them. This faith in the coming Messiah, The Seed, brought eternal life to each believer. Under the New Covenant, if a person recognizes that Jesus Christ is the Lamb of God Who came to take away sins, he needs to apply the blood of Jesus, the Lamb, to his life by faith. God will not destroy him if God sees the blood of Christ when He looks at him!*

We are saved by faith. **It was faith that motivated the Israelites to put the blood of the <u>Passover</u> lamb on their doorposts. If they had not believed, they would not have obeyed.** *It is faith in the Lamb of God that motivates us to accept Him as Lord and Savior! If we don't really believe, we won't surrender to Him! It's not actions or deeds; it's faith in The Seed!*

Jesus fulfilled the feasts of Israel according to their appointed times. Luke 19:28-44 The very first <u>Passover</u> was the inauguration of a new calendar for Israel—a new life called for a new calendar! Israel would have its very own twelve months, and the month of Nisan would be the first. On the tenth day of Nisan, the lambs were taken into households of the Israelites to be examined for spots or blemishes. *The Son of God was taken into Jerusalem to be examined for three days by His Own people for wrongdoing.* **Luke 20:1-8, 19-40**

After the period of examination was complete, if, and only if, a lamb was perfect, it would be slain at twilight on the fourteenth day. At the exact hour that the <u>Passover</u> lambs were being slain, *the perfect Lamb of God was put on the cross to die. He, too, had passed the examination. His people could find no defect in Him at all.* **Luke 23:4, 15, 22; John 18:38; 19:6**

The innocent little lambs took the punishment that the people deserved. *The innocent Lamb of God took the punishment that I deserved and that you deserved.* **John 15:25**

As a result of faith in God, the Israelites were delivered from bondage and slavery in Egypt forever, never to go back! Pharaoh didn't really want to let them leave his control, but he had to! God was in control! *God is in control! We too, can be delivered from bondage and slavery to sin, never to go back, if we will put our faith in the Lamb of God. Satan doesn't want to let us free from our slavery to sin, but he has to!* **Colossians 1:13**

2. The <u>Feast of Unleavened Bread</u> (picturing Jesus' burial) was celebrated from the evening of the fourteenth day through the twenty-first day of Nisan (also called Abib). For seven days the Israelites were to remove any and all leaven from their houses. A person who ate anything that was leavened during those seven days was to be cut off from the nation of Israel. This celebration commemorated God bringing all the Israelites out of Egypt. Leviticus 23:6-8; Exodus 23:15; 34:18; Numbers 28:17

Once God's Angel of Destruction had gone through Egypt killing all the firstborn, except those of Israel who had obeyed God and put blood on their doorposts, Pharaoh said quite plainly to Moses and Aaron, *"Get out of here, all of you!"* So the people got out! They didn't even take time to leaven their dough. They had been released from slavery and they were leaving!

They were able to leave quickly because God had prepared them. The Israelites had been told to stand with their walking shoes on, ready to go, while they hastily ate the lamb. This was because as soon as they were delivered from the Angel of Destruction, they would be leaving the land of slavery and bondage. They needed to be prepared to move immediately and far! *What a wonderful picture of true salvation! Once we are rescued from our bondage to sin, we are to move immediately and distance ourselves far away from it! We can't live in the land of sin any longer! The <u>Feast</u>*

of Unleavened Bread is a picture that shows us that sin should not be the way of our lives once we are saved because Jesus has broken the power and bondage that sin had over us.

You see, God doesn't *just* **forgive us of our sins and thereby protect us from His wrath that** *must* **come against all sin. He does more than that. He takes us out of sin! Matthew 1:21 He doesn't leave us in Egypt!**

Once the people left Egypt, they needed to depend upon God to feed them. He fed them bread in the wilderness. That bread was called "manna" and was like a flaky wafer. Exodus 16:14 It was a picture of the True Bread that God would also send from heaven. *Jesus is the Unleavened Bread of Life. He is all we need, and we are to feed on Him daily!*

Although leaven itself is not sin, it is a picture of certain qualities of sin. Just as leaven causes bread to rise by permeating and corrupting the entire lump of dough, so too, sin entered the world through one man and infected the entire "lump" of humanity! Not only are we to put sin away from our own life, we are to put it away from the assembly of the church! Sin refuses to sit quietly in the pew! Everyone is in danger when sin is ignored! **I Corinthians 5:6-8; Romans 5:12**

As the <u>Feast of Passover</u> *was a picture of Jesus' death, so the* <u>Feast of Unleavened Bread</u> *is a picture of His burial! Jesus was dead and buried in His tomb while the* <u>Feast of Unleavened Bread</u> *was celebrated!*

His burial showed us that He truly died. When we truly believe in Him and are saved, something supernatural happens to us—the "old man," who was our slave driver causing us to sin, is killed! When we are saved, the Holy Spirit supernaturally identifies us with Christ's death, burial, and resurrection. As Christ truly died, so our old man truly dies. He no longer has <u>any</u> power over us whatsoever! Did you hear that? <u>He no longer has any power over us whatsoever!!!</u> The old man forced us to sin. We were slaves to him. But once the old man dies, he is just like leaven in that he has no place in our lives anymore. We are new creatures when we are in Christ! **Romans 6; Galatians 2:20; Ephesians 4:22-24; Colossians 3:9-11; II Corinthians 5:17**

Quite likely, the Israelites would have been crossing the Red Sea during the days that God would later appoint for them to proclaim as the holy convocation of the <u>Feast of Unleavened Bread</u>**. They were leaving the land of bondage and would not be going back! God delivered them by His Mighty Hand.** *So too, we proclaim our identification with Christ, our Deliverer. As the Jews passed through the waters of the Red Sea, we were given a type or picture of water baptism. When we are water baptized, we are giving the world a picture of the death of the old man that used to rule us! It's the old man's memorial service and there is nothing good to be said in his eulogy! Actually, even water baptism itself is a visual picture of the Gospel!*

I am reminded of the old hymn, "I have decided to follow Jesus! No turning back! No turning back!"

3. The <u>Feast of First Fruits</u> *(picturing Jesus' resurrection)* **was celebrated on the day following the Sabbath of the** <u>Feast of Unleavened Bread</u>**. God told His people,** *"When you enter the land which I am going to give to you and reap its harvest, then you shall bring in the sheaf of the first* *fruits of your harvest to the priest. And he shall wave the sheaf before the* LORD *for you to be accepted."* Leviticus 23:9-14; Exodus 23:16; 34:22; Numbers 28:26

Not only does the _Feast_ commemorate the great event of God bringing His people into the Promised Land of Israel, it also points forward to two great realities that were wrought when Jesus was raised to life on the exact day that the _Feast of First Fruits_ was celebrated! The _Feast_ is celebrated because it is a promise—a wonderful promise of the harvest to come! I Corinthians 15:20-23

> *1. Jesus was the first of many brethren – the church*
> Think of a tomato plant that is growing in your back yard. How did it get there? It began with a dead seed that was buried. The seed came to life, and you saw its life manifested as a plant. One day you look and you see a blossom. You know that this blossom is going to turn into a tomato. It's the first one. Jesus was the first "blossom" on the plant and therefore, the first "tomato." Jesus was the first member of the church! Individual believers are "blossoms" that come along after the first. Individual believers are all the "tomatoes" that follow that very first one, Jesus! Jesus was the first fruit of the tomato plant. John 12:24

> *2. Jesus was the first to be raised in a new glorified body*
> In July or August finally one of those tomatoes is completely red and ripe. You pick it and eat it. So good! Jesus was the first "tomato" to ripen on the vine. He is the first one to receive His new glorified body. Each believer is individually ripening on the vine and will someday also receive a new glorified body. Jesus is the promise of a whole harvest of glorified bodies. Believers are that harvest to come!

II. _Feast of Pentecost_

The _Feast of Pentecost_ was celebrated fifty days (seven complete Sabbaths) after the Feast of First Fruits. _Shavuout_, which means "weeks", is the Hebrew name for the _Feast of Pentecost_. There were seven weeks between Passover and _Pentecost_. _Pentecost_ is the Greek word for the day it was celebrated, which was the fiftieth day. "Pente" means "fifty." Leviticus 23:15-22

The early summer wheat crop was ready to harvest. The people were to make their wheat into fine flour and bake two loaves of bread with leaven to be given to the LORD as their first fruits of that early wheat harvest. They were to be made of two-tenths of an ephah (approximately one-fifth of a bushel). These were not small loaves! The priest would wave these two loaves as an offering before the LORD.

Looking backward this _Feast_ would be a reminder of the great event that happened in the third month after Israel was delivered from Egypt. That great event was God giving His people His Law at Mount Sinai. His people agreed to His terms and entered Covenant with Him there. Exodus 19

God told Moses that He would come to him in a thick cloud and let the people hear His voice speaking to Moses so that the people would always believe in Moses as their leader. God told Moses to gather the people and get them ready. On the third day, the LORD God came down on Mount Sinai and called Moses up to Him.

This was not a casual meeting. God made sure it was full of frightening fanfare and terror. He came in a blazing fire and smoke and a thick cloud. There was thunder and flashes of lightning! There was darkness and gloom and whirlwind.

There was also a very loud trumpet sound that was not coming from any of the people's trumpets! It kept getting louder and louder! The whole mountain was being covered with smoke, and it was shaking violently. Moses spoke, and God answered him with a voice of thunder. God's voice was so terrible and awesome that those who heard it begged that no further word should be spoken to them. Can you just imagine!!! They trembled with fear! Even Moses was full of fear and trembling! Hebrews 12:18-21

Interestingly, God kept warning the people not to try and come any closer than the base of the mountain. If they did, they would perish. Now, although I can't imagine there were too many brave souls who would have wanted to even try, God was making a point. The people *did not* have access to God. They were not able to enter into His presence.

God then wrote His Law on tablets of stone for the people to possess so they could obey Him. When Moses came down from the mountain with those tablets he found the people had forsaken God and were worshiping a disgusting calf that Aaron made for them. Moses saw that things were out of control so he stood in the gate of the camp and called out, *"Whoever is for the LORD, come to me!"* The sons of Levi gathered to him. At Moses' command the sons of Levi put about 3,000 men to death that day.

Looking forward the _Feast of Pentecost_ was also a picture of the promise of The Seed, Who would come in God's Holy Spirit and indwell believers forever. God painted a perfect picture for man, complete with intricate details, so he would be sure not to miss the coming of The Seed. In the New Covenant, no longer would God's Law be written on tablets of stone. Now He would write His Law on their hearts, on tablets of flesh inside of every believer. Jeremiah 31:33

When the day of _Pentecost_ came after Jesus' ascension there was also a gathering of the people just as there had been almost 1,500 years earlier. A smaller group of about 120 persons was waiting together in a house for God. They had come to Jerusalem to celebrate the _Feast of Pentecost_. They were waiting for the promise of the baptism of the Holy Spirit given by Jesus just before He left them and ascended to His Father. Acts 1:1-8; 2

Reminiscent of that great event on Mount Sinai so many years before, there was a noise from heaven that was like a violent rushing wind. It filled the whole house where they were sitting. There was a big difference, though. These believers had not come to Moses' terrifying Mount

Sinai. They had come to the heavenly Mount Zion. Where previously they did not have access to God, now they could be ushered into His presence! Hebrews 12:22-24

Before, the blazing fire of God, rising awesomely into heaven, had covered the top of Mount Sinai; now there were tongues like fire distributing themselves over the believers' heads! Suddenly they were all under the influence of the Holy Spirit, and they began to speak with other tongues as the Holy Spirit was giving them the ability to speak out!

Just as the crowd of people had watched Moses meet with God, a huge multitude came together in amazement and marveled at what they saw! God wrote His Law on the hearts of 3,000 people who believed in The Seed that day. On that great day of _Pentecost_ 3,000 people were made alive, where as 3,000 died on that ancient day at Mount Sinai. II Corinthians 3 compares the Old and the New Covenant. The Law (Old Covenant) came with death, but the New Covenant came with life!

It is interesting that the ones who were for the LORD and came to Moses were the ones that God made into priests before Him. The Levites were the ones who gathered around Moses. God declared that only those from the tribe of Levi could be priests unto Him. In the New Covenant, God makes all believers priests. The entire Kingdom, the Kingdom of God, become priests to Him.

The mystery of the two loaves that the priest waved before God was now revealed! The leaven in the bread represented sin. One loaf represented the Jews, and the other loaf represented the Gentiles. The Jews were no more righteous than the Gentiles. Romans 3:9-10 They were both made acceptable in the sight of God through their faith in The Seed, Jesus. When the priest waved the two loaves as an offering before the LORD, it was a picture of Jew and Gentile together being accepted by God in Christ Jesus. It was a picture of the coming Church, the body of Christ! Ephesians 2:11-22; I Corinthians 12:13

As the original and each subsequent _Feast of Pentecost_ began at the time of the early summer wheat harvest, so too was that great _Pentecost_ almost 2,000 years ago. The 3,000 believers on that day were only the first of the New Covenant fruits of the harvest that is now underway. We are still in the time of harvest. The wheat is ripe and needs to be brought in. We don't have much time left…

III. _Feast of Tabernacles_

The _Feast of Tabernacles_ consists of three festivals: _Feast of Trumpets_, _Day of Atonement_, and _Feast of Booths_. All three take place in the fall and look forward to the coming of Messiah.

1. The _Feast of Trumpets_ was celebrated on the first day of the seventh month of the Jewish year. The Israelites were to have a rest—a holy convocation. They were to blow the trumpets which were made of rams' horns. The blowing of the shofar (ram's horn) was symbolic of

asking God to remember and think about His Covenant commitment to them as a people. It reminds the Israelites of His certain promise, as well. Leviticus 23:23-25; Numbers 29:1-6

When the prophets spoke, their messages were often warnings. So too, it was traditional to use the sound of the blowing of the shofar as a call to alarm—a time to prepare themselves for what was ahead (usually judgment!). Numbers 10:9-10; Joel 2:1, 15 It was the duty of the Hebrew to hear and respond to the sound of the ram's horn. He must never ignore it! Ezekiel 33:1-6; Jeremiah 6:17

Looking back, the _Feast of Trumpets_ commemorates the time when Joshua led the Israelites into the land that God had promised them. It was to be a day of rest for the people. And as Joshua led the people conquering the inhabitants of the land of Canaan, so indeed, they were resting, for it was God Who was fighting the battle for them! Joshua 3; 24:13; Nehemiah 4:20

Looking forward, the _Feast of Trumpets_ was a picture of the time when God would call His wife, Israel, back to the land He had promised her. Do you hear a trumpet? Have the people started coming back to Israel? Oh, yes! In 1948, Israel even regained her status as a nation before the eyes of the world. God is stirring the hearts of the Jews to return to their homeland. They are coming back by the droves. The sound of the shofar was a long slow sound that reached far away from its source. I believe the sound of the shofar is right now ringing in the souls of the Jews in all four corners of the earth. I pray they will respond because Messiah is coming!

God will sound a trumpet that will announce the coming of the Day of the LORD, a time in the future when God will begin to send forth His judgments. The trumpet will herald to the people that the _Day of Atonement_ is also coming soon so they need to get prepared for the days ahead! Zephaniah 1:14-16; Isaiah 27:13

2. The _Day of Atonement_ or _Yom Kippur_ takes place on the tenth day of the seventh month and follows the _Feast of Trumpets_. The people are to humble their souls and present an offering by fire to the LORD. They are not to do any work on this day. The day is set aside to make atonement on their behalf before the LORD. Leviticus 23:26-32

On this most solemn and important day, no one except the high priest was allowed in the Tabernacle. He had a very important task to perform on the _Day of Atonement_. He would offer blood to God as atonement for the Holy Place itself and for the sins of the people. God required blood because blood contains the life of the flesh and the penalty due for sin was the sinner's life. It was through the substituted blood of this animal that God allowed atonement to be made for the people. Leviticus 16; 17:11, 14

The high priest started out his day with an extremely detailed consecrating hygiene which God required. Then he took two male goats and one bull from the congregation. He offered the bull for a sin offering for himself and for his household. The high priest was a sinner too, just like the people. Next he took the two goats to present before the LORD at the doorway of the

Tabernacle. The high priest cast lots for the goats to decide which one was for the LORD and which one would be the scapegoat. He would offer the LORD'S goat as a sin offering, but the scapegoat would be dealt with later that day. The scapegoat would be presented alive to the LORD, to make atonement on it, and then sent into the wilderness.

Then the high priest would take fire from the altar and incense and bring it inside the veil which partitioned off the Holy of Holies from the rest of the Tabernacle. The cloud of incense created by the fire coals covered the Mercy Seat (Propitiatory Seat) so that the high priest would not die because he saw God. Exodus 33:20

Next the high priest would sprinkle some of the blood from the bull of the sin offering for himself and his household toward the Mercy Seat seven times.

Next he would slaughter the goat of the sin offering for the people. He would then come back inside the Holy of Holies and sprinkle the blood of the goat seven times on the Mercy Seat and in front of the Mercy Seat. This was because the Tabernacle was among the people in the midst of their impurities, therefore it had to be atoned for as well.

The high priest's next task was to go out to the altar where the animals were slain daily. He was to take some of the blood of the bull *and* of the LORD'S goat and put it on the horns of the Altar on all of its sides. Again, he was to sprinkle blood seven times with his finger. This was to cleanse the Altar from the impurities of the sons of Israel.

When he had finished atoning for the Tabernacle and the Altar, he would offer the scapegoat. He would lay both of his hands on its head and confess all the sins, iniquities, and transgressions of the sons of Israel over it. Symbolically, the sins of the people were being transferred onto the goat. The goat was then led into the wilderness by the hand of a man who stood in readiness. Once in the wilderness, the man released the goat who symbolically bore all of the Israelites' iniquities into a solitary land.

Next the high priest would cleanse himself all over again and then offer up in smoke the fat from the bull and the goat. Their hides and refuse were taken outside the camp to be burned.

In the picture of the LORD'S goat, it is so easy to see our dear Savior offered instead of us, and His blood, which contained His perfect life, offered instead of ours. Hebrews 9:11-28

But what about the scapegoat? What did that show the Israelites? It showed them the Lamb of God Who came to *take away* the sins of the world. Jesus too, bore our sins outside the camp. He took our sins on Himself and took them away from us. He carried them into the wilderness so we would not bear them any longer. God doesn't just save us from the penalty of our sin, He saves us from our sins themselves. He changes us and causes us to walk in a manner worthy of Him. We won't sin as the habit of our life any longer! Praise God and Praise His Scapegoat, Jesus, our Savior!!!

Prophetically the _Day of Atonement_ has not yet been fulfilled. It has to do with the nation of Israel, not the church. Yes, Jesus provided atonement through His finished work on the cross for anyone and everyone who would believe in Him—God showed that clearly in His Passover picture. Yet, the nation of Israel did not recognize the time of their visitation by their Messiah. They rejected Jesus and His death as a substitute for theirs. So God quit dealing with the Jews in the same way He had previously. God then brought the Gentiles into His plan and created the church. He grafts individual believers, both Jew and Gentile, into His olive tree.

Israel as a nation has been set aside for awhile. But is God finished with Israel completely? No!!! Romans 11 He is most certainly not finished with His people. He will come one day (the _Day of Atonement_) and every single one of them who are alive at that time will have their eyes opened, and they will look upon Jesus and mourn over Him as the death of an only child because they killed Him. Zechariah 12:10 In that day, the entire nation of Israel will receive and embrace their atonement! They will be cleansed and then be grafted back into their own olive tree alongside of the church! Amazing! Ezekiel 36:25-33; Zechariah 13:1 For Israel, the picture of the scapegoat is yet to be fulfilled!

3. _Feast of Booths_. This part of the _Feast of Tabernacles_ has not yet been fulfilled prophetically either. It is called "_Sukkot_" in Hebrew. It is to be celebrated in the seventh month starting on the fifteenth day and lasting for seven days. The Israelites were to have their crops gathered in by the fifteenth day of the month. Leviticus 23:33-44; Deuteronomy 16:13-15

It was to be a feast of the LORD. On the first and eighth day, the people were to have a holy convocation and do no work whatsoever. In between they were to be making offerings to the LORD by fire. They were to take the foliage of beautiful trees, palm branches, and boughs of leafy trees and willows of the brook and make temporary booths to live in. They were to decorate their "homes" with the fruit found on these trees. For seven days they lived in those booths and rejoiced before the LORD.

Looking back, the _Feast of Tabernacles_ commemorated the 40 years that the Israelites lived in tabernacles, or booths, in the wilderness. The Israelites were totally dependent on God during that time, for food and water, for clothing, for shelter, for life! The Israelites were to celebrate as they remembered the LORD'S provisions for them. They were to remember that during those 40 years He was all they needed; He provided everything they required for daily living—they were simply to rest in Him.

While Herod's Temple stood in Jerusalem, the Jews would celebrate with all they had. The city of Jerusalem was lit by beautiful menorahs (lamps). The people would sing psalms of praise to God while the sound of instruments of every kind filled the air around them. The priest would bring water from the pool of Siloam and pour it over the altar on the very last day of the _Feast of Booths_.

Notice the involvement of both _Water_ and _Light_ during the _Feast of Booths_. Jesus presented Himself before a great crowd and called out to the people, "_If any man is thirsty, let him come_ *to Me and drink. He who believes in Me, as the Scripture said, 'From his innermost being shall flow rivers of living water.'"* John 7:37-39 Guess which day Jesus called out His offer of water? It was on the last day of the *Feast of Tabernacles*—the day that the priest performed the ceremony of pouring water over the altar! Jesus was the True Light of the world. He made Jerusalem sparkle like a costly stone with His light, yet the people refused to see…   John 1:1-14; 8:12; I John 2:8

Looking forward, this *Feast of Tabernacles* is a picture of the 1,000 years when Messiah, The Seed, will rule and reign with a rod of iron over the earth. Zechariah 14:16-19 During that time all the nations of the earth will be required to come to Jerusalem yearly and celebrate the *Feast of Booths*. If any of the nations refuse, Jesus will withhold rain from its land. They will have no water! Just as the Israelites were dependent upon God while in the wilderness, now the whole earth will see that God is the one Who provides everything—water, bread, clothing, shelter, rain… The Israelites will live in their land, Israel, during this time. They will be God's people and God will be their God! Ezekiel 36:28

When Jesus starts His Millennial Reign, it will also be the beginning of a Kingdom which will have no end, an everlasting Kingdom. Daniel 2:44; 7:14 After the 1,000 years are over, His saints will live for the rest of eternity in the new Jerusalem on the new earth. God will actually dwell with man. God will live on the new earth in the new Jerusalem!

In this city, we also see the True Light and the Living Water. Revelation 21:23; 22:1 The Glory of God illumines the city, and Jesus is its Lamp (Menorah). As much fanfare as the people of Israel tried to create when the priest poured water from the pool of Siloam over the altar, it was *nothing* compared to the Water of Life that will pour forth from the throne of God!

4. Exodus 32
While Moses is on the mountain with God, the people of Israel break the Covenant they had just made! And they break it in a big way! Aaron actually makes a calf out of gold and the people say, *"Here is the 'LORD' your 'God', O Israel!"* How very tragic it is to see how quickly the people turned aside from God and His ways!

POINT OF DEPTH

God told the Israelites to make tassels for the corners of their garments. He told them to do this generation after generation. His purpose was to help them remember all the commandments of the LORD so they would do them and not follow after their own eyes and heart. Numbers 15:37-41 There's that old heart condition again!

To this day, if you go to Jerusalem, you can see Jews at the Wailing Wall wearing these tassels. The Wailing Wall is part of the original Herodian Temple wall. Titus besieged the city and destroyed Herod's Temple in 70 AD. The Jews go to the wall and pray and wail over Jerusalem. By the way—there is excavating going on under the wall. The excavators are searching for the Ark of the Covenant from the Holy of Holies!

POINT OF CONNECTION

God gave His people the Law to keep them locked up from the full influence of sin in their lives until the time The Seed would arrive. Galatians 3:23 The Law also served the purpose of leading God's people to The Seed. Galatians 3:24 Everything in the Old Covenant was a picture of the Covenant to come—Jesus! Because of their deceitful and desperately wicked hearts they were not able to keep the Law. Jeremiah 17:9; Hebrews 8:6-12

When the Israelites sinned, they made a sacrifice for their sin. Their sacrifice became the covering for their sin. Leviticus 17:10-11; Hebrews 9:13-14, 22 The Law required them to make their sacrifices in the Tabernacle. They were not allowed to have an altar or worship any other place.

When an Israelite would bring an animal to the Tabernacle for a burnt offering to atone for his sin, he would lay his hand on the head of the animal. Leviticus 1:1-9 This was a picture of his sins being transferred to the animal; and, more importantly, it was another foreshadowing of mankind's sins being transferred to Jesus Christ, The Seed, the Lamb of God.

5. **Numbers 13:1-3, 17-33; 14:6-10, 26-39**
Shortly after Israel had broken Covenant with God…
　↓
　　Which was shortly after they had entered Covenant with God…
　　↓
　　　Which was shortly after they had exited Egypt…
　　　↓
　　　　Moses sends 12 spies into the land of Canaan to check out this land that God was taking them into.

Does the number 12 sound familiar? Remember, it's all part of one story. Yes, there is one spy from each of the tribes of Israel.

As Israel's secret agents, they scout the land for 40 days. When they come back to the people and Moses, they have news and fruit! They tell the people that most certainly it is a land that flows with milk and honey, just like God said it did.

I imagine that right here they probably passed out the grapes, pomegranates, and figs to everyone while they gave them the bad news! *"The people of the land of Canaan are big, scary guys! No way are we going back there! Especially to overpower them! Absolutely no way!"*

Well, that's what ten of the spies (or should I say grasshoppers) said. Two of the spies, Joshua and Caleb, agreed with the first ten spies about the size of the people of the land. *"Yes! They are humongous!"* But they weren't afraid of them. Instead they feared God. They trusted in their God Who had promised the land to the Israelites in the first place! They said, *"The LORD is with us, so don't fear the people!"* However, the people wouldn't listen. In fact, they set out to stone Caleb and Joshua!

The awful result was that the people of the nation of Israel had to wait and wander in the wilderness for 40 years because of their disobedience. They didn't believe God would deliver them from the giants in the land. They had to wait 40 years because of their unbelief. Unbelief is sin. **Hebrews 3:17-19**

The wilderness where they wandered for 40 years is horrific! It's barren and uninhabitable. **But God had promised that The Seed would come through the nation of Israel, so God took care of them even in that wilderness**. For 40 years their shoes did not wear out. For 40 years their clothes did not wear out. For 40 years God fed them manna and quail. For 40 years God lead them through the wilderness.

God promised that Israel would live in the land of Canaan and so they would. What He promises, He fulfills—whether man obeys or not! But if man disobeys there is a consequence—he will pay for sinning. If a man will believe, God will redeem him from sin. Believers will not pay the wages of death because Jesus paid it for us. But—there are still consequences to disobeying God.

POINT OF CONNECTION

Isn't it amazing? Just a matter of a few weeks before, the Israelites had seen God Himself. Remember? He had scared them with His presence and thunder and lightning flashes, a trumpet and a smoking mountain. And rightly they should have been scared! How could they possibly be more afraid of a few grape farmers than of *God***!!! But they were. Again, how very, very tragic; how desperately they needed a new heart—one that** *could* **stay faithful to their God. Deuteronomy 5:29; Jeremiah 17:9; 31:31-33**

6. Deuteronomy 28:1-15, 58-66
Deuteronomy was the last book that Moses wrote. He gave the nation of Israel all of God's laws, statutes and commandments one last time before they entered the land of Canaan. Remember, they had been wandering for 40 years and all the older generation had died off. Moses is making

sure they know that the Law they are to follow is a Covenant of blessings and cursings. If they obey the Law (and thus obey God), God will bless them and prosper them and give them life. If, however, they disobey or break the Law, God will curse them and give them adversity and death. It's the peoples' choice!

Just read **Deuteronomy 28** with the cursings listed and think about what has happened to the Jews in history. Can you see **HIStory**? This chapter explains the Holocaust to us. It explains why the Jews are persecuted in the lands where they flee. It is no accident what has happened to the Jews! They are receiving the cursings of the Law because they broke their Covenant with God!

POINT OF DEPTH

Not long after the Israelites had been redeemed from Egypt, they were grumbling over the conditions they were in. They had been through a situation in Marah where they only had bitter water, but God had taken care of it for them. God had commanded Moses to throw a tree into the waters, and the waters would become sweet. God healed the bitter waters and made Himself known to the people as Jehovah-Rapha, the LORD Who heals. Exodus 15:22-27

Then they came to a place where they had *no* water. Again, God took care of their need. He told Moses to take the Rod of God (his staff) and strike the rock at Horeb (Mount Sinai). God said He would stand before him there on the rock and would make water come out of it so that the people could drink. Moses did exactly that and God fulfilled His Word. The people had the water they needed. Exodus 17:3-6

In the extremity of the desert, they came to a place in the wilderness of Zin where they again had no water. The people grumbled at Moses and blamed him for their situation.

Moses and Aaron left the people and went to meet with their God. The Glory of the LORD appeared to them and God told Moses to take the Rod of God and gather all the assembly of the Israelites. Then Moses was commanded to speak to the rock that was before their eyes, and it would bring forth water for the congregation. (This was a big congregation so there was going to be a lot of water soon!)

Moses was not in a good mood. In fact, he was in a frustrated, disobedient, rebellious mood. He called the people rebels and sarcastically asked if they wanted him and Aaron to supernaturally produce water for them from the rock!

Before the people could answer, Moses disobeyed and out of anger struck the rock twice with his rod. Yet God still provided for the needs of His people—water did come out. It had nothing to do with Moses' power. It had everything to do with God.

Although God provided water from the rock, He was not pleased with Moses and Aaron because of their unbelief. Because they did not treat God as Holy in the sight of the sons of Israel, Moses and Aaron would not be allowed to enter the land they had been waiting for. Numbers 20:2-12, 24; Deuteronomy 32:48-52; 34:5

Why was God so angry with Moses and Aaron? The New Testament explains it for us. That rock was a picture of the Lord Jesus Christ and His cross! The rock was Christ. The people were drinking from Christ, the Spiritual Rock! Deuteronomy 32:3-4; I Corinthians 10:1-4, 11; John 7:37-39

By dying for us, He obtained all we needed for life. He is the Water of Life. The rock was smitten and out came satisfying waters.

What happened to them happened as an example for us! Think about this with me for a moment. When Moses struck the rock at Horeb, that was a picture or type of Christ's crucifixion. We are saved through that *finished* work! When we are saved, we enter through the blood of Jesus into life! After that, we have everything we need. Jesus does not need to be crucified again! He can't be crucified again! He died once for all!

Moses striking the rock twice is like crucifying Christ a second time! That just can *not* happen! It would put Him to open shame because it would be saying that Jesus couldn't and didn't accomplish everything He should have the first time!!! Hebrews 6:6

After we die to ourselves and enter into Covenant with Jesus, we simply continue to drink from Him through the Holy Spirit. When Moses struck the rock again, he was not treating God as Holy and he blurred the picture God was showing us! God couldn't let Moses get away with that because it would be confusing to those of us on whom the end of the ages have come! When God punished Moses, He cleared up His picture for us!

When I went to Israel the first time I saw a lot of people getting baptized. Some do it every time they go to Israel. It seems to me that if Moses was not supposed to strike the rock again because that was a picture of the crucifixion of Jesus, then why would God want us to get baptized more than once? Isn't baptism a picture of the death, burial, and resurrection of Jesus Christ and our union with Him in that new life? And that is a once-for-all act.

HIStory Event 10
...GOD Brings the Nation of Israel into The Land

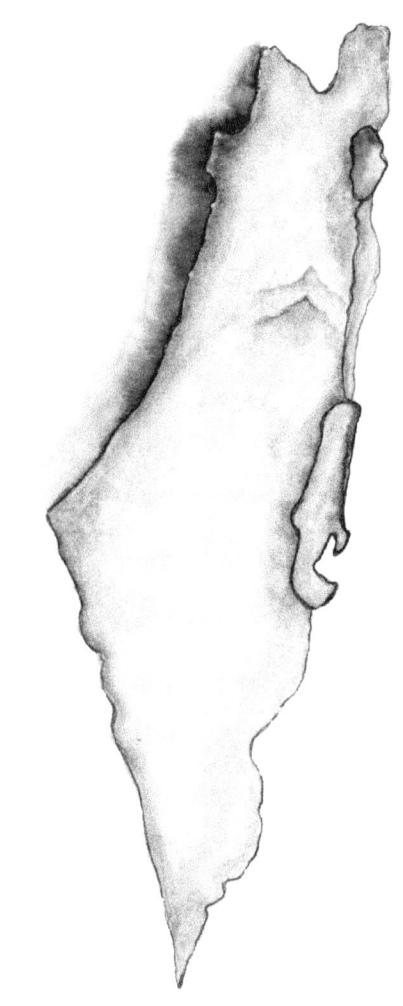

JOSHUA

The nation of Israel has been following God in the wilderness for 40 years. Finally God leads them to Moab, across the River Jordan from Canaan. There, God commissions Joshua as Moses' replacement. Moses reminds Joshua that he must always and only follow the LORD their God as he leads God's people. Israel will dispossess the nations living in the land of Canaan and dwell there herself because it is God's land and He has promised to give it to Israel! For the most part, Israel obeys God under the leadership of Joshua and she is blessed.

READ AND OBSERVE

1. Deuteronomy 34:9; Joshua 1:1-9
2. Deuteronomy 11:29-30; 27; Joshua 8:30-35
3. Joshua 10:42; 23:1-3, 6-8, 14-16; 24:29, 31

READ AND ANSWER

1. Deuteronomy 34:9
To whom does Moses pass the leadership of the nation of Israel?

Joshua 1:1-9
When Moses died, what did God tell Joshua to do?

      1.

      2.

      3.

Just as God spoke to Moses, so God spoke to Joshua. Just as God was with Moses, so God was with Joshua. Would God ever fail Joshua and Israel? Would God ever forsake Joshua and Israel?

What did God tell them to be?

What did God tell them to be careful to do?

What would be the result if they obeyed God?

How would the people know what God wanted them to do?

Were they to be afraid of man or anything else?

2. Deuteronomy 11:29-30
Where were they to go when they entered the land to possess it?

What were they to place on Mount Gerizim?

What were they to place on Mount Ebal?

Deuteronomy 27
God had given Moses instructions about what the people were to do when they entered the land. In **Deuteronomy**, Moses gives God's instructions to the people just before they enter the land. What were they to set up on Mount Ebal?

What were they to write on those stones?

Why were they to do this? (Remember, it's all one story—**HISTORY**!)

What were they to build by those stones?

They were to offer sacrifices on the altar. Then what were they supposed to do?

Moses also gave instructions to Simeon, Levi, Judah, Issachar, Joseph, and Benjamin. These tribes were to represent the blessings of God on Mount Gerizim. Where were Reuben, Gad, Asher, Zebulun, Dan, and Naphtali to stand? What would these tribes represent?

Joshua 8:30-35
When Joshua and the people entered the land God promised to give them, did Joshua follow Moses' instructions?

What did Joshua do? List what he did step-by-step.

1.

2.

3.

Can you imagine how long it would have taken for Joshua to write a copy of the Law of Moses on those stones? Who watched him as he wrote God's words on those stones?

Next, all the people took their places either by Mount Gerizim or Mount Ebal. Then what did Joshua do?

What a great thing! To stand and hear the Word of God read in its entirety!!! How often do churches even sit down and read a portion of it? Shame belongs to the visible church in the world!

3. Joshua 10:42
Why was Joshua able to conquer the kings of the land that he had just brought the Israelites into? Remember, these were the kings that had scared ten of the twelve spies!

Joshua 23:1-3
When Joshua was old, of what did he remind the people?

Joshua 23:6-8
When Joshua was old, what did he remind the people to do?

Joshua 23:14-16
What was absolutely, certifiably true of the good words the LORD had spoken to Israel?

What was absolutely, certifiably true of the threats the LORD had spoken to Israel?

READ AND REASON

1. Deuteronomy 34:9; Joshua 1:1-9
Moses dies and passes the leadership of the nation of Israel on to Joshua. Joshua and Caleb are the only two people still living who were from the generation that left Egypt. God now would talk to Joshua as the leader of His chosen people.

There will be many, many things that will happen to this chosen group, but the most important thing to remember is that **the world has been promised The Seed through Israel**. They were waiting… the world was waiting… until the appointed time!

2. Deuteronomy 11:29-30; 27; Joshua 8:30-35
Before Moses died, he told the people what they must do when they entered the Promised Land. On the day that they crossed over the Jordan into the land God had promised to give them they were to take large stones and write God's Law on them. They were to take these stones and place them on Mount Ebal. They were to build an altar there to the LORD from stones which had not been touched with any iron tool. They were to be uncut stones. There they were to offer burnt offerings to the LORD their God. They were also to offer peace offerings and eat there and rejoice before the LORD!

Moses reminds them that they are a people *for* the LORD. Notice the word "for." These people were to serve the LORD'S purposes—not their own. They had entered a Covenant with God 40 years earlier at Mount Sinai. They had agreed to obey all that God said to do, and He had agreed to bless them. But the Covenant also required that if the people disobeyed God He would have to curse them. Moses gives the people instructions for a memorial ceremony of this Covenant that they were to perform once they entered the land of Canaan.

Moses instructed that six of the tribes—Simeon, Levi, Judah, Issachar, Joseph, and Benjamin—were to stand on Mount Gerizim to bless the people. Representing the curse, the tribes of Reuben, Gad, Asher, Zebulun, Dan, and Naphtali were to stand on Mount Ebal which was across a valley. The Levites were to say to all the men of Israel with a loud voice, *"Cursed is the man who disobeys our God's commandments."* Then all the people would answer and say, *"Amen."*

When Joshua led the people into the land, he obeyed the instructions of God. I want you to catch the scene here. They built the altar made out of uncut stones and offered sacrifices on it. Then in the presence of all of Israel, Joshua wrote out a copy of the Law of Moses. (When is the last time you wrote out part of the Bible by hand?)

Everyone was there. The Levitical priests carried the Ark of the Covenant of the LORD; the elders and officers and judges were standing on both sides of the Ark. All the people, both native and stranger, were gathered for this momentous event, half standing in front of Mount Gerizim and the other half in front of Mount Ebal.

Picture this → two mountains, perfect acoustics and millions and millions of Israelites. The Levites would call from Mount Gerizim and then the people would respond with *"Amen!"* Can you imagine the volume of sound, the beauty of it all, and the anticipatory excitement caused by the wonder, the awe, the splendor of the God of Israel and His ways?

Finally, Joshua read before all the assembly every single word that God had spoken to them through Moses. In other words, he read the entire Bible that was in existence up to that point; what we today call **Genesis**, **Exodus**, **Leviticus**, **Numbers**, and **Deuteronomy**! (The Jews call this the Torah.) How many times has your church or group that you fellowship with offered God the time of listening to Him while the Torah was read out loud? (Interesting note: The little ones were not in the nursery during this time! **Joshua 8:35** They were right there listening to the Word of God!)

3. **Joshua 10:42; 23:1-3, 6-8, 14-16; 24:29, 31**
Israel conquered most of the land, because the LORD, the God of Israel, fought for them. After many days, God gave rest to Israel from all her enemies. There was rest from war. When Joshua was ready to die, he called for Israel and charged them to remember what God had done! He reminded them that all God's good words had come true and so would His threats! He warned them to obey!

Joshua eventually died, along with the elders who had ruled the people under Joshua. They were living in the land that God had promised to give them. Portions of Israel belong to the tribes, even today.

The people were obedient and served the LORD, for the most part, under Joshua. Because they had obeyed, they had enjoyed years of victory! But when Joshua died, the people rebelled, and their victory would be changed to defeat!

POINT OF CONNECTION

Have you ever thought that it didn't seem fair that God took the nations out of the land and gave it to the Israelites? After all, what had the nations done that was so wrong? God's Word has an answer to that!

God brought Abram out of the Ur of the Chaldeans to give him and his descendants the land of Canaan to possess. Genesis 15:7 The reason God could give the land to Abram was because it was God's land! He owned it and could give it to whomever He pleased! Leviticus 25:23

He told Abram that there would be an interruption to their dwelling in it. He said they would be going to a land that was not theirs (Egypt) for 400 years. During that time the Amorites would occupy Canaan. God caused the Amorites to occupy the land so that it would not become overgrown with vegetation or overtaken by wild animals. However, in the fourth generation, Abram's descendants would return to the land God had given them. Genesis 15:13-16 God tells Israel that it would take those 400 years for the iniquity of the Amorite to be complete.

The abominations of the Amorites defiled the land. Leviticus 18:24-28; 20:22-24; I Kings 14:24 Our God is a patient, long-suffering God. He puts up with sin much longer than He has to. In fact, He doesn't *have* to put up with sin at all, but He does. He gave the Amorites year after year to repent and obey the LORD God. They never did. So after 400 years, God said, "That's enough!" Then He cast them out of the land! Deuteronomy 9:5 You see, it's not a fairness issue. It's a mercy issue. Israel didn't deserve to live in the land either, but God chose to extend mercy to them. Romans 9:15

122

HIStory Event 11
...GOD Sends Judges to Rule Over Israel

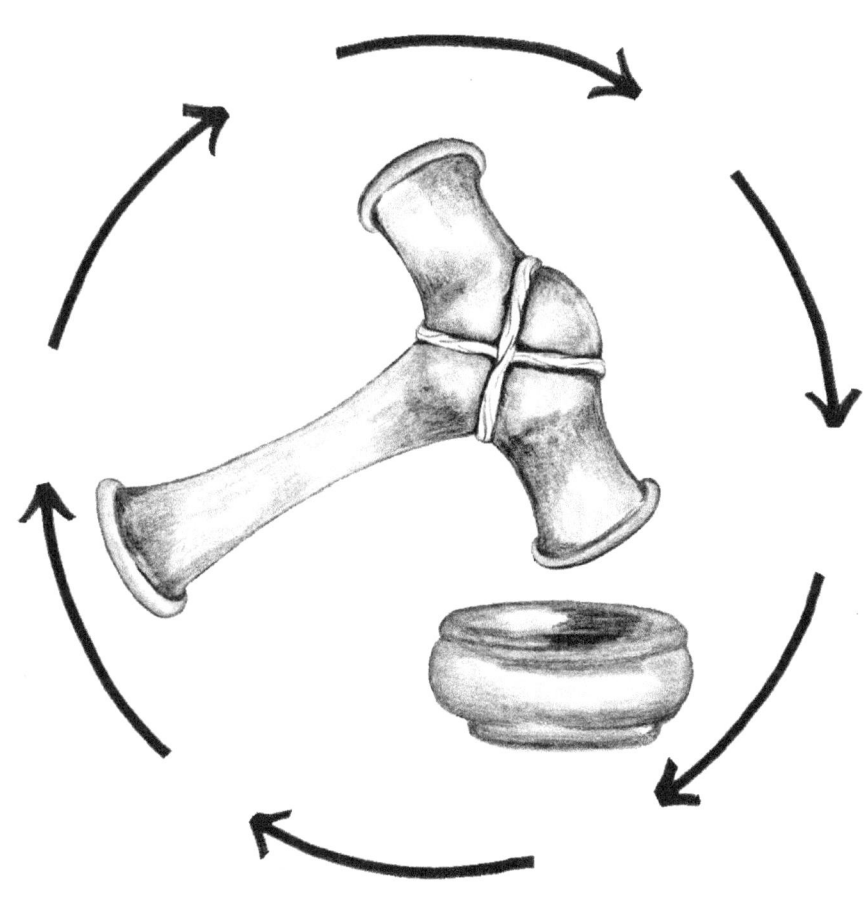

JUDGES

After Joshua died, the nation of Israel stopped paying attention to the Word of God. The result was a new generation that did not even know God or the things He had done for Israel; a people that did what was right in their own eyes!

During this dark and awful 350-400 years, God would raise up one judge after another to lead His people. While the judge was alive, God was with His people, but when the judge died, the people would sin even worse than before and God was bound by His Covenant to judge them!

READ AND OBSERVE

1. Judges 1-2

READ AND ANSWER

1. Judges 2:10
When Joshua died, a new generation arose. What two things did this generation not know?

    1.

    2.

Judges 2:11-12
Evidently this new generation did not listen to the Word of God. It would also appear that the generation before them had stopped recounting the works of God. As a result of this, what did this generation do?

    1.

2.

3.

Judges 2:12
How did God feel about what they did?

Judges 2:1-3
Did the Israelites have a right to worship whomever they chose?

Why or why not?

Did God have a right to be angry?

Did God have a right to do what He did?

Why or why not?

Judges 2:14-15
What exactly did God do in His anger?

   1.

   2.

   3.

Judges 2:15-20
After the people were severely distressed (their judgment for forsaking God and worshiping false gods) what did God do?

What did those judges do?

Did Israel listen to the judges?

While the judge was alive, God was with him and would deliver the people from their enemies. What did the people do when the judge would die?

What would God's response be?

The people went through a cycle of sin and punishment during the times of the judges. Try to list the cycle below. Don't worry if you don't come up with exactly eight. Just try and get the main ones so you can see the cycle.

      1.

      2.

      3.

      4.

      5.

      6.

      7.

      8.

Read and Reason

1. Judges 1, 2

After Joshua died and the elders leading under him died, a generation arose that didn't know the LORD or the work that He had done for Israel. Evidently they had stopped listening to the Word of God being read. Evidently the leaders were not even reading it anymore! The result was that Israel did evil in the sight of the LORD. They forsook God and started serving other gods.

Who were those other gods? They were the gods of the peoples that the Israelites had surrounded themselves with. God had told them to make no covenant with the inhabitants of the land, to tear down their altars to their false gods, and to drive the people out of the land. But they didn't obey completely and left many of the inhabitants in the land. Incomplete obedience is exactly the same as disobedience. Disobedience always brings a consequence.

God had "covenanted" with the people. They had agreed to obey all that He said but they broke their Covenant with Him. So God kept His side of the Covenant. He had to curse them. God was angry, and rightly so! He brought enemies against Israel. His hand was against Israel for evil just as He had spoken to them, and just as He had sworn to them Israel fell before her enemies.

Then the people would cry out to God for deliverance. God would be moved to pity by the groaning of the people. He would raise up a judge for them and be with the judge. God would deliver His people from their enemies all the days of the judge. Then the judge would die, and the people would return to their old ways and act even more corruptly than before. Then the anger of the LORD would burn again and He would send in nations against them once more. Do you see a pattern developing here? It was a cycle of sin and consequences!

For 350–400 years, this cycle would repeat itself in Israel:
1. Israel would sin. They would not fully obey God. They would worship other gods.
2. God would sell them into the hands of enemies.
3. Their enemies would oppress them.
4. Israel would cry out to God.
5. God would raise up a judge—also called a deliverer—and God would be with him.
6. Israel would be delivered during the life of the judge.
7. The judge would die.
8. Israel would sin even worse than before.

And on and on it would go. They were in a downward spiral. This was a dark, evil time in the **HISTORY** of Israel. Yet God continued to save Israel because of His Name, because of His Word, because of His Promise—The Seed!

POINT OF DEPTH

During the days of the judges there was a famine and the story of Ruth unfolds. Woven into that story is the truth of the teaching of the Kinsman Redeemer. If someone needed a deliverer from a situation, they needed their kinsman redeemer. The Hebrew word for kinsman redeemer is "go'el." This title gave the bearer the right and authority to buy back a relative or his land from a desperate situation.

One example would be land which had been lost through a death or a debt. Another would be the situation Ruth was in. Ruth needed a husband. Boaz was her kinsman redeemer. He bought her and took care of her.

Every single person on earth is in a desperate situation. The wages of sin is death and all men have sinned. Every unsaved person is a slave to sin and needs a kinsman redeemer to pay the price for his release and take care of him.

Believers have a Kinsman Redeemer; He is Jesus, the Christ! He is our kinsman because He became human like us. He is our redeemer because He paid the price for our release with His Own precious blood. Sin can no longer hold any believer in bondage, nor can death be master over anyone who has trusted in the payment Jesus made! He bought us and will take care of us for all of eternity. Leviticus 25:23-28; 47-55; Numbers 27:8-11; Deuteronomy 25:5-10; John 8:34-36; Romans 6; Ephesians 1:7-8; Colossians 1:13-14; Hebrews 2:14-16; I Peter 1:18-19; Revelation 5:8-10

Ruth

The book of Ruth (a Gentile woman who chose the God of Abraham as her God and subsequently became part of the lineage of The Seed) took place during the time of the judges. The reason Naomi, Ruth's Hebrew mother-in-law, left Israel and went to Moab in the first place was because there was a famine in Israel.
There was a famine in Israel because Israel disobeyed God—
God was true to His Covenant so He cursed Israel; He withheld His rain from them.
If Israel obeyed, it would be the head and not the tail.
Everything would go very well.
If Israel disobeyed, it would be the tail and not the head.
There would be famine, pestilence, death, and other cursings!
Deuteronomy 28:13, 44

Elimelech took his wife, Naomi, and his two sons into the land of Moab because of the famine. While they were there, their two sons married Moabite women, Orpah and Ruth. Then, in God's sovereignty, Elimelech died along with his two sons, leaving Naomi widowed with her two widowed Moabite daughter-in-laws.

When Naomi hears that God has visited His people back in the land of Israel (in giving them food) she decides to return. Her two daughters insist on going with her because they love her. However, Naomi painfully tells them to return to their own families in Moab and seek new husbands there. Orpah listens to her mother and leaves weeping; Ruth however stays with Naomi and makes a covenant vow to her.

Ruth had chosen to take care of Naomi, and in so doing would seek refuge under the wings of the LORD, the God of Israel. God had chosen to take care of Ruth by leading her to her kinsman redeemer, Boaz. Boaz would take care of Ruth from the moment he met her to the day they were wed. Their relationship is an amazing picture of what Christ has done for the church and how He will provide for His people Israel, because both Ruth (Gentile) and Naomi (Jew) receive a redeemer.

In the last few verses of Ruth we see the lineage of The Seed continued. The lineage starts with Perez, the son of Judah, through Boaz, and right up to David.

HIStory Event 12
...Israel Rejects GOD as her King

I Samuel

I Samuel covers the life of Saul, Israel's first king. The people did not want God to be their King any longer and rejected Him. They begged Samuel, God's last judge, for a human king to rule them so they could be like the other nations.

God's purpose for the nation of Israel was to be a kingdom of priests, a holy nation, a light to the other nations. They were to show the world Who God really was and lead all the other nations to Him. Instead, they were the ones being led! They were following the ways of the nations—the nations who would not admit that God was the LORD <u>at</u> all—much less the LORD <u>of</u> all!

Saul was a tall and handsome man, a seemingly perfect choice (albeit fleshly) for the nation of Israel's king. Though Saul obeyed a few times at the beginning of his reign, he proved time and time again to be disobedient to the LORD. Samuel rebuked and reproved Saul—but it was to no avail. God had sought someone else out to be king—someone "after His Own heart."

God's choice for a king over His people was David. As David was exalted, Saul's jealousy grew, and David spent much of his time in the wilderness fleeing Saul's rage. This game of "cat and mouse" continued until the death of Saul.

II Samuel

After Saul's death David became Israel's second king. He took the city of Jebus in battle (later named Jerusalem) and made provisions to build a temple for God there. However, God forbade David from building the temple; instead Solomon, David's son, would build it. God made a Covenant with David and promised that his kingdom and throne would endure before Him forever. The Seed that God promised back in Genesis would come from the lineage of David.

I Kings

I Kings commences with Solomon becoming king in his father David's place. After Solomon's sinful reign, the kingdom of Israel is torn in two by God. Solomon's servant, Jeroboam, becomes king over the ten northern tribes of Israel. Solomon's son, Rehoboam, becomes king over the two southern tribes of Israel. I Kings continues with story after story recounting the deeds of the kings of Israel (mostly evil) through the kings of Ahaziah (NK) and Jehoshaphat (SK).

II Kings

II Kings takes up where I Kings leaves off. It was a dark period of time for both Israel and Judah. They continually sought after the idols of the nations around them. Though there were a few bright shimmers of hope (like Josiah), the people's hearts were set to do evil and follow other gods. Though God sent His prophets to warn them, they would not listen. Eventually God sent Assyria and took the Northern Kingdom into captivity. Though the Southern Kingdom saw this, they did not repent either. Therefore, God kept the Covenant and took them into captivity, but in His mercy promised that they would return to the Land He gave them.

Read and Observe

1. **I Samuel 8:1-8; Exodus 19:6**
2. **I Samuel 9:1-2; 13:9-14; 15:9-11, 17-23; 16:14**
3. **I Samuel 16:1, 13; II Samuel 2:10-11; I Samuel 13:14; I Kings 15:5; II Samuel 12:1-13; I Samuel 15:20-21**
4. **II Samuel 7:8-16**
5. **II Samuel 7:1-2; I Kings 5:5; 11:1-13**

Read and Answer

1. I Samuel 8:1-8
When Samuel was old, what did the people ask for?

What was the reason the people gave to Samuel for wanting a king to rule over them?

How did Samuel feel about this request?

What did Samuel do?

What did God tell Samuel to do?

Why?

Exodus 19:6
What was God's purpose for Israel?

    1.

    2.

2. I Samuel 9:1-2
God gives Israel what they want. What was their "king to be" like?

I Samuel 13:9-14
How did Saul act?

What did he not keep?

What would God have done if Saul had kept the commandment of the LORD?

What would God do because Saul had not kept the commandment of the LORD?

I Samuel 15:9-11, 17-23
When Saul was not willing to destroy the Amalekites completely, how did God feel?

How did Samuel feel?

What was the mission on which God sent Saul?

Did Saul fulfill that mission?

When Samuel confronted him, what did Saul say?

What is the same as "not obeying the voice of the LORD"?

As God continues to speak through Samuel, He makes His point. Have you ever ignored the voice of the LORD—whether He spoke to you through His Word during a sermon, or song, or simply a thought? God says ignoring Him is evil in His sight!

What does the LORD take the most delight in?

What is disobedience or rebellion the same as?

What is insubordination the same as?

Because Saul rejected the Word of the LORD, what did God do?

I Samuel 16:14
What did God do concerning Saul?

      1.

      2.

3. **I Samuel 16:1, 13**
David would be Saul's replacement. Who picked David?

I Samuel 13:14
How did God choose David?

Just a reminder → why did God replace Saul?

I Kings 15:5
In contrast to Saul, what did David do?

II Samuel 12:1-13
David was not perfect, but when he was confronted with his sin, what did he immediately do?

I Samuel 15:20-21
How was this different than Saul's reaction when Samuel confronted him with his sin?

4. **II Samuel 7:8-16**
God again identifies whose family line The Seed will come from. Whose family is identified?

5. **II Samuel 7:1-2**
Why did David have rest from his enemies?

When David was enjoying his rest from his enemies, what did he notice?

I Kings 5:5
What did he intend to do about it?

Who was to build it?

I Kings 11:1-13
Solomon, David's son, built the Temple for the L ORD. However, he didn't continue to follow the Word of the L ORD later in his life. How many wives did Solomon have?

From where did he take his wives?

What had the L ORD said about those nations?

Why did God tell the nation of Israel to not associate with those nations?

What happened to Solomon's heart as a result of his 700 wives and princesses and his 300 concubines? (This should have come as no surprise to Solomon. God had warned him beforehand!)

Where did his heart turn to?

What did Solomon do in the sight of the L ORD?

What did Solomon build for his wives?

How did the L ORD feel about what Solomon was doing?

What did the L ORD tell Solomon He was going to do?

Did God tear the kingdom out of Solomon's hands right away?

Why not?

Did God tear the entire kingdom out of Solomon's hand?

Why not? (Hint: Remember the promise of The Seed! Remember whose family God last identified for us that The Seed would come from!)

READ AND REASON

1. I Samuel 8:1-8; Exodus 19:6
Samuel was the last judge. He was also a prophet and a priest. His sons were next in line, but the people didn't want his sons to judge them. The Israelites were wicked and wanted a king like the other nations. They wanted to be like everybody else. Everybody else had a king—they wanted a king! What was so wrong with that? *Everything!!!* Remember God gave them the Law and the Tabernacle to make them *different from* every other nation on the face of the earth! They were to be a light to the Gentile nations so they could know God and become like He wanted them to be. Instead, Israel was trying to become like the nations!

God was grieved. God told Samuel, *"Go ahead and anoint a king. They haven't rejected you, Samuel. They have rejected Me as their King."*

Do you see how much The Seed, the Savior, is needed? We humans need a heart that wants to follow God's ways instead of one that wants to separate ourselves from Him.

2. I Samuel 9:1-2; 13:9-14; 15:9-11, 17-23; 16:14
God gave them Saul—the people's choice. He was handsome and tall… and he disobeyed God! Saul rebelled against God's specific command. God says rebellion is the same as the sin of witchcraft. God rejected Saul from being king because Saul rejected the Word of the LORD. From then on, Saul was miserable.

3. I Samuel 16:1, 13; II Samuel 2:10-11; I Samuel 13:14; I Kings 15:5; II Samuel 12:1-13; I Samuel 15:20-21
God gave them David—God's choice. He also was handsome, but he had a heart after God's Own heart! The Spirit of the LORD came mightily upon David from the day that he was anointed with oil by Samuel. In fact, God tells us that David did what was right in His sight, and did not turn aside from anything that He commanded him all the days of his life, except in the matter of Uriah the Hittite. Nathan, God's prophet, confronted David over his sin, and David repented.

I want God to come upon me mightily.
I want to be controlled by His Spirit in a mighty way → not to do mighty things,
but to walk in the exact center of His will to please Him, to obey Him more perfectly. Amen.

4. II Samuel 7:8-16

Adam and Eve
⇓
    Abraham
        ⇓
        Judah
            ⇓
            David
                ⇓
                The Seed

God promised Adam and Eve that The Seed would come and save men. He chose Abraham to carry the line of The Seed. Abraham's descendant, Judah, was chosen from the 12 sons of Israel to bring The Seed. God told Judah that the scepter would not depart from his hand. David was chosen from the tribe of Judah. God made a Covenant with David and promised him that The Seed, the Messiah, would sit on David's throne. The Seed would have an everlasting Kingdom, and He would come through David.

> ## PSALMS
>
> Many of the Psalms deal with persecution, as David was hunted down by Saul in the wilderness. Still others deal with repentance toward God and a plea for forgiveness. The coming of The Seed was prophesied, Israel's future was foretold, and there were accountings of the nation of Israel's history. Whatever the subject, one thing is for certain, these Psalms are God's Word put in musical form meant to bring Him Glory as they (the Psalms) reflect His character and attributes.

5. II Samuel 7:1-2; I Kings 5:5; 11:1-13
David had been a bloody warrior from his youth to his old age. David had conquered many peoples and enjoyed many victories. David had obeyed God, and God had blessed Israel.

After the LORD had given David rest on every side from all his enemies, David decided he wanted to build a house for God. David told Nathan, the prophet of God, that he, the king, was living in a house of cedar, while the Ark of God was dwelling with tent curtains.

The Israelites were no longer following their traveling Tabernacle. During the time of the judges, the Ark of the Covenant had been taken to Philistia. The Philistines sent it back (because it was causing them all sorts of grief!), but it had never been put back in its rightful place in the Tabernacle. **I Samuel 5:1-7:2**

God responded to David's desire to build Him a house by telling him, "You have been a man of blood." God didn't tell David that was wrong. God made David a man of blood for a purpose, but it wasn't to build a Temple. God told David that his son would build the Temple for Him instead. **I Chronicles 22:8-10**

David's son, Solomon, was the next king over Israel. Solomon was the one that God chose to build His Temple in Jerusalem (the main city in the nation of Israel). There was peace and glory during his reign.

He was wise and wealthy, but not wise enough to obey God! He still disobeyed God and multiplied wives, horses, and silver to himself. There had to be a consequence for his sin. There always is because God is Holy. He has to punish disobedience. In 931 BC, God tore the kingdom of Israel in two because of Solomon's sin.

POINT OF DEPTH

Below I have several marked passages of Scripture printed out for you. Read them through noticing what Hebrew word is used and what it means. (The numbers come from *Strong's Exhaustive Concordance of the Bible*.**) Watch, because sometimes one is translated interchangeably with another. Basically, I want you to notice what they all have in common.**

<u>4390 mala</u> – **filled, endowed, completed, armed**

2450/2451 chokah – wisdom, expert, skilled

<u>8394 tebunah</u> – **discernment, reasoning, skill, to act wisely**

1847 daath – **knowledge, skill, concern**

995 BIN – **act wisely, consider carefully**

<u>8085 shama</u> – **to hear**

<u>3820/3824 lebab</u> – **inner man, mind, will, heart**

Exodus 28:3
"You shall speak to all the skillful persons whom I have <u>endowed</u> with the spirit of **wisdom**, that they make Aaron's garments to consecrate him, that he may minister as priest to Me."

If a person is full of skill, i.e. skillful, it is because God put skill in him by giving him the spirit of wisdom. Here, God gave someone skill to do a job that would enable another person to serve God. The skill is to make Aaron's garments so that Aaron could be consecrated, set apart and able to minister to God.

Exodus 31:1-6
"Now the LORD spoke to Moses, saying, 'See, I have called by name Bezalel, the son of Uri, the son of Hur, of the tribe of Judah. I have <u>filled</u> him with the Spirit of God in **wisdom**, in <u>understanding</u>, in *knowledge*, and in all kinds of craftsmanship, to make artistic designs for work in gold, in silver, and in bronze, and in the cutting of stones for settings, and in the carving of wood, that he may work in all kinds of craftsmanship. And behold, I Myself have appointed with him Oholiab, the son of Ahisamach, of the tribe of Dan, and in the <u>hearts</u> of all who are **skillful** I have put **skill**—that they may make all that I have commanded you.'"

Here God chose one man, Bezalel, and filled him with the Spirit of God in wisdom. This is the same wisdom that God gives to make people skillful. It is further explained to us that God gave Bezalel the Spirit of God in understanding, in knowledge and in all kinds of craftsmanship. God also gave skill to Oholiab. Why? Because God had a job He wanted done, He equipped certain men to do it! He gave them the skill needed to be able to obey the commands of God! In this case, it was to make certain things for the Temple so that men could worship God in the way God desired.

I Kings 3:7-12
"'And now, O LORD my God, Thou hast made Thy servant king in place of my father David, yet I am but a little child; I do not know how to go out or come in. And Thy servant is in the midst of Thy people which Thou hast chosen, a great people who cannot be numbered or counted for multitude. So give Your servant an **understanding** <u>heart</u> to judge Your people to DISCERN between good and evil. For who is able to judge this great people of Yours?' It was pleasing in the sight of the LORD that Solomon had asked this thing. God said to him, 'Because you have asked this thing and have not asked for yourself long life, nor have asked riches for yourself, nor have you asked for the life of your enemies, but have asked for yourself DISCERNMENT to <u>understand</u> justice, behold, I have done according to your words. Behold, I have given you a **wise** and DISCERNING <u>heart</u>, so that there has been no one like you before you, nor shall one like you arise after you.'"

This passage is familiar. Solomon asks for wisdom and he gets wisdom! But notice that the wise heart God gives him is the same wisdom He gave to other skillful and wise people. God gave Solomon skill to do something for Him. What? Judge the people in justice. The wisdom came for a purpose. The purpose is always going to be to serve God!

I Kings 4:29
"Now God gave Solomon **wisdom** and very great discernment and breadth of mind, like the sand that is on the seashore."

Again we see that God gave Solomon wisdom or "made him skillful." His skill was not to make artistic carvings, but instead, it was to have great discernment. God gave him "breadth of mind" or "width of heart." God gave Solomon the discerning knowledge to know what to do to accomplish the job God had for him → to judge His people as their king. That's why Solomon asked for it in the first place! I Kings 3:8-9

I Kings 7:14
"He was a widow's son from the tribe of Naphtali, and his father was a man of Tyre, a worker in bronze; and he was filled with **wisdom** and understanding and *skill* for doing any work in bronze. So he came to King Solomon and performed all his work."

Here God filled a widow's son with wisdom (expertise and skill) and understanding (discernment, skill, reasoning to act wisely) and skill (knowledge, skill, and concern). What was he to do with all this wisdom? He was to perform the work of the LORD in the building of the Temple of his God!

I took piano lessons as a young girl. I hardly ever practiced. It was a terrible waste of my parents' money. I couldn't even play a simple song. In fact, at my first (and last!) piano recital I started out my song with all the wrong notes! Boy! Did they sound awful! So I got up, went back to my seat, opened my music book, found the right notes and went back to the piano and tried it again → but to no avail! I simply was not a pianist!

Throughout my adult years I have regretted never learning the skill of piano playing. As I watched others in my church, I coveted their skill. I even thought half-heartedly about taking lessons as an adult. All I did was think about it though! I didn't have the right motives anyway. I just wanted to "perform" like the others! Oh, I would have called it service to the LORD, but it wouldn't have been. It would have been attention for me!

Then we started attending a different church. There was a woman there who played as though the piano was part of her. She could play any song in any key at anytime! She was amazing! But what I really loved about her playing was that she always sang as she played and she led you right into worshiping the LORD with her.

I thought of the nasty little motive that had lived in my heart for so many years and quietly thanked God that I never did learn how to play because I would not have given Glory to Him like she did. I would have taken whatever glory I could have for myself.

Then, one day, this lovely lady offered me the deal of a lifetime! She knew that my husband and I were full-time missionaries. She knew I was awed over her playing. She offered to teach me how to play by "ear" for free! I told her right away, "Thank you, but no. I have tried to play before and it's just no use. I barely graduated from John Thompson's First Grade Book for Piano!"

She said, "Sharon, music was designed by God. Music is all about math, and math, too, is designed by God. If you learn His ways and you play for Him, you will be able to play."

"Hmmm…" Boy, did I ever want to play. And this time, my heart motive was right. I had seen a godly example and I wanted to do nothing more than what she had done. I wanted to help people worship God. So we started lessons. She was able to give me one lesson a month for ten months.

That very first lesson was life changing for me. She taught me how to play "Amazing Grace" using chords. I had never been able to play *any* song before and now, here I was singing and thanking God for His grace through this song anytime I wanted to! She prayed for me and said she believed that God was going to give me the ability to play the piano.

Instantly my mind shot to the truth about Solomon, Bezalel, and Oholiab's wisdom! God had given them a gift of wisdom, of skill, of understanding, and of knowledge to be able to do the job that He had for them to do, in order for them to serve God in the way God wanted them to!

I prayed, "Enlarge my heart, O LORD, like You enlarged theirs! Give me wisdom to play this piano for You and You alone. Please use me, God, in Your Kingdom!" I knew that my spiritual gift of teaching had been given to me according to the will of God at the time of my salvation, but this was different; I was asking God to give me wisdom, understanding, and skill to play for Him.

Well, shortly after my second piano lesson I was in Chattanooga, Tennessee for a Precept Ministries Institute of Training. Although I was traveling alone, I met people right away. I asked a couple of ladies if they knew whether there was a piano someplace that I could practice on. They did not know of one. I was going to be there for almost two weeks, and I wanted to keep using the chords I had recently learned so I wouldn't forget them. Plus, I just so enjoyed meeting with the LORD and praising Him through the piano. By now, after two lessons, I could play two songs, "Amazing Grace" and "What a Mighty God."

That evening for dinner I sat with these same two ladies I met earlier. When we were done eating, they excused themselves from the table and said they were going to practice. They had found a piano in the main auditorium. I asked what they were practicing for. They informed me that they had talked to Jack Arthur and asked if they could lead morning praise and worship sessions for anyone who would want to come. I was elated! I wanted to come! So I asked them what time the sessions would be. They thought around 7:30 a.m.

Then they just stood there and looked at me. I waited for them to say something. Finally they said, "Are you coming?" "Where?" I asked. "To practice with us!"

Since they didn't know whether I could sing or not, I was surprised, so I replied, "You want me to sing with you?" They looked at each other quizzically and then answered me, "Well, you can sing, too, if you like, but you're going to play the piano for us."

"What??? Oh, No!!! You don't understand!!! I can't play the piano. I have only had two lessons and I only know how to play two songs. And I don't actually play either of those songs very well."

"But we've already set it up with Jack to have morning worship sessions throughout the conference." I replied, "Do you mean *the* Jack Arthur?" Although I tried in vain to convince them that this could not work because I could not play the piano, they would not listen.

Finally, I consented to go to the auditorium to show them very graphically just how *much* I couldn't play the piano. I thought, "Once they hear my little wimpy chords, they will realize what a foolish thing they have done!"

We got to the auditorium and I played the two songs I knew. Actually, they weren't unimpressed at all. They were thrilled. I didn't know what it was going to take to convince them that I couldn't play!

Then one of them said, "Hey, do you know this song?" and started singing a praise song. I didn't know it, of course, and emphatically said, "Gals, you just don't seem to understand. *I can not play the piano!*" I put my hands on the keyboard to show them, knowing that nothing but wrong notes would sound.

But, completely to my shock (although not so much to theirs since they were convinced that I could play) the notes that my fingers hit were the right ones! I couldn't believe what I was hearing. I was playing the exact song she was singing and I was playing in the same key! Amazing!!!

This, of course, did not help to prove to them that I couldn't play. So my other new friend started singing a different song and said, "How about this one?" I again put my fingers on the keyboard and found that I was playing along with her. Amazing! Yes, it was a miracle. I knew that I couldn't play. I knew it had to be God! By this time, they believed my humility had been a ploy and that I could really play anything I felt like playing. As we stayed there and worshiped God for over an hour, I played song after song.

Twice that evening, my flesh rose up and shouted out to me, "Hey, Sharon, not bad!" When I entertained that thought, instantly all that came out of the piano were notes that hurt my ears. Then I would immediately humble myself before God again, and I would start back playing the notes correctly. I couldn't help but think of Peter when he was walking on the water. When his eyes were on Jesus, he was fine, but when he put his eyes on himself and the situation around him, he fell *flat* (sorry about the pun!) Matthew 14:29-30

Well, needless to say, I was overjoyed at what God had done. I knew it was a special gift from Him for that special time. Perhaps He was giving me a taste of what He had in store for me.

I came home from that conference elated and excited to share with everyone the miracle that God had performed. I wondered once or twice whether this gift would stay or leave me once I was back at home. It left. But I remembered and I told of the mighty power of God whenever anyone would listen.

Within a couple of weeks after I was home I felt like God was asking me to come to the piano, so I went. I thought He was telling me to play something, to just put my hands on the keyboard like I had done in Chattanooga, so I did. The loveliest chord sounded. I didn't know what it was, of course, but it was beautiful. I moved my hands and another great sounding chord was played. Suddenly, I was playing a song, a real song, and one that I had never heard before.

I had asked God to enlarge my heart, to give me wisdom to play and He was! I stopped right then and told God again that I was His servant. Whatever He wanted to do through me with the piano was fine. I would simply obey.

I had no idea the name of the chords I played that day. In fact, at that time, I didn't even know *if* they *were* genuine chords. So I took out a piece of paper and wrote down every note that my fingers were on; thumb on B, pointer finger on C, middle finger on E$^\flat$, pinky on G, etc.

Then I would play the notes over and over again. It was beautiful to my ears. Suddenly there were words in my head. Words about God—words that spoke of Who He is—words from HIS WORD! I wrote them down, too.

I went to my third piano lesson with my scribbled notes and chord "wannabes." I showed them to my teacher. After playing them on the piano she said, "Sharon, not only are these chords real—they are complicated. You have written a song in a very difficult key." Then I just sat there, letting the truth wash over me. God had answered my prayer. Once again, God had shown me He was God!!!

After that, God started calling me to the piano regularly and I would just put my hands on the keyboard. I was always amazed at the gorgeous sounds that came out. Each time they were different because each time there was a new song!

God said to sing to Him a new song! Psalm 33:3; 40:3 Well, each time He gave me notes He also gave me His words from His Bible. And that is exactly what I would do. I would sing them back to God over and over. My piano teacher would ask me every month, "What has God given you this month?" I was always anxious to show her! The thing that pleased me the most was that the songs were all about Him, not about man—just like His Word—because they *were* **His Words!**

The Spirit had given me the spiritual gift of teaching to be used in the body of Christ. I Corinthians 12 He had given me the ability to explain the Scriptures so as to give understanding to those who were listening.

The Lord had provided the ministry to use my spiritual gift. The ministry was teaching my children the Bible. It was also teaching Bible students three times a week plus monthly workshops on Saturdays.

God gave the effects of that ministry. Leading "pew people" to the Lord was His design. Many, many faithful church members were being called to a confrontation with the Word of God. Many realized that their "faith" had been in good works, church attendance, giving, baptism, even their membership in church. Upon that realization, they were able to enter into the Holy of Holies for the very first time by placing their faith solely in the finished work of Jesus Christ!

What God was doing with me through the songs made so much sense! He was giving me another avenue of ministry using the same spiritual gift. The words in the songs were all about Him. They were teaching tools! They were His Word.

God placed me in situations where I could teach people the songs. Words to a song stay in your mind long after they have been sung. God certainly knew what He was doing, and I was just flabbergasted every time I thought about it!

Oh, how I wish that everyone knew about Jesus! Oh, how I wish that everyone would bend his or her knee to the God of the Universe! Someday everyone will. Until then, "Thank You, God, for using me in any way at all!"

Point of Connection

God is the King of His people. He has made them and ruled over them and delivered them. However, God prophesies that they will reject Him as King over them and set a king over themselves like the rest of the nations → a man. God is *not* telling the Israelites in Deuteronomy that it is okay for them to have a human king over them! He is simply prophesying that they will reject Him once they are in the land. Deuteronomy 28:36 And, of course, they do. I Samuel 8:7

Because He is going to allow them to reject Him as King and place a human king over them, God, in His grace, gives them certain requirements that will help them not to fall into sin as deeply as they would otherwise. Of course, this would mean that they would have to actually obey His requirements!

Look at what He tells them to do. Deuteronomy 17:14-20
1. The king must be an Israelite.
2. The king must not multiply horses for himself.
3. The king must not cause the people to return to Egypt to multiply horses for themselves.
4. The king must not multiply wives for himself.
5. The king must not greatly increase gold or silver for himself.
6. The king must write for himself a copy of the Law in the presence of the Levitical priests.
7. The king must keep the copy of the Law with him every day.
8. The king must read the copy of the Law every day.

God had a reason for each of these requirements.

1.
Why do you think He said the king must not be a foreigner? Think about this with me. What was God's purpose for the nation of Israel? First of all, Israel would produce The Seed that would be the Savior of the world. Secondly, Israel was to be a light to the nations so they could find God, their Savior!

How was Israel to be that light? By being holy, set apart, different from the other nations. If the people set a king over them who was a foreigner, he would bring in all the ways of that other nation and Israel would look just like everybody else! That just wouldn't do because God had a plan!

2 and 3.
Why wasn't the king supposed to multiply horses for himself or cause the people to return to Egypt to multiply horses either? What was the purpose of having horses? It wasn't to trail ride! Horses represented the "war-power" of a nation. God wanted to fight Israel's battles for them because He was God! He wanted His people to depend upon Him. That brought Him Glory! If they depended on their horses and they won a battle, where would all the glory go?

4.
Why wasn't the king supposed to multiply wives to himself? God wanted people to see a picture of what their relationship to Him was supposed to be through the structure that He ordained in marriage. That picture consisted of one man and one woman. Two individuals joined in marriage became one flesh. If the king married many wives, his heart would be turned away from God. The man would end up serving his many wives instead of God. As usual, God was concerned with His Glory being seen. Mankind was to serve one God—the LORD.

5.
Why wasn't the king supposed to greatly increase silver and gold for himself? Wealth can translate into being independent from God. If the king had wealth that he had accumulated

for himself, he would feel the need to protect it himself. Again, the king would not be dependent upon God, and God would lose His Glory.

6, 7, and 8.
The last requirements for the king were of utmost importance. They were the fail-safe element of ruling the people correctly.

The king needed to write out the Law by hand *himself!* It goes without saying that the king would know God's Law and ways better if he took the time to actually write it out himself. And of course, the king would never be able to plead "not guilty" because of ignorance! Keeping the Law with him daily and *reading* it daily would equip the king to rule the people, Israel, wisely…if the king would only obey what he knew!

If Solomon had obeyed God's requirements for a king, what a difference it could have made! He chose wisdom above everything else when God offered him a gift. He wanted to rule Israel wisely, yet in the end, he disregarded that wisdom and chose foolishness!

Solomon loved many foreign women. I Kings 11:1-5 God had told the nation of Israel *not* to associate with them. Remember, Solomon had written out the entire Word of God. He *knew* better!!! God even told him that those wives would turn his heart away from God, but Solomon held fast to his wives rather than to God! Solomon broke Covenant with God.

Solomon went so far as to build "high places," for each of his foreign wives to burn incense and sacrifice to their own gods. I Kings 11:6-8 How detestable! The man that God allowed to build His Temple turned around and built altars for other gods! I hate it!

Solomon did what was evil in the sight of the LORD and did not follow the LORD fully, as his father, David, had done. I Kings 11:33 God was angry with Solomon because He had appeared to him twice and commanded him not to go after foreign gods. I Kings 11:9-10 (Don't ever be jealous of Solomon because God appeared to him twice. God has appeared to us in His Word, in His Son, through His Spirit!)

Because Solomon did not keep Covenant with God, God would tear the kingdom of Israel from his hands. I Kings 11:11-13 Because of the promise that God had made to David, and for the sake of Jerusalem, God did not tear *all* the kingdom away from Solomon. And because of the promise that God had made to David, He didn't rip the kingdom in two during Solomon's lifetime.

What about us?
- How wise are we? Do we obey the voice of God or do we ignore Him? Do we even know what God has said?
- What do we read daily? The internet? The newspaper? A novel? The comics?
- What do we keep at our side daily? Our grudges? Our lusts? Our smartphones and tablets? The keys to our almighty "stuff"?

> What are we married to? Our jobs? Our bodies? The world? Our own ways?
> What have we multiplied to ourselves? Wealth? Health? Power? Friends?
> What have we built in our lives? Altars of time? Tradition? Rebellion?

God requires a holy people because *He* is Holy. He has to judge our disobedience!

Proverbs, Ecclesiastes, Song of Solomon

Solomon, David's son, authored these books (most, but not all of the Proverbs).

Proverbs is a collection of wisdom, including exhortations to do what is right—to obey God's Law and to be upright and diligent in everything.

Ecclesiastes looks at the labors and decisions of man on earth and what they accomplish in light of death. Solomon's conclusion is that all is vanity on the earth; therefore "fear God and keep His commandments."

Song of Solomon is a song of love between a man and his wife. God shows us pure dedication and love in this song. Many see this book as a poetic depiction of the relationship of God to Israel (His wife) or of Christ to the Church (His bride).

Point of Depth

The first time I visited Israel (which was also the first time I traveled overseas) I was by myself. The year was 1997, a year of great unrest for Israel. I went into El Al Terminal as a novice and naive traveler and was interrogated for three excruciating hours by three exasperated agents. Two were very, um, shall we say, "stern" with me. The third wasn't smiling, but at least she wasn't yelling at me!

Don't get me wrong—I was not at all upset with any of them, nor with El Al. I believe El Al is probably the safest airline in the world and because God's people, the Jews, are the most terrorized people in the world, I condone and bless every one of their measures (at least the ones I know about) in providing safety for every one of their passengers.

The interrogators took me into the back room, and eventually into the *back*, back room! Three separate and very slow times they each took every single piece of my luggage and contents apart, including my brand new camera and my curling iron. They gave me back the *parts* of my new camera and eventually informed me that my curling iron would *not* be traveling to Israel as planned.

At one point in the interrogation, when the two "stern" ones left the interrogation room, I was left alone with Miss "at least she's not yelling at me." I had been praying to God for strength and wisdom throughout the entire ordeal. Suddenly a thought came into my mind to talk to her. "Okay" I thought, "I'll try." I looked at her name-tag. It said "JAEL." So I ventured, (as friendly and confidently as I could) "How do you pronounce your name?" She said immediately, "Yah-el." She hesitated, and then in Hebrew-accented English fired a question at me, "Okay, you say you are a Christian. I am in the Bible. Who am I?"

At this point, I was ungenerously thinking, "Great! Just great! Your name couldn't have been Mary or Sarah! It had to be YAH-EL! *Who* is Jael!!!"

Then I prayed, "Father, I think You want me to talk to her. *I have read Your whole Bible*, and if her name is really in there, then I should have it written on my heart somewhere because that is what You have promised to do! Will You tell me who 'Yah-el' is, if she's in the Bible?"

Now, I wish God always answered as quickly and as clearly as He did at that moment, but I accept that He doesn't, and am grateful that He does even once in awhile! It popped into my head and out of my mouth something like this: "Judges! Tent-peg lady! You gave him milk!" (You can go to Judges 4 and read the account of one of Israel's great victories and Jael's part in it if you like!)

I was amazed to see Jael's eyebrows relax and her mouth drop open as I told her 'who she was'. She exclaimed, "You *do* know your Bible! You *are* a Christian!" At that moment, I realized God was orchestrating the entire situation and I knew He was sovereignly going to speak to Jael through me.

I peacefully replied to her, "No, Jael. I am not a Christian because I know the Bible. I am a Christian because God, the God of Israel, the One Who wrote the Bible, saved me and made me His child". God had given me an open door that no one could shut. I had an opportunity to witness to a Jew, one of God's special chosen treasures! It was wonderful!

I know that God could have given me the information about Jael whether I had ever read the Bible or not because He is God and He can do anything and everything, but I also know that is not how He usually works. This time, because I had read His entire Word, He simply brought back to my remembrance information He had spoken to me earlier through His Word.

There is a common myth among people that the Bible is too big to read.
The myth is a lie. It is not true at all!

The key to freedom from the lie in this case is faith in God's Word and obedience to Him. Deuteronomy 8:3 *"He humbled you and let you be hungry, and fed you with manna which you did not know, nor did your fathers know, that He might make you understand that man does not live by bread alone, but man lives by everything that proceeds out of the mouth of the LORD."* Do you live by eating a little bit of food once a day, or once a week, or once a month, or once a year? No, you eat regularly and consistently. So, too, you need to feed on His Word daily—and not just for a few minutes here or there! Job 23:12 says, *"I have not departed from the command of His lips; I have treasured the words of His mouth more than my necessary food."* Food is necessary for physical life and health, the Word of God is necessary for spiritual life and health!

Decades ago I was presented with the exhortation that many, if not most, Christians have never read the Bible through even once, much less regularly. I grew up believing that was quite a high and lofty ideal. I believed only preachers or very dedicated individuals would ever be able to do it!!! As I was hearing the exhortation, I realized that I was someone who had been taken captive by believing a lie from the pit of hell!

I had believed that the only way to even try to accomplish reading the whole Bible would be to use a guide and even then, *it would take me an entire year*! Trouble was, every time I started one of those "through the Bible in a year" schedules, I would eventually miss too many days, then I would feel stress and start to wonder if I could ever catch up. Sound familiar? Feeling a bit like a failure, I would ultimately quit and then wait to try again another year—because you know the *"only correct time"* to start reading the Bible with one of those guides is in January, don't you? Oh, boy!

I went home after receiving that exhortation determined to read through my Bible as literature. After all, what other book would you even expect to get anything out of if you stretched it out over the course of an entire year? Why, it's silly to even think about doing it. Unless it's a cookbook!!!

I started in Genesis (at the entirely wrong time of year, I might add) and read all the way through to Revelation in *only a few weeks*. And I found that I enjoyed it (what an understatement!) more than I could have ever imagined. Many times I couldn't put down God's Word because I was so engrossed and interested. I loosely counted up the hours I had spent reading and realized it wasn't all that many. (I won't tell you yet just how many.)

Hmmm... I had an idea! I decided to exhort my Bible study students in the same way that I had been exhorted! I told them how I had even learned interesting things in Leviticus! (Because of course, another one of Satan's lies is that parts, if not all, of the Bible are dry and boring or just too hard.) I told them how beneficial it was to read through an Old Testament book in just a few days because I could see how verses were simply referring back to something I had read just a night or so ago. I told them how I had started to cross-reference my own Bible myself whenever that would happen.

I told them the story of the fruit I saw from reading God's whole Word when I went to Israel and was interrogated by the El Al interrogation agents. My classes all loved the story I told them about Jael but still were not convinced they could ever really read the *whole* Bible, because they were believing the lie that it is *too big of a book for normal people to actually read!* Satan has filled the world, tragically, even the church, with the lie that the Bible is just *too big* to read—it would take too long! What is really *too big* is *Satan's lie*!!!

I then delivered the clincher, my last hope to persuade them. I said, "Just guess how long it would take. How long do you think?" Most said about one year. Some ventured to guess below that universal figure, but not too much lower.

I then said very quietly, "It only takes 60 to 70 hours to read the Bible." They couldn't believe it and responded, "No way could it possibly take less than many months!" I encouraged them, despite their unbelief, to just start reading it! God wrote His Bible as literature—He expects it to be read that way. It's not an encyclopedia!!! You don't just look up bits and pieces of it for information as it suits your need!

How about you? Did you know that the Bible can be read aloud in 77 hours? That means you can easily read the Bible all the way through silently to yourself, and it will take *less* than 77 hours! This should give you an idea of how long it will take you each and every time you read the Bible all the way through, because I am certainly not advocating reading it through just one time! You need to read it through as literature for the rest of your life—over and over and over again. (And, of course, it is a given that you must study it, as well.)

A few math facts are in order. I am using the 77 hour figure which, remember, comes from reading it aloud. Reading it silently to yourself will take even less time than the figures below. Ready? Here goes! If you read the Bible for 1 hour every day, it will only take you 77 days, or only 2 ½ months, to read it through. If you read the Bible for ½ hour (30 minutes) each day, it will only take you 154 days, or 5 months, to read it through. If you read the Bible for 15 minutes a day, it will only take you 308 days, or 10 months, to read it through. If you want to read through the Bible, *and you are determined to stretch it out to an entire year, <u>you must be willing to limit yourself to only reading it for 12 ⅗ minutes per day!!!</u>*

The truth is out!!! We are free to read God's Word!!!
You can read through the Bible in way less than one year!!!
You can read the Word of God all the way through many, many times in your life—
for the rest of your life!!!
You can live by every Word that proceeds out of the mouth of God!!!
Not only can you—you must!!!

When I told my students that if they only read the Bible for 15 minutes a day they would finish in 10 months they were amazed. That was less than the "through the Bible in a year" guide. By the way, I was not, and am not, suggesting to only read for 15 minutes a day; you need to spend serious reading hours, just like you would with any book you might read. The promotion of those kind of 'guides' may lead one to think it is so hard to do that practically the *only* way one can read the entire Bible is to use a schedule! That's garbage—and that is the place where I put my old guide!

The Bible is not an encyclopedia, although it has more information than one. Nor is the Bible a recipe book, although it gives you the Bread of Life. Therefore, you cannot read it like you would an encyclopedia or cookbook. You need to read it as a piece of literature—a Masterpiece to be exact!

One year, my husband, who was Director of WORD Center Ministries in Iowa, felt God wanted us, as a body, to read the entire Word of God out loud—Genesis to Revelation—round the clock for as long as it would take. The purpose was not a competition or a gimmick; rather, it was to dedicate the property God had given us by continuing to dispel the lie that Satan had entrenched in so many people—"Reading the Bible is just too huge of a task!"

We started at 6:00 PM Thursday, November 30, 2000, and finished at 11:37 PM on Sunday, December 3, 2000. During those 77 hours and 37 minutes, 88 different people came to read a portion of God's Word. The room where "The Reading" took place was available for anyone to come early, or stay later, to listen.

It was indescribable to be drenched (or delightfully drowned) in the Water of His Word hour after hour. Spirit and Life itself affected men, women, and children alike, as The Living Word spoke to all who came to listen to Him. It was more than an experience… it was a matter of being consumed by the Power and Love of God Almighty, Himself.

As The Reading continued throughout the hours, crescendo after crescendo echoed the cries of God's goodness. More than once, tears were common to all who were in the room. More than once, a pause in the reading reflected a heart that had been pierced by His living, active, and oh, so sharp, Word! More than once, I lowered my head, closed my eyes, and thanked this great and fearful God for His mercy and goodness to me.

I pray that you will see the importance of God's Word and be motivated to spend more time with Him in it. I pray that His Spirit and Life will consume you. I pray that you will seek Him in His Word daily. I pray that you will immerse yourself in His testimonies continually. May you never, ever be the same…

WORD Center Ministries is founded on, and grounded in, the WORD of GOD. We attempt to help people listen to God in His Word (the Bible) by teaching them how to study the Bible itself and by giving them the tools needed to study the Bible for themselves.

"The first step in studying the Bible is to read it." How can something which can elicit "Duh!" as a response be so profound?

154

HIStory Event 13
...GOD Splits the Kingdom of Israel in Two

Read and Observe

1. I Kings 11:26-40, 43; 12:1-24

Read and Answer

1. **I Kings 11:26-40, 43; 12:1-24**
Who was Jeroboam? How was he connected to Solomon?

Who was Rehoboam? How was he connected to Solomon?

What did God give to Jeroboam?

What did God give to Rehoboam?

What promise did God give to Jeroboam concerning his kingdom?

Read and Reason

1. **I Kings 11:26-40, 43; 12:1-24**
In 931 BC, when God took the kingdom of Israel and ripped it in two because of Solomon's disobedience, He gave one part to Jeroboam and one part to Rehoboam, David's grandson. God is faithful to His promise. He said that The Seed would come through David and that David would always have an heir on the throne.

If Solomon had not disobeyed, God would not have ripped part of the kingdom from David's house. If God did not keep His promises (Praise Him that He always does!), then He would not have ripped away only part of the kingdom—He would have ripped the whole thing out of Solomon's hands!

Here's how God brings it about: Jeroboam, one of Solomon's servants, is told that he will be given 10 of the 12 tribes of Israel to rule over. He is told that he will not have all the tribes because God has promised that The Seed, the Messiah, would come through the tribe of Judah through the lineage of David. God even makes him an offer. If Jeroboam will listen to all that God commands and walk in His ways, and do what is right in His sight by observing His statutes and commandments, then God will build him an enduring house and give those 10 tribes of Israel to him permanently.

When Solomon dies, his son, Rehoboam reigns in his place. Almost immediately, he gets advice from the assembly of people, including Jeroboam, who is not king yet, although God has promised him he will be. The people want Rehoboam to lighten their load in serving the king. They say, "Your dad broke our backs working for him. You need to loosen up a bit!"

Rehoboam goes to the elders for counsel. They advise the king to grant the people their petition. It's good counsel, but Rehoboam doesn't take it. He goes to some of his buddies from his childhood and asks them what they think. They tell him the opposite of what the elders have advised. They say rather than lightening the yoke, that he should make it much, much heavier. Rehoboam follows the poor counsel of his peers and puts pressure on the people.

Rehoboam did not listen to the people because God was fulfilling His Word that He spoke to Jeroboam. When the people heard the bad news, they rebelled and found themselves a king. Guess who? Right. They made Jeroboam king over them.

So God tears Israel into two kingdoms just like He said He would do. God is Sovereign over the affairs of mankind. He does *His* will among the peoples. He has the right to. He is God!

For the sake of understanding **HISTORY**, we will follow both parts of the kingdom, but only one at a time. God gave the tribe of Judah to Rehoboam, Solomon's son. Judah, along with Benjamin, became known as the Southern Kingdom. God gave the other ten tribes to Jeroboam, Solomon's servant. These ten tribes became known as the Northern Kingdom. We will follow **HISTORY** of the Northern Kingdom first.

POINT OF DEPTH

The story of Rehoboam receiving good and bad counsel from the elders and his peers (and the subsequent division of the kingdom of Israel), is one that I've heard a lot, *but* without proper context. So many times I've seen people focus on the drama unfolding and come to this conclusion: "Let us learn from the sin of Rehoboam—we should listen to counsel given by elders and not from our peers."

There are two problems with that conclusion.

1. **It is *not* an absolute truth, *nor* is it doctrine, but merely an event. We should never pull doctrine from events—only from clear, repeated teaching!**

2. **Obtaining counsel is *not* the main point of this story. God's sovereignty *is* the main point of this story. Solomon had sinned, so God appointed it for Rehoboam to listen to the bad counsel of his peers. I Kings 12:15 God was simply fulfilling His Word.**

That, my friend, is what this story is all about, not just the division of the Northern and Southern Kingdoms of Israel, but the complete and total control and sovereignty of our God. He told Solomon that because of his sin the kingdom would be divided in the days of his son, and so it was... He does whatever He pleases and He stands over His Word to perform it!!! Psalm 115:3; Jeremiah 1:12

Also, keep in mind that although the kingdom has been divided, the Covenant and Law has not. Both the northern and southern tribes are required to appear in Jerusalem for the Feasts of the LORD and to make sacrifices to the LORD. The Covenant Promises God made to them are still intact for both the kingdoms. Though The Seed will come through the southern tribe of Judah, that Seed will be for the whole nation of Israel. Not only that, but we will see that The Seed will be the One Who will eventually rejoin both kingdoms into one. Ezekiel 37:15-28

Over the next few Events we will look at both the Northern and Southern Kingdoms. Here is a chart with a simple breakdown on some of the facts.

Northern Kingdom	Southern Kingdom
Generally referred to as: Israel	Generally referred to as: Judah
Capital – Samaria	Capital – Jerusalem
King – Jeroboam, Solomon's servant	King – Rehoboam, Solomon's son
10 tribes – Reuben, Simeon, Manasseh, Ephraim, Issachar, Zebulun, Gad, Asher, Dan, Naphtali	2 tribes – Benjamin, Judah
Disobeys God, plays the harlot	Disobeys God, plays the harlot
God sends prophets to the northern tribes calling them to repent!	God sends prophets to the southern tribes calling them to repent!
Ignores and kills the prophets God sends	Ignores and kills the prophets God sends
Israel will not repent!	Judah will not repent!
God sends Assyria to take the Northern Kingdom into captivity – 722 BC	God sends Babylon to take the Southern Kingdom into captivity – 586 BC

HIStory Event 14
...GOD Sends Prophets to the Northern Kingdom of Israel (Israel)

Read and Observe

1. I Kings 12:25-33; 13:33; II Chronicles 13:8-9
2. I Kings 13:1-6; II Kings 23:15-20

Read and Answer

1. I Kings 12:25-33; 13:33; II Chronicles 13:8-9
Where did Jeroboam live when he first became king of the Northern Kingdom?

What was he worried would happen?

What did he decide to do to prevent his people from returning south to Jerusalem to offer sacrifices to God?

What did the people do?

Did Jeroboam obey the Word of God concerning who could be a priest?

Did Jeroboam obey the Word of God concerning *where* the Feasts of the LORD were to be celebrated?

Did Jeroboam obey the Word of God concerning *when* the Feasts of the LORD were to be celebrated?

Did Jeroboam obey the Word of God concerning *anything*?

2. I Kings 13:1-6
Who came by one day while Jeroboam was standing next to one of his altars to burn incense?

What did this man of God do?

What did he prophesy against the altar?

Did he name the person that would fulfill this prophecy?

What would be the sign that the man of God's words were from God and would most definitely happen as prophesied?

Did the sign take place?

II Kings 23:15-20
It is now 300 years later. Who is king at this time?

What did King Josiah do?

Was the prophecy fulfilled?

Read and Reason

1. I Kings 12:25-33; 13:33; II Chronicles 13:8-9
As I have said, in 931 BC, God tore the kingdom of Israel in two. Ten of the twelve tribes of Israel became the Northern Kingdom under the rule of Jeroboam, one of Solomon's servants. The Northern Kingdom was sometimes (early on) referred to as "Ephraim" because Jeroboam first built Shechem in the hill country of Ephraim and lived there. He went out from there and built Penuel. Samaria eventually became the capital of the Northern Kingdom. *The Northern Kingdom was sometimes (later on) referred to as "Ephraim" because in 733 BC all ten northern tribes were taken captive by Assyria except Ephraim and western Manasseh. In 722 BC the rest of the Northern Kingdom was destroyed.*

Jeroboam had a problem, though. The Israelites needed to follow the ceremonies of the Law which required them to go to Jerusalem three times a year to the Temple. The Temple in Jerusalem was the only place that Jews could worship, sacrifice, or keep feasts. Jeroboam was worried that the people from the ten tribes God had given him would defect to the Southern Kingdom if they went down to familiar Jerusalem. Now, did he have a legitimate concern? Not if he obeyed God—but he didn't! God had given him those ten tribes, and God promised to let him keep them if he would simply obey!

So what does Jeroboam do? How smart is he? Well, it seems he must have forgotten that it was God Who gave him his position as king, and it was God Who could and would take it away! Jeroboam decided to take matters into his own hands and fix everything. He thought he had a great idea. All he had to do was arrange it so the people didn't have to go south to Jerusalem to worship God. You can tell where this idea was leading!

He made two golden calves and he told the ten northern tribes, *"It is too much for you to go up to Jerusalem. Behold your gods, O Israel, that brought you up from the land of Egypt."* He set one in Bethel and the other one he put in Dan. Just in case that preposterous little ploy wasn't enough, he also built houses on high places (altars in the hills for foreign gods).

But he wasn't done yet; he would need priests to take care of all the ceremonial stuff. So… he just made his own! God was very clear to Moses that *only* Levites could be priests, but Jeroboam was on a roll. Why be burdened with all those cumbersome rules? He would make priests from all the people who were not of the sons of Levi! His rule was simply, *"If you want to be a priest, let me know! I'll give you a title!"*

As far as that goes, he thought, *"Why be stuck with God's calendar?"* He would just go ahead and devise his own feast days too! After all, he was the king, wasn't he?

Well, needless to say, idolatry increased abundantly in the Northern Kingdom. So God sent prophets calling the people to repent. The king and the people stopped up their ears and would not listen to the prophets, and instead, they stoned them.

Amos

Amos was just a shepherd from Tekoa and lived in the Southern Kingdom of Israel. God called him to the Northern Kingdom of Israel to deliver a prophet's message to those who were His.

Amos' fiery message was first directed to the nations literally surrounding Israel and then at Judah, but the Israelites did not see the ever tightening circle like a noose gathering around their neck. They did not realize that they, too, were the target of God's blistering rage over their own sin.

God made sure that Israel knew it was the Lord GOD Who was bringing this calamity upon them. **Amos 3:6**
He also reminded them why! **Amos 2:6**

HOSEA

Hosea was sent to the Northern Kingdom, but Israel would not listen!
The prophet's own life with his wife, Gomer,
was a picture of God's ways with His wife, Israel.

God married Israel,
but she soon rejected Him and became a harlot, sleeping daily with the world.
Despite her loathsome behavior,
God was faithful to her and would not give up on her.
He bought her out of the slave market of sin and took her home with Him,
but He shut her up until a future time
when He would go in to her once more as a husband.

Jesus paid the price to buy Israel back for God.
Israel is now shut up during the age of the church,
but God is not finished with Israel.
He will indeed go back into her as a husband
when the Redeemer Himself comes again, this time in full Glory!
The people had eyes, but they would not see themselves in the life of Gomer.

2. I Kings 13:1-6; II Kings 23:15-20

At God's word, a man of God came from Judah to Bethel while Jeroboam was standing by the altar to burn incense. (God controls people, time, places, and events simply by His Word! Doesn't God just take your breath away!) God's prophet cried against the altar, *"O altar, altar, the LORD says that a son will be born to the house of David by the name of Josiah. He will sacrifice and burn the bones of the priests who burned incense on you!"*

Three hundred years later, God's words through the prophet came true. King Josiah came to Bethel and dug up the bones of the very priests who had sacrificed on that ungodly altar and burned them on the same altar! Then he broke down the altar and the high place, burned them and ground them into dust!

Josiah noticed a monument there in Bethel and asked about it. It was the grave of the man of God who came from Judah and proclaimed the very things that Josiah had done against the altar of Bethel. Josiah told everyone *not* to disturb the bones of the prophet from Judah!

Josiah finished his campaign by slaughtering the priests who were living at that time and burning their bodies on the altar as well. God's Word is sure. He stands over His Word to perform it.
Jeremiah 1:12 It will not go back to Him without accomplishing exactly what He sent it for!
Isaiah 55:11 If He says it will happen → *it will!* He is in charge of everything—every single thing!

JONAH

Jonah's story is familiar to many, yet we need to study the book of Jonah with fresh eyes. Jonah disobeyed the LORD's command to preach repentance to the wicked city of Nineveh. God sent calamity on Jonah until he obeyed. When he finally cried out the news of Nineveh's imminent destruction, the Ninevites repented (and he was not even finished walking through the city).

Because of their repentance, God had compassion and relented concerning the calamity He had declared He would bring to them. Jonah was angry that God had compassion on the city of Nineveh and the LORD rebuked him.
Both calamity and compassion come from the LORD;
and every conversion is the work of the grace of God.

Think with me for a moment.
Jonah was not sent to the Jews. Instead, he was sent to Nineveh in Assyria. It's interesting to consider that about 50 years later God sent the Northern Kingdom to Assyria as a judgment because they broke Covenant with Him, and yet here He is sending the Word of Righteousness to the nation that will be housing Israel during her captivity... perhaps to lessen the severity of Assyria's treatment toward the Jews? God's love for Israel is amazing!

Sadly, Assyria did not stay in her repentant state for long and God would eventually dispense His judgment on her, as well.

POINT OF DEPTH

We have a much more sure word of prophecy than the ancients ever did. Are you listening? Are you believing? Are you obeying? You'd better be, because God is *still* standing over His Word to perform it!!!

HIStory Event 15
...GOD Sends Assyria to Take the Northern Kingdom into Captivity

READ AND OBSERVE

1. II Kings 17

READ AND ANSWER

1. II Kings 17
Why did the nation of Assyria come up against Israel?

When the verse says *"the sons of Israel had sinned against the LORD their God, Who had brought them up from the land of Egypt from under the hand of Pharaoh,"* what important event is it referring to? (When God delivered Israel from Egypt, to what mountain did He take them and what did He give them there?)

Israel did not keep her Covenant with God but went after other gods. God had the right to destroy her for their disobedience, yet He was patient with her. But He warned her that if she did not repent He would indeed destroy her—He would keep His Covenant with her! When He sent prophets to warn her, did she listen?

Who was Israel to fear?

Did they?

READ AND REASON

1. II Kings 17

God sent prophets, one after another, patiently urging His people to obey Him and love Him. They stiffened their necks and continued to reject Him while clinging defiantly to their idols. They even sacrificed their own children by fire and offered them to foreign gods!

In 931 BC, God had divided Israel into two kingdoms. Then for almost 200 years He continually pleaded with them to confess and repent and come back to Him. Now, He would take action. He would no longer wait to keep His Covenant with His people. They had done evil in His sight repeatedly. He would take them out of the land and send them into exile.

God brought the Assyrians down to invade the land in 722 BC. King Hoshea, who was king over Israel in Samaria, was carried away into exile to Assyria along with most of the people. The Assyrians left some of the Jews, but took most out.

Once the king of Assyria took Israel out of the land, he brought in other people to inhabit it. Men came from Babylon, Cuthah, Avva, Hamath, and Sepharvaim and settled in the cities of Samaria in place of the sons of Israel. Of course they did not fear the LORD (or they would never have moved into God's neighborhood uninvited!), and they brought their idols into the land. God wasn't pleased. He sent lions among them to kill them.

So the squatters told the king of Assyria about it. They thought their problem was just that they didn't know the ways of the "god" of this land. The king had a plan: *"Just go get one of the priests of Samaria that we sent into exile, bring him back and have him teach you new guys how to fear his 'god.'"* So they brought back a priest to Bethel. (Now, if you remember, the priests from Samaria were simply "anyone who wanted to be one," they were not from the tribe of Levi and thus had a position that did not belong to them, so they were not even true priests!)

The nations tried to learn how to keep God off their backs by learning His ways, but they didn't have a righteous teacher. The priest from Samaria forgot to tell them one little thing…God's Name is Qanna. He is a jealous God. He will not let you worship any other god but Him! The other nations were still making their own gods but trying to fear the LORD on the side. They even made a whole bunch of brand new high priests, just to be safe. Sounds so much like today—people doing things their own way, running their own lives…

POINT OF CONNECTION

The Jews had no dealings with the Samaritans. Yet, the Samaritan woman (who came to draw water from the well and found Jesus, the Living Water there instead) referred to *"our Fathers"* **who** *"worshiped in this mountain."* **John 4:9, 20 Samaria is close to Mount Ebal, the barren mountain of cursing, and Mount Gerizim, the lush mountain of blessing. She was referring to Mount Gerizim when the people had stood in the valley and said,** *"Amen"* **in response to the stating of the laws of God from the mountaintop. Deuteronomy 27**

Ever wonder why the Jews hated the Samaritans? It was leftover emotion from all the years of the Northern and Southern Kingdoms' enmity towards one another. Also, the king of Assyria had left a few of the Israelites living in the land. They intermarried with the Gentiles that he brought in and served their foreign gods. II Kings 17 They were no longer pure Israelites. To the Jews, the Samaritans were a half-breed mongrel race who served God *and* idols. That's why they had nothing to do with them.

When God tore the kingdom of Israel in two because of Solomon's sin, He gave ten tribes to Jeroboam, Solomon's servant. I Kings 11:26-40 Jeroboam went north with those ten tribes and established the Northern Kingdom. He fired all the Levite priests from their duties and

appointed new priests. His requirements? *"Any who would, he ordained."* I Kings 12:25-33; 13:33; II Chronicles 11:14-15; 13:9

Jeroboam made Israel sin, and she continually refused to repent. So God finally brought in another nation to take Israel captive. The king of Assyria took the Northern Kingdom out of the land. The king of Assyria didn't want a lot of weeds to grow on his new property so he brought other prisoners of war from Gentile nations he had conquered and settled them in the land of Israel. They would be his caretakers of the land—a nice way of saying "slaves."

But the Gentile nations had a problem. They did not fear the LORD God so He sent lions into the country and killed some of them! The Gentiles were smart enough to figure out *Who* had brought on the lion plague so they contacted the king of Assyria and told him the situation. *"The exile nations [us] that you have brought in to live in the land of Samaria do not know the custom of the 'god' of this land, so 'he' has sent lions in to kill us!"*

The king of Assyria had a plan! Why not bring back one of the priests that he had taken out of Israel into exile! That way he could teach the Gentiles living in Israel the custom of the "god" of that land! It was a plan all right, but it had its problems. First of all, bringing a "priest" back in to Israel wasn't really bringing a priest of God at all. All these guys had going for them was a signed certificate in their wallets from their disobedient king!

And secondly, when the Gentiles did bring one of these "priests" back to Israel to teach them the ways of the "god" of the land, he was handicapped in helping them—he had not been following and obeying the ways of God personally because he didn't know the ways of God!

Consequently, the priest taught them what he knew but didn't inform them of the repercussions of continuing to worship other gods! And they did exactly that. So while the nations were afraid of the God of the lions, they still worshiped their own gods on the side! And if that wasn't bad enough, they also decided to shore up the amount of priests in the land by appointing from among themselves a whole new team of priests!

HIStory Event 16
...GOD Sends Prophets to the Southern Kingdom of Israel (Judah)

Read and Observe

1. II Kings 21:10-18
2. Jeremiah 1:4-10, 12
3. Jeremiah 2:8-9, 13
4. Jeremiah 3:6-11; Ezekiel 16:51; Jeremiah 4:4; 9:25-26; Romans 2:28-29; Colossians 2:11
5. Jeremiah 5:1-3, 7-13, 18-19, 30-31; 6:10, 27-30; 8:7-12; 11:1-8, 14; 16:21; 22:1-9
6. Jeremiah 17:9-10; Deuteronomy 5:29
7. Jeremiah 25:12; 29:4-10

Read and Answer

1. II Kings 21:10-18
Now that Israel was taken into captivity in Assyria, it seems logical that Judah would pay attention and make sure the same thing didn't happen to her. Did she?

Did God send prophets to warn her that if she did not repent the same thing would most certainly happen to her—that she would be taken captive too?

2. Jeremiah 1:4-10, 12
What had God appointed Jeremiah to be?

Why was Jeremiah not to be afraid?

How would Jeremiah know what words to speak for God?

What does God do when His Word goes forth?

3. Jeremiah 2:8-9, 13
What did the priests do wrong?

What did the rulers do wrong?

What did the prophets do wrong?

Because of what they did, what would God do?

What had the people done wrong?

    1.

    2.

4. Jeremiah 3:6-11
Israel was faithless to God. God punished her. Did Judah learn from Israel's mistake?

When Judah returned to God, was it for real or was it in deception?

Compared to each other, which nation was more sinful?

Ezekiel 16:51
Judah made Israel appear righteous. How did she do that?

Jeremiah 4:4
What did God call for Judah to do?

Explain what "removing the foreskins of your hearts" means.

What would happen if they didn't?

Jeremiah 9:25-26
What would God do to those who were circumcised physically, yet uncircumcised of heart?

How did God describe the nations?

How did God describe Israel?

Romans 2:28-29
What is true circumcision?

Where does it take place?

Who does it?

What does that make a person once their heart has been circumcised?

Colossians 2:11
When is it that a person's heart is circumcised?

What is cut away?

How is it cut away?

5. Jeremiah 5:1-3
What does God tell Jeremiah to look for in the streets of Jerusalem?

What will God do if Jeremiah finds such a man?

Is a man's righteousness evidenced by what his lips speak?

Is a man's righteousness evidenced by his deeds?

What had the people of Jerusalem done?

> 1.
>
> 2.
>
> 3.

Jeremiah 5:7-9
Should God *punish* the people because they forsook Him for other gods?

Should God *pardon* the people because they forsook Him for other gods?

Jeremiah 5:10-13
What does God decide to do?

Will He destroy Jerusalem completely?

What is not in the prophets that needs to be?

Are the people fearing God?

Jeremiah 5:18-19
When God's punishment is severe on Jerusalem, what can they know and have hope in?

If anyone should ask why God punished Jerusalem so severely, what would the answer need to be?

Jeremiah 5:30-31
What was the appalling and horrible thing that happened in Jerusalem?

How did the priests rule?

How did the prophets prophesy?

How did the people feel about it?

Jeremiah 6:10
Jeremiah wanted to warn the people, but could they hear the truth?

Why not?

Jeremiah 6:27-30
God put His people in a crucible (melting pot) and started a hot fire beneath them. His purpose was for them to release their impurities, to let go of their sins, just like silver in a crucible was supposed to do. Did they?

What does God call them?

Jeremiah 8:7-12
What did God's people not know?

Why were God's people not wise?

What was the message of the priest to the people?

Was that message true?

What did God's people not know how to do?

What would be the result of their not being ashamed over their sin?

Jeremiah 11:1-8, 14
God made a Covenant with His people in the day He brought them out of Egypt. Do you remember what the conditions were? If the people disobeyed God, what would happen to them?

What did God warn them over and over again to do?

Did they?

Instead, what did they do?

What kind of heart did they have?

God warned His people over and over again, but they would not listen. Eventually God would not listen to them! What does God tell Jeremiah not to do? Amazing, isn't it?

Jeremiah 16:21
What would God's punishment cause His people to know for certain?

Jeremiah 22:1-9
What one thing did God require from His people?

If they disobeyed, what would happen to them?

If anyone went by Jerusalem and saw her destroyed and asked why God had done this to Jerusalem, what was the answer to be?

6. **Jeremiah 17:9-10**
How does God describe the heart condition of men?

Deuteronomy 5:29
What kind of heart did God want His people to have?

What would this heart do for them?

What would be the result?

What kind of heart did they have? Remember **Jeremiah 17:9-10**

7. Jeremiah 25:12
How long would Judah be in captivity in Babylon?

What would happen to Babylon after that time?

Jeremiah 29:4-10
What does God tell His people to do in Babylon?

Why?

How long were they going to be there?

Should they listen to anyone who might say anything different?

READ AND REASON

1. II Kings 21:10-18
In 931 BC God tore the kingdom of Israel in two because of Solomon's sin. We have already looked at the Northern Kingdom, consisting of ten tribes. Now we will turn our attention to the Southern Kingdom, where the last two tribes, Judah and Benjamin, remain. The Southern Kingdom is often referred to as "Judah." Its capital was Jerusalem. Its king was Rehoboam, Solomon's son. Of the 20 kings that reigned over Judah, 8 (for the most part) followed God and 12 did what was evil in His sight (only slightly better than Israel's record–100% evil kings!)

Manasseh was such an especially evil king that God declared He would wipe Jerusalem as one wipes a dish. God was going to destroy her because Manasseh did abominable things and made Judah sin with idols.

God sent prophets to Judah over and over again, just like He did with Israel. Judah wouldn't listen to God's prophets either. We are including the prophets who have books in the Bible named after them, but don't be mistaken, He sent *many* others! He was gracious and merciful beyond our comprehension!

Isaiah

Isaiah was a prophet sent by God with a message to the Southern Kingdom of Israel (Judah), and to its capital city, Jerusalem, on Mount Zion. Isaiah talks about the sinful condition of Israel, God's judgment He would send to her, the One God would send to save her from that judgment, and a remnant He would gather from the nations to which He exiled her.

God sent Isaiah during the same time He sent Amos and Hosea to the Northern Kingdom of Israel. Isaiah prophesied before, during, and after the Assyrians took the Northern Kingdom captive in 722 BC. God's message to Judah was severe and final: "Judah needed to repent of her sins and return to God and His ways!" She did not repent and finally God sent Babylon to take her captive according to His Covenant with Israel.

There are two major themes in Isaiah:
<u>The Holy One of Israel—The King</u>
<u>Zion—The Holy One's (the King's) intended royal habitation.</u>

The Holy One of Israel intends to dwell in Jerusalem, Zion, with His people. He is holy and cannot dwell with sin; therefore, His people and His city need to be purged of their sin. In addition, the nations surrounding Zion, the earth, and all of Creation need to be purified. God will thoroughly cleanse His creation. Purification will be a painful process because mankind refuses to release its sin.

The purification includes:
<u>Painful Cleansing—Justice and Judgment</u>
<u>Healing Salvation—Redemption and Restoration</u>

(Isaiah)

Because the Holy One of Israel intends to dwell in Zion, the book of Isaiah moves—

From the necessity of purifying judgment,
To the inevitability of purifying judgment,
To the actual judgment,
Then beyond the actual judgment to healing,
And beyond healing to God's Glory!

God will first judge and then save! The Holy One will purge His Holy Hill, Mt. Zion. Once the purification process is complete the Holy One of Israel will dwell in Zion with a remnant of believers who will inherit God's Glorious Holy Kingdom of Zion!

Micah

Micah prophesied to both the Southern and the Northern Kingdoms of Israel.
His message was two part:
<u>Israel's sin and the consequence</u>
<u>God's judgment and God's promise of restoration to His people</u>

Micah speaks much of the idea of shepherding, first calling the false shepherds of Israel into account with the LORD, and then picturing the Glorious Shepherd, the One from God, Who would come and redeem the remnant of His people from the hands of the nations (the very hands God, Himself, sent them into because of their sin against Him). In the end, when God's judgment has done its work, He will call to the remnant of His people, and they will finally see their sin, repent, and come back to the LORD their God. He will then, with His Own hands, eternally care for the remnant of His people, making them into a great nation.

God sent Isaiah and Micah to Judah to speak for Him. Judah did not listen.
God did not speak to Judah for the next 60 years.

Obadiah

Obadiah receives a vision from the Lord GOD concerning Edom (part of present day Jordan) and the news is not good. Obadiah hears from God that He will summon all the nations against Edom including Edom's own allies. Every nation will be against him and no one will escape God's vengeance.

Why is God sending the nations of the earth to battle against Edom? It is because he treated Israel with great disdain. Edom stood on the sidelines during a time of deep humiliation for, and violence against, Israel. Edom didn't even stay on the sidelines though; he got in the game by cheering on Israel's destroyers and actually cutting down Israel's fugitives running from the massacre and imprisoning his survivors. God declared hundreds of years earlier in a Covenant with Abraham that He would bless those who bless Israel and curse those who curse Israel.

Edom cursed Israel and the book of Obadiah shows God's Covenant response of cursing Edom. The Day of the LORD is drawing near! When it comes, what Edom did to Israel will happen to him. There will be restoration for Israel and justice and judgment to all the nations.

Joel

Joel uses a literal locust plague to warn Israel to repent. If she won't repent, then a fate worse than the locusts will befall her. Joel uses the plague to prophesy of the coming, terrible Day of the LORD. Joel gives Israel an admonition to tell and retell the vision to each subsequent generation. What is to be told and retold?

"What you are experiencing (the locust plague) is judgment; you are sinning and God is judging you! You need to repent from your sin because there is a much worse judgment coming in the Day of the LORD!!!"

Nahum

One hundred years after Jonah preached repentance to the city of Nineveh (and they did repent) God now sends His prophet Nahum with a message of destruction. The city of Nineveh, the capital of Assyria, long ago "repented" of its repentance and has once again made itself God's enemy by coming against God's people, Israel. God will come as a powerful, wrathful avenger of His people. The attack on Nineveh and its devastation are the inevitable result of tyranny against God and His people.

2. Jeremiah 1:4-10, 12
God appoints Jeremiah as a prophet to faithless Judah. He gives him quite a task, but He tells Jeremiah not to be afraid of the people because God is with him to deliver him. First, he is "to pluck up, to break down, to destroy, and to overthrow;" second, he is "to build up and to plant." He is to speak God's Word, and God will stand over it to perform it.

3. Jeremiah 2:8-9, 13
The priests and prophets have been ruling the people apart from God's Word. Therefore, God is going to contend with them. God says that the people He chose to bring The Seed into the world had done two terrible evils:
1. They forsook God. In other words, they rejected God—said they didn't need Him.
2. They hewed broken cisterns for themselves. In other words, they tried to take care of themselves and run their lives without God. They chose independence from God. They chose their depraved life over the life God had for them!

Habakkuk

Habakkuk cries out to God for righteous judgment, so God names the destroyers He is going to bring on Jerusalem—the Chaldeans from Babylon are coming to wipe out Judah! Habakkuk is afraid but remembers that the righteous lives by faith.

4. Jeremiah 3:6-11; Ezekiel 16:51; Jeremiah 4:4; 9:25-26; Romans 2:28-29; Colossians 2:11

Israel, the northern ten tribes, went after other gods. God sent her away into Assyria. Yet, Judah, the two southern tribes, would not learn from Israel's mistake! Instead of returning to God, she sinned even more wickedly than Israel. Compared to Judah, Israel appeared righteous!!! And when Judah did "come back" to God, it was only in deception. She had not truly repented. Her heart condition was no better. Judah needed to have that hard covering over her heart removed! Her heart needed to be circumcised, yet that would not happen until the New Covenant when Jesus Christ came to do it for her through His Spirit.

5. Jeremiah 5:1-3, 7-13, 18-19, 30-31; 6:10, 27-30; 8:7-12; 11:1-8, 14; 16:21; 22:1-9

God tells Jeremiah to roam through the streets of Jerusalem. Even now, He would pardon Judah if righteousness was found. Righteousness is not found! The people say they are living according to God's ways, but they will not take correction from Him. They will not repent! The people love the godless rule of the prophets and priests! God's Word has become a reproach to them! I wish that didn't sound so much like today!

So God decides that He will definitely punish them. He has to avenge Himself. And yet, even then, He will not destroy all of Judah. Why not? Because He has made a Covenant promise that He will bring The Seed, the Savior, through Judah. So He will leave a remnant.

God is about to put Judah into the refiner's fire. There will be *many* stubborn and rebellious ones who will not release any dross. They will be rejected and cast off. God even tells Jeremiah to *stop praying* for their deliverance, to stop trying to intercede for them, for He will not even listen anymore. His mind is made up. They are going into exile! He is going to make man know that His Name is the LORD! I pray that the LORD has not made up His mind about America's judgment. I hope He still hears our prayers on her behalf. She needs to repent of her independence from God…

The other nations will know why Judah has been taken out of her land. It is because she forsook the Covenant of the LORD and bowed down to other gods and served them.

6. Jeremiah 17:9-10; Deuteronomy 5:29

That same old heart condition is mentioned again. Men are born with a heart that is more deceitful than anything else! It is desperately sick and impossible to cure. God searches the heart and sees the despicableness in it! He alone can change a man's heart.

7. Jeremiah 25:12; 29:4-10

Jeremiah gives instructions to the Jews to settle themselves in Babylon and pray for its welfare. As Babylon prospers, so will the Jews. He warns them that false prophets will come. God says not to even listen to them, because *He* did not send them! He promises they will come back to Israel in 70 years.

Zephaniah

In Zephaniah, God pronounces judgment against the entire earth, on Judah and Jerusalem, and on the surrounding nations. He urges the people to seek the LORD, righteousness, and humility so that perhaps they may be hidden in the Day of the LORD'S anger—the pervasive theme in Zephaniah. God also promises to preserve a remnant who will do no wrong and once He has taken care of Israel's sins, He will take away her troubles and give her renown and praise from her former enemies.

Jeremiah

Jeremiah tells Judah that God is going to fulfill **Deuteronomy 28**. They have disobeyed God so He will be faithful to His Covenant by taking them out of the land of Canaan into captivity. Jeremiah delivered the unalterable news that Babylon would most certainly demolish Jerusalem; in fact, God tells Jeremiah many times to not even pray for Jerusalem—He is not going to change His decision!

But he also delivered <u>two great promises of God:</u>
Yes, Judah would be taken captive to Babylon.
<u>But also, Judah would only be there for 70 years.</u>
<u>Then she would come back to Jerusalem.</u>
Yes, God would keep His Covenant promises
which would mean that Judah must go into exile to Babylon.
<u>But God promised He would make a New Covenant with Israel.</u>
<u>One that was different from the old one.</u>
<u>One that would cause her to obey God so He would never have to curse her again!</u>

Jeremiah stayed in Judah during the kingdom's exile to Babylon.
However, he sent the scroll of his writings to Babylon for the exiles to read.
Daniel read it while he was there and noticed the promise of 70 years!
The books of Daniel and Ezekiel were written from Babylon.

Point of Depth

Why did God take the nation of Israel out of the land for 70 years? Why not 32 years or 154 years? Why did God choose 70?

First of all, we need to remember that the land belongs to God! He gave it to Israel to live in, but they had to obey Him! In Leviticus, God told the people through Moses that they were to give His land a Sabbath. For six years they were to sow the fields and work the land and gather in the crop, but on the seventh year they were to let the land rest. Leviticus 25:1-7, 23

What were they supposed to eat during the seventh year? God had it all under control! He ordered the land and the plants to provide three years worth of food during the sixth year! That way, the people would have enough food to eat during the seventh year and would even be taken care of during the eighth year while they were waiting for the harvest to come in! Leviticus 25:20-22

Oh, why do we doubt the ways of our God! He has thought of every last detail!

Israel broke the Sabbath for the land. During the days they were living in the land, there had been 490 years in which the people were not faithful to give the land its Sabbaths. Doing the math shows there should have been 70 different years of rest for the land during that time. But Israel had disobeyed and not given the land its Sabbaths.

God was faithful to His Covenant with Israel. Because they did not give the land its Sabbath rests, He took them out of it for 70 years. God will have His way! He is God! The land was owed 70 years of Sabbath rests. God would simply take those rebellious people of His out of the land for the number of years it took to fulfill His Word → 70 years! Leviticus 26:2-6, 14-17, 33-35; Jeremiah 25:12; 29:10; II Chronicles 36:15-21

Point of Depth

The book of Jeremiah is a book for the church today. The accusations made against Judah equally indict us.

The people who spoke for God, His priests and prophets, did not even know Him. Plus, when they would prophesy and say the message was from God, in fact, it had come from Baal. The shepherds did not have a heart after God's Own heart. They were not feeding the sheep with knowledge and understanding of God. Jeremiah 2:8; 3:15 I wonder just exactly how many pulpits today are filled with messengers of Satan.

The priests were saying, "Peace! Peace!" But there was no peace! The people were sinning. They had broken Covenant. Destruction would surely come upon them from their Covenant-keeping God! It was horrible then, and it is horrible now, when shepherds rule on their own authority rather than God's, and when prophets prophesy falsely. It is appalling that the people love it so! Pulpit upon pulpit teaches week after week that, *"Everything is fine. Just do the best you can. God is love. God is love. God is love."* But the end of disobedience will always be judgment! Jeremiah 5:2, 30-31; 6:10

Yes, God is love. And just as much, *God is Holy!* He has to punish all ungodliness! Judgment begins with the house of God! We are to judge ourselves! We are to examine our lives to see if we are keeping the Covenant we have entered. We have entered the New Covenant—the one that causes us to walk in His ways and to keep His statutes!

The people said they were following God, yet their deeds denied it. Our deeds, not our words, show the truth of what kind of people we are. The people had no delight in God's Word, so how could it direct their ways? Today's "church" is a stench in the nostrils of God, not a sweet aroma of Christ. The people say they love Him, yet they will not even give Him the smallest sacrifice of their time to seek after Him. They think He has plenty of their time just because they take the time to go to church meetings!

Jeremiah accuses the people of sinning, yet they stand before God in the Temple and say, *"We are delivered."* Oh, how like "church" people today! They are sinning and then coming to services on Sunday or serving in ministries throughout the week without repentance thinking they are safe! Jeremiah 7:1-20

Their safety is a delusion. Safety doesn't come from being baptized, or regular attendance, or giving, or deeds of service. When will they study the Word of God and find that those deeds are as filthy rags before Him? They are not safe if they are sinning as a way of life *no matter* what other "churchy" and "righteous" things they are doing!

If the church today was doing what it should, then it would be asking an awful lot of people why they are *not* walking in His ways and *not* keeping His statutes and yet still calling themselves Christians! No, friends, despite what you hear from the pulpits, there is no peace in the "church" today!

If a person is truly in Covenant with Jesus Christ, His Spirit will cause that person to walk righteously as a way of life. Then, and only then, will that person have peace. God says to go back and look at Shiloh and see what He did to it because of the wickedness of the people. Jeremiah 7:12-15 God says we are to look and see how He has dealt with sin in the past in order to learn from it! We are to remind people—warn people of God's judgment!

Will you be a watchman on the tower and warn others of the danger they are in? Even if they do not listen, you must warn them!

POINT OF DEPTH

Why was Josiah, king of the Southern Kingdom, all the way up north in Bethel? He was on a national morality campaign! II Kings 22; 23:1-28; II Chronicles 34 Oh, how I wish our president would go on one!

You see, it all began when Josiah was about 26 years old. He had been reigning over Judah since he was 8 years old! Imagine any 8 year old you know and picture him reigning over a nation! This 8 year old was different. He followed in the steps of his father David and did right in the sight of the LORD!

After he had reigned for 18 years, he told his scribe, Shaphan, to tell Hilkiah, the high priest, to hire workers to restore the Temple. God's Temple had fallen into disrepair. Yet, I wonder how everyone's own personal homes were doing!

While all this was going on, Hilkiah made a great find! Hilkiah found a dusty old scroll which is the Book of the Law and he gave it to Shaphan! Imagine that—finding the Word of God in the House of God! Doesn't that sound incredulous? The Word of God had been lost *in* the House of God!

Oh, how I wish that were not so familiar today. It's not that we don't have plenty of Bibles. In fact, many churches even have convenient "pew" Bibles available. By the way → is that so you will have one if you forget your own? Or is that so you don't have to lug yours around? We need to be convicted of our conveniences!

> We may have the Book, but we don't KNOW the Book.
> We may sometimes read parts of the Book,
> but we don't diligently STUDY and CONSUME the entire Book.
> We don't consider God's Word MORE important than our necessities in life!
> We don't want to admit that the Word of God IS necessary for life!

Shaphan took the Book of God and read it to King Josiah. When Josiah heard the words of the Book, the voice of God, he immediately tore his clothes and wept. He saw that the wrath of the LORD was great against Judah because they had not listened to the words of the Book of God to do according to all that was written in it. The people were not reading and obeying God's commands although that was the agreement the Israelites made when they entered into Covenant with God at Mount Sinai. He gave them His Law and they said, *"All that the LORD has said, we will do."*

They hadn't done all that the LORD had said. But God would do all that He said. He promised to bless them if they obeyed and curse them if they disobeyed.

Had they disobeyed? What do you think? Inside the Temple of the LORD the people had put vessels to worship Baal, Asherah, and the hosts of heaven. The priests were idolatrous. The women would sit inside the house of God and weave hangings for a wooden symbol of a female god, Asherah. There were actually male cult prostitutes operating out of the house of God! *Aughhh*! The people were taking their children and burning them before the false god, Molech!

Yes, the people had disobeyed. Josiah believed what God said in His Book and he *knew* that God's wrath would have to fall on them. He realized they were cursed!

Josiah told Shaphan to take the Book to Huldah, the prophetess. She affirmed that God indeed was burning with anger against His chosen people because of their disobedience. However, she said to give a special message to the king himself.

God told Josiah, through Huldah, His prophetess, *"Because your heart was tender and you humbled yourself before the LORD when you heard what I spoke against this place and against its inhabitants that they should become a desolation and a curse, and you have torn your clothes and wept before Me, I truly have heard you. Therefore, I will gather you to your fathers, and you shall be gathered to your grave in peace, neither shall your eyes see all the evil which I will bring on this place."* II Kings 22:19-20; II Chronicles 34:27-28

Does your heart hear God's Word? Is your heart tender to it?

What does it mean to be tender to God's Word? Think about what your skin feels like when you have injured it. It becomes "tender" to the touch. If something touches it, you react immediately. You cannot ignore it. I will ask you again, *"Is your heart tender to God's Word? Do you respond immediately to it? Or do you ignore it?"*

LORD,
I ask You to make Your children's hearts tender,
Oh, so tender, to the touch of Your Word!

God stayed His hand of judgment on Israel until after Josiah died. He spared Josiah from experiencing His wrath because his heart was tender and responsive to God's Word.

So Josiah took his national morality campaign across the country. Good for him! Good for Israel! Josiah obeyed God's Word and went out and cleaned up the land! There was a revival in the land during the days of Josiah.

I find it interesting, but cheerless, to note the contrast between those days and now. Nowadays, people pray and pray and pray for God to send revival to their land. I think they expect it to come like a gift-wrapped package to their mailbox. Then, all Josiah did was to obey…

POINT OF DEPTH

Do you think God only objects to idols when they are made out of wood or precious metal and look like a statue of a person? Would you be offended if I were to suggest it is entirely possible that you worship an idol, a god other than God?

God says, "No one can serve two masters. If you try you will just end up hating and despising one while you love and hold to the other." God is speaking to me, and He is speaking to you. Luke 16:13; Matthew 6:24

An idol is *anything* that takes the place that God should have in your heart! The place that God should have in your heart is the *whole* place! An idol could be sleep! An idol could be money or the love of it, the possession of it or the pursuit of it. An idol could be anything you think is worth "holding" onto! An idol could be your family, your job, or your position. It could be your health, your own body, or your education. An idol could be a friendship, a relationship, or an emotion. It could be TV, internet, video games, your lawn, or your car. If you are holding onto and loving any of these things, God says you hate and despise Him.

James calls "friendship" with the world (desiring and enjoying its ways) adultery! Do you long after the ways of the world? Do you long for position, power, authority, and love? Would you mind if God took all those things away from you? Would you resent Him?

Some people are miserable day in and day out because they are trying to serve two masters. They want to do "the right things" and be part of the church, but they also want to fit in at work and in our neighborhoods. God has made it clear that if we truly try to live a godly life we will be persecuted and neither liked nor admired by the world.

Do you realize that God hates your idols and my idols just as much as He hated the idols of Israel? Do you see that it breaks His heart when you reject Him as your God? Are you sorry when you break His heart with your sin? Does your heart beat the same as His? Do you know Him so it can?

By saying the "sinner's prayer" many have simply signed a life insurance policy! The question is, can they afford the premiums?

It won't be long and then He will come. Will you be found faithful? As for me and my house, we will serve the LORD…

HIStory Event 17
...GOD Sends Babylon to Take the Southern Kingdom into Captivity

Read and Observe

1. II Chronicles 36:5-21; II Kings 24-25; Jeremiah 24; 19-20; 29:1-14; Daniel 1:1-4

Read and Answer

1. II Chronicles 36:5-21; II Kings 24-25
God had warned His people and sent His prophets; now He sent His wrath to them. He brought Nebuchadnezzer, the king of Babylon against Israel. What did King Nebuchadnezzer make the dethroned king of Israel, Zedekiah, do?

Why do you think Nebuchadnezzer made Zedekiah swear allegiance by God? Is it possible that Nebuchadnezzer knew that God was orchestrating all these events?

What did Zedekiah do? (Look for his heart condition.)

Why had God sent word to Judah through His messengers again and again?

What did Judah continually do when God spoke to them?

What did God finally do?

Jeremiah 24
Who are the good figs?

What will happen to them because God considers them good?

Who are the bad figs?

What will happen to them because God considers them bad?

Who decides whether they are good or bad figs?

What promise do the good figs have regarding their land?

What promise do the good figs have regarding their heart?

Jeremiah 19-20
Who was the potter's jar?

Who would break the potter's jar?

Why?

Jeremiah has been speaking the message that God gave him to give. For Jeremiah, what has been the result of giving this message?

What is the result for Jeremiah if he doesn't give the message?

Will the LORD be with Jeremiah when he gives God's message? How is that described?

Jeremiah 29:1-14
Jeremiah writes a letter in Jerusalem and sends it to Babylon. What does the letter instruct the people to do?

How long will the people be in Babylon?

How does God describe the plans He has for His people?

When will these plans come about? (Remember the promise of The Seed.)

When will God listen to His people?

When will God's people find Him?

What will have to happen to their hearts before they can search for Him?

READ AND REASON

1. II Chronicles 36:5-21; II Kings 24-25; Jeremiah 24; 19-20; 29:1-14; Daniel 1:1-4
Because of God's compassion, He sent word to Judah time and time again, but they mocked His messengers, despised His words, and scoffed at His prophets. Finally, the wrath of the LORD arose against them until there was no remedy! So He brought up the Chaldeans to destroy Jerusalem and its people. The people He had chosen to be a light to the nations would now be destroyed by the very people who should have seen their light and repented. But Israel had not been that light...

Babylon, under the control of Nebuchadnezzar, came up three times at God's command to take the city of Jerusalem.

>1st siege on Jerusalem – 605 BC **II Kings 24:1-4**
>Daniel and other noblemen were taken
>
>2nd siege on Jerusalem – 597 BC **II Kings 24:10-16**
>Ezekiel and 10,000 were taken
>
>3rd siege on Jerusalem (final siege) – 586 BC **II Kings 25:1-21**
>Jerusalem, her Temple and her walls were destroyed, and the vessels of the Temple were taken to Babylon

The Babylonians now were in control of Israel. She may have rejected God as her ruler, but she would not continue to rule herself! God had sold her into captivity.

Daniel

Daniel was taken captive in the first siege on Jerusalem in 605 BC. He and some of the royal family and nobles of the sons of Israel were taken to Babylon to serve in the king's court. He wrote the book of Daniel while he was there.

Jeremiah had sent his scroll to Babylon for the exiles to read. While Daniel was reading it, he observed the number of years which was revealed for the completion of the desolations of Jerusalem, precisely 70 years! **Jeremiah 25:12; 29:10**
So he immediately gave his attention to the Lord God to seek Him by prayer and supplications with fasting, sackcloth, and ashes. Daniel confessed his sin and the sin of his people. **Daniel 9:1-27** Why don't you try praying his prayer for your nation?

Daniel also received several visions which told the future part of HIStory! God told Daniel specifics about his own people, the Jews. He revealed to him how He would specifically fulfill **Deuteronomy 28**. God told Daniel the Medo-Persians would conquer Babylon and therefore rule over Israel, as well. God told Daniel that the Greeks, by conquering the Medo-Persian Empire, would rule over Israel next. The Romans, by defeating the Greeks, were the next in line to rule over Israel. The history of nations is determined by God's plan and time-schedule, not by a nation's own strength or power!

Then God revealed to Daniel what would happen in the last seven years of Israel's history (which she has not yet experienced). He said the last three and one-half years of Israel's history would be like nothing that has ever happened before. It is horrific to ponder! Babylonian troops had put fishhooks in the mouths of the Israelites and dragged them across the wilderness to Babylon! Yet God told Daniel the last three and one-half years of Israel's history would be worse than that (or even the holocaust!)

Then God told Daniel about the end. He told him that everyone would be resurrected either to everlasting life or everlasting contempt. Daniel didn't understand everything completely, but God promised him that his visions would not be sealed up forever. God said that in the end time they would no longer be concealed. We are living in the end times. Study the book of Daniel. Your eyes will be opened!

Ezekiel

The book of Ezekiel, like Daniel, was written from Babylon. Ezekiel was taken captive to Babylon in the 2nd siege on Jerusalem in 597 BC along with all the captains and the mighty men of valor, and all the craftsmen and the smiths—10,000 people. Nobody remained in Jerusalem except the poorest people of the land.

The book starts with a spectacularly formidable vision; one that no one has yet been able to accurately imagine. Yet Ezekiel saw it and described it in great detail for us—it was the likeness of the Glory of the LORD. God calls Ezekiel "son of man" throughout the book and commissions him in **Ezekiel 2-3**. Ezekiel is sent to a rebellious people, the sons of Israel, and will perform sign after sign for the people to see and understand. God informs him that Israel will not listen to him, yet they will know that a prophet has been among them.

Israel was committing false, vile worship even in God's Own Temple, but the law of God's house is absolute holiness, so He had to leave—and leave He did! Ezekiel heartbreakingly saw the Glory of the LORD slowly rise up from His Mercy Seat in the Holy of Holies, and hover over various parts of His house in which His own people were committing loathsome, adulterous acts against Him. Then the Glory of the God of Israel departed from His Temple, went up from the midst of the city, and stood over the mountain east of Jerusalem. But the Glory would return one day; a promise found in **Ezekiel 33-34**. And when it did there would be a New Covenant—one that would ensure their obedience to the Holy One of Israel!

Ezekiel prophesied about Judah and Jerusalem, about the nations, about Israel's restoration, and about the Temple of God in Jerusalem. He told them in no uncertain terms that there was judgment to come; it could not be stopped. Then he told them about God's restoration for Israel that was just as unshakable!

LAMENTATIONS

The book of Lamentations contains the language of grief of the people of Israel—
grief over their exile and the state of their existence.
Israel expresses her despair which began with the attack on Jerusalem,
but even more so, she confesses her sins as evil and wicked before the LORD.
She acknowledges that He is the One Who has brought this calamity upon her.
Israel mourns and cries out for help as her enemies mock her.
She remembers that the LORD'S lovingkindnesses never cease.
They are new every morning. Great is God's Faithfulness!

POINT OF DEPTH

Belshazzar, who was the grandson of Nebuchadnezzar, took the cups and furniture that had been plundered from Solomon's Temple and had a drunken orgy using them. He was making the statement that his gods were more powerful than this God of Israel. While he was in his drunken celebration, a hand appeared on the wall of the room and began writing a cryptic message. "Mene mene tekel upharsin." It basically meant "you have been weighed and found wanting." Daniel 5

Have you ever seen a set of justice scales? It has a base at the bottom with a pole from it that balances two sides which hang loosely. To weigh something, the object was put on one side of the scale. Then, very carefully, weights would be added to the other side until both sides hung at the same level.

God is saying that He has put His righteousness on one side of the scale. His righteousness causes that side of the scale to lie on the tabletop because it is so heavy. Then He says that He put all Belshazzar's righteousness on the other side. There was not enough weight on Belshazzar's side to even move God's side at all. Belshazzar had been weighed and found to have no weight. He was not worth anything.

Belshazzar was slain that very night. He had been weighed and found wanting.

You, too, will be weighed. Will you be found wanting?
You are accountable for what you know. What have you done with what you know?
Your own righteousness cannot balance His scales.

*God promises that He will wrap us with a robe of righteousness
and garments of salvation when we are saved. Isaiah 61:10
Do you have the weight of His righteousness in you?*

POINT OF DEPTH

During the captivity, the exiles (the Diaspora) encountered problems. They had no Temple so they couldn't make any sacrifices. They were living among the Gentiles—the Babylonians to be specific. They started intermarrying with the Babylonians. They had to eat different foods. They learned new customs along with a new Aramaic language. Hebrew, their mother tongue, was dying out from lack of use.

So they stopped and reevaluated the Law. They thought it could use a little updating—perhaps *just* a smidge here and there!

A major division alienated the exiles into two groups—the liberal Jews and the Orthodox Jews.

The liberal Jews developed a Jewish mysticism. They reinterpreted Jewish belief in the light of their new pagan teaching. They had a fascination with the spirit world. (Sounds like today, doesn't it!) They saw a competition between light and darkness. They felt God was in control, but that He was remote and not in the presence of His people.

As a result of the thinking of the liberal Jews, others panicked. They didn't want their children to start believing this mysticism so they formed synagogues. The idea was actually a really good one. It would have been perfect if they only would have done what Ezra did after the Temple was rebuilt. When Ezra was teaching the people he exclusively used the Word of God.

"Synagogue" means "to gather together." A minimum of ten Jewish men could establish a synagogue in any particular community. A leader was appointed for each synagogue who was called "Rabbi" or "Teacher."

Here's where this idea began to manifest its inherent problems. The Rabbi would come up with his own commentary on Scripture. Now, the Rabbi might have understood the Torah (the first five books of the Bible) or he might not have! Either way you now had people listening to commentary rather than to the Word of God itself. So the result *had* to be a departure from the Truth! Sound anything like today?

The commentaries of many of the Rabbis were written down in a book called the "Midrash." They got this idea from the Greek libraries. The scribes were the ones who wrote the Midrash in the 4th century BC.

Another book was also written. It was called the "Mishnah" and contained the Rabbi's legal opinions on the Law. (Doesn't the word "opinion" tell you all you need to know about the danger of this process?) The Rabbi's oral interpretation of the Law was written down and *that* became more important to the people than the *Word* of *God*!

It literally breaks my heart to hear so many "church" people today talking about all sorts of books they have read—books about the world, about themselves, even about God—but who *will not* take the time God demands of them to study His Word. We don't need books *about* the Bible! We need *The Bible!!!* You don't need someone else's opinion about the Word of God. You need to know what God *says* in the Word of God!

The Word of God is pure, unadulterated *Truth*. If you don't know what He says, then you won't know when you hear a lie! And if you can't recognize a lie, you might believe it. And if you believe a lie, you will sin.

The Midrash and the Mishnah together became known as the Talmud. The Talmud became a substitute for the Word of God. Do you have a substitute for the Word of God? What is it? Get rid of it, and get into the Word—to the Law and to the Testimony! Isaiah 8:20

God had told the Jews all about The Seed and His coming in His Word, but they didn't recognize *Truth (The Seed)* when He came because they had thrown out the Word of God. Today is no different...

Point of Connection

God reveals to Daniel the future of the nation of Israel. In Daniel, chapter two, this revelation is recorded in a skeletal form and then some flesh is added to it in chapters seven through twelve.

In Daniel 2, God gives Nebuchadnezzar dreams that trouble his spirit and give him insomnia. The king orders the magicians to tell him what the dreams had been and then to tell him what the dreams had meant. Obviously they couldn't. They were only men.

So they tried twice to get Nebuchadnezzar to tell them his dreams. Then they would "be able" to interpret them for him. *Yeah, sure they could!* Nebuchadnezzar said, *"No way! Either tell me the dream and its interpretation or be prepared to lose your limbs → all of them!"*

The Chaldean magicians do make a truthful statement in verses 10-11. They inform the king that *no one* could possibly do this thing. *"Why, you'd have to be a god! And gods don't live here on earth that we could actually go to them and ask them!"*

Nebuchadnezzar says, *"Okay! Fine! Die! All of you!"*

Well, Daniel and his friends were on Nebuchadnezzar's death list, so Daniel does what the magicians could not do. Daniel goes to *his God* and asks Him to tell him what the dreams were and what they meant. God does just that.

Before Daniel ran to tell the king what God had shown him, he calmly kneeled down and thanked God for revealing the dream and its interpretation to him. I love that! I have to admit, I wonder if my flesh would have been screaming, *"Thank God later! Tell the king in a hurry before he kills you!"* Daniel, however, remembered Who was in control! Daniel then proceeds to tell the king what his dream was about but not without first informing the king from where he got his information—The God of Heaven!

Nebuchadnezzar had been thinking about what would happen in the future. God showed him through his dreams. He dreamed of a single great statue, large and of extraordinary splendor, standing in front of him. Its appearance was terrifying!

The head of the statue was made of fine gold. Its chest and arms were made of silver, while its belly and its thighs were made of bronze. The statue's legs were iron, but its feet were a mixture of iron and clay.

Nebuchadnezzar watched in his dream while a Stone that was cut without hands struck the statue on its feet and crushed them. Then the entire statue was crushed all at the same time. It became like chaff from the summer threshing floors, and the wind carried it away so that not a trace of it was found. *But*, the Stone that had struck the statue became a great mountain and filled the whole earth.

Daniel informs the king that the gold head of the statue is Nebuchadnezzar and his Babylonian Empire, but that his kingdom won't last. The Medes and the Persians, represented by the chest and arms of silver, will come as allies against Babylon and defeat her.

The Medo-Persian Empire will be defeated by Greece, the bronze belly and thighs of the statue. Greece will rule the world… for a while. Greece will lose her power when the Romans conquer her. The statue's iron legs represent Rome. Even Rome, who would be ruling when Christ (The Seed) came, would not endure as ruler over all the earth.

The feet of the statue were made partly of iron and partly of clay. God revealed to Daniel that there would be a divided kingdom after the strong iron rule of Rome. There were ten toes and those ten toes would be ten kings. Those ten kings would ultimately be crushed by the Stone that God sent. The Stone would crush all the kingdoms. God would set up an everlasting Kingdom. It would endure forever. That Kingdom has not yet come on the face of the earth, but it will!

Do you remember the "ancient" game of "Pac-man"? Remember how it gobbled up one thing after another? Well, that is what happens to the nation of Israel. She disobeys God, so He sends in a Babylonian Pac-man to gobble her up. She is still inside of Babylon when God sends a Medo-Persian Pac-man to gobble Babylon up. Now Israel is inside of Babylon, who is now inside of Medo-Persia. But God is not done yet.

Next, He sends a Grecian Pac-man to gobble up Medo-Persia → who has Babylon inside of her → who still has Israel inside of her! Fourthly, God sends a Roman Pac-man to gobble up Greece, who has wolfed downed Medo-Persia, who has ingurgitated Babylon, who has swallowed up Israel! Got it? Good! Whew!

I guess, to keep using the Pac-man illustration, we could say that the final Pac-man, Jesus Christ, the Stone, will ultimately swallow, chew-up and spit out all the kingdoms except Israel —Israel, He will forgive and cleanse.

In chapters 7-12 of Daniel, God, piece by piece, adds more information concerning the future of Israel. Watch for these nations in God's Word. He refers to them often. He decided He would give them power over other nations and over Israel. He prophesied exactly that and then He made it happen! Isaiah 37:26

And yet, the nations themselves would be responsible to God for their attitude towards Israel. They were still to remember that Israel was God's nation and that the *only* reason they had any control over her whatsoever was by God's hand, not theirs. They were simply servants of God's.

If they mistreated God's people or if they took glory for themselves and said their gods were more powerful than God, they would pay. And they would pay dearly.

Point of Connection

The Glory of the LORD fills the Tabernacle
At the end of Exodus we see God filling the Tabernacle with His Glory. So much so that Moses was not able to enter the tent of meeting because of the cloud that had settled on it. God had come to dwell in the midst of His people. Exodus 29:43; 40:34-35

The Glory of the LORD leaves Israel
Later, at one of Israel's many points of disobedience, God's Glory left the presence of Israel. Eli, God's priest, had two rebellious sons who took the Ark of the Covenant into battle against the Philistines. The Israelites were soundly defeated and the Ark was taken captive to Philistia. Eli and his two sons died. When Eli's pregnant daughter-in-law gave birth to her son she called him Ichabod saying "the Glory of the LORD has departed from Israel." I Samuel 4:17-22

The Glory of the LORD fills the House of the LORD

Solomon later built a Temple for the LORD. The House of God was dedicated and consecrated to Him with great ceremony. God showed His acceptance of the House by filling it with His Glory. It was so great that the priests couldn't even minister because of the thick cloud of Glory in the House where God had said that He would dwell! I Kings 8:10-13

God's Glory, sometimes called the "Shekinah Glory," remained in the Temple until the sin of His people became so great that He had to move out of His Own House!

The Glory of the LORD departs from Israel

Ezekiel is living as an exile in Babylon when God commissions him to speak to the Jews, whether they listen or not! Nebuchadnezzar had successfully attacked Jerusalem twice—the first time was 605 BC, and the second was 597 BC. Ezekiel had been taken captive to Babylon in the second siege. There was one more siege to come in 586 BC which would completely destroy Jerusalem. They have seen the wrath of God come on them, yet they still will not repent. God's decision has been made. He will judge—and judge them harshly! Ezekiel 2:3-5, 7; 3:4-9, 26-27

The Jews are rebellious and stubborn, even more rebellious than all the other nations! They refuse to listen! God, through Ezekiel, gives them a stinging prophecy of their own future. It is horrible what will happen to them. In fact, God says, *"Because of all your abominations, I will do among you what I have not done, and the like of which I will never do again."* **Fathers will eat their sons and sons will eat their fathers! God will execute His judgment on them and they will be scattered to every wind of the world! Ezekiel 5:5-10**

Verse 11 is a key verse to understand what is happening in the book of Ezekiel. God orders that the Jews be taken out of the land. But because the Jews have defiled His Sanctuary with all their detestable idols and all their abominations, God, Himself, is going to leave, too. He is going to withdraw, first from the Temple of His Sanctuary, and then from the city of Jerusalem itself! Ezekiel 5:11

By His Spirit, God takes Ezekiel to Jerusalem and shows him what the Jews are doing in His Own Temple and in His Own City.

- **Ezekiel 8:3-6**
  He shows Ezekiel the entrance of the north gate of the inner court. There, in God's House was a seat for an "idol of jealousy." To the north of the altar gate was the idol of jealousy at the entrance. Unbelievable! In God's Own House, where He should be sitting on His Mercy Seat, the people were instead worshiping an idol sitting on its own seat! Should God have to leave because an idol has taken His place??? God tells Ezekiel, *"Keep watching! There is more!"*

- Ezekiel 8:7-13

  In the inner rooms of the Temple, God shows Ezekiel the false, disgusting carvings of creeping things and beasts and detestable idols. And who is worshiping these carvings? Why, it's none other than God's Own elders! They are offering incense to other gods in God's Own House with the lights turned out! And they have the audacity to say, *"The LORD doesn't see us doing this. After all, He has abandoned us!"* Aughhh! Then God gives Ezekiel the next bad news, *"Prepare yourself, Ezekiel. It gets even worse."*

- Ezekiel 8:14-15

  God now takes Ezekiel to the actual entrance to the house of God, and there, the women of Israel are sitting and weeping for Tammuz! Tammuz was believed to be the reincarnation of his father, Nimrod. Tammuz is also known as "Osirus" or "Adonis." He is pictured on seals as a protector of flocks against wild beasts. This "weeping for Tammuz" lasted for 40 days preceding the pagan Spring Equinox Festival. The women were grieving over his death in hopes that he would come back to life, representing a renewal of nature. Can it get worse? God tells Ezekiel that it does. Then He shows him…

- Ezekiel 8:16

  He takes Ezekiel to the inner court and there, at the entrance to the Temple of the LORD, between the porch and the altar, were about 25 men with their backs to the Temple of the LORD and their faces toward the east. They were laying down worshiping the sun!

- Ezekiel 8:17-18

  God has had it! He says to Ezekiel rhetorically, *"Wasn't it bad enough to sin the terrible sins they sinned against Me? Wasn't it bad enough that they polluted the land with their abominations? Wasn't it bad enough that they wouldn't repent?"* No, I guess it wasn't bad enough because they went one step further and committed their horrible abominations right in God's Own House!

  I want to give you a graphic example of what they had done to God. Israel was God's wife; she committed adultery against Him. That, in itself, was bad enough, but then she actually took her lover to God's bedroom and flagrantly made love to him right there in front of God, her husband. I can't imagine the pain God must have felt… and the anger…

Starting in chapter 9 of Ezekiel, we see the Glory of the LORD beginning to depart—first from His Sanctuary, then from His Temple and then from His City… Ezekiel 9-11

Before God leaves, He calls for destroyers to execute those Jews who are part of this awful sin against God. A mark is put on the forehead of every person who sighs and groans over all the abominations which are being committed in the city. The executioners are given orders to utterly slay everyone who does not have that mark, whether it is an old man or a young man, a maiden or a women, or even a little child. And He commands that the execution begin in His Sanctuary! Judgment begins with the house of God! I Peter 4:17

Now, heartbreakingly, we see the Glory of the God of Israel departing from the Holy of Holies and hovering over the entrance of the east gate of the LORD's house. Ezekiel 10:4, 18, 19

In verses 22-23 of Ezekiel 11, we see the Glory of the God of Israel going up from the midst of Jerusalem and standing over the mountain which is east of the city.

Yet in verses 14-21 of Ezekiel 11, before God actually leaves, He gives His people a promise of a New Covenant. He is leaving because they sinned against Him. They sinned against Him because they could not keep the Law He had given them. They could not keep the Law because their hearts were wicked and evil. They were slaves to sin. Because they broke the Law, God had to scatter them from the land of Israel He promised to them.

In this New Covenant, God would give them one heart to obey Him. He would put a new spirit within them—one that would seek after God. He would take their heart of stone out of their flesh and give them a heart of flesh so they could walk in His statutes and keep His ordinances. This heart of flesh would be sensitive and responsive to the finger of God. Their old heart of stone never even felt or noticed His touch. In this New Covenant, God would be their God and they would be His people.

As God departs from His Temple, He promises to send the New Covenant to them. He is promising to send Jesus to them! He is promising The Seed!

The Glory of the LORD returns to Israel

The Glory of the LORD does return to Israel when Jesus is born. Jesus' parents brought Him to the Temple to present Him to the LORD; He was only eight days old. Luke 2:21-22

Simeon, a righteous and devout man, was looking for The Seed. God brought Simeon into the Temple by His Spirit and when he saw this tiny baby, he took Him in his arms and announced to the people that the Glory of God had returned! God Himself was among them once again. Luke 2:25-35 Anna, the prophetess, also gave witness that He was indeed The Seed. Luke 2:36-38

He came to His Own, and His Own did not receive Him. God was back with Israel tabernacling among them in the flesh. He was full of Glory as the only begotten of God, full of grace and truth, and yet their eyes would not see Him. They would not see His Glory. John 1:11, 14

Jesus teaches the nation of Israel for three long years. A few people believe, but most turn their backs on Him when He offers to let them enter into the New Covenant with Him. Instead of receiving Him—they murder Him.

The Glory of the LORD departs from Israel

Finally, it is Jesus' last week. He goes into the Temple one last time to teach the people. When He leaves, He informs them He will not be back again to the Temple. They will not see Him as the Glory of Israel until He comes again in all His Glory at the end of the age. O Jerusalem... How Jesus wept for you... Matthew 21:23; 23:37-39

The Glory of the LORD returns!

God's Glory does return after Jesus leaves the earth. He sends His Holy Spirit to indwell all believers. The Holy Spirit causes believers to walk in God's ways and to obey Him—conforming each one into the image of God's Own Son, Jesus. True believers give Glory to God simply by being observed by the world! II Corinthians 3:18

The Glory of the LORD returns to Israel!

Jesus is coming again! He will return to the earth in all His Glory. The whole earth will see Him. All the tribes of Israel will see Him and mourn because they will realize that this Jesus that they crucified was indeed The Seed. And, just as He prophesied, they will say, *"Blessed is He Who comes in the Name of the LORD!"* **Revelation 19:11-16; Zechariah 12:10; Revelation 1:7**

The Glory of the LORD remains!

Ezekiel finishes his book with a description of the new Temple that will be in existence during the Millennial Reign of Christ. In this Temple the Glory will stay forever! It will never leave. And just as we saw the Glory of the God of Israel leaving to the east, we see the Glory of the God of Israel coming back from the east. Ezekiel 43:4

God tells Ezekiel, "This is the place of My throne and the place of the soles of My feet, where I will dwell among the sons of Israel forever. And the house of Israel will not again defile My Holy Name." Why won't they? Because they will enter a New Covenant with God—a Covenant where God keeps both sides of the Covenant and <u>causes</u> <u>them</u> <u>to</u> <u>obey</u> <u>Him</u>—a Covenant where God gives them a new heart—a Covenant where God gives them Jesus, His Holy Son—The Seed to bring them Life! Ezekiel 43:1-9

HIStory Event 18
...GOD Promises a New Covenant...
THE SEED!

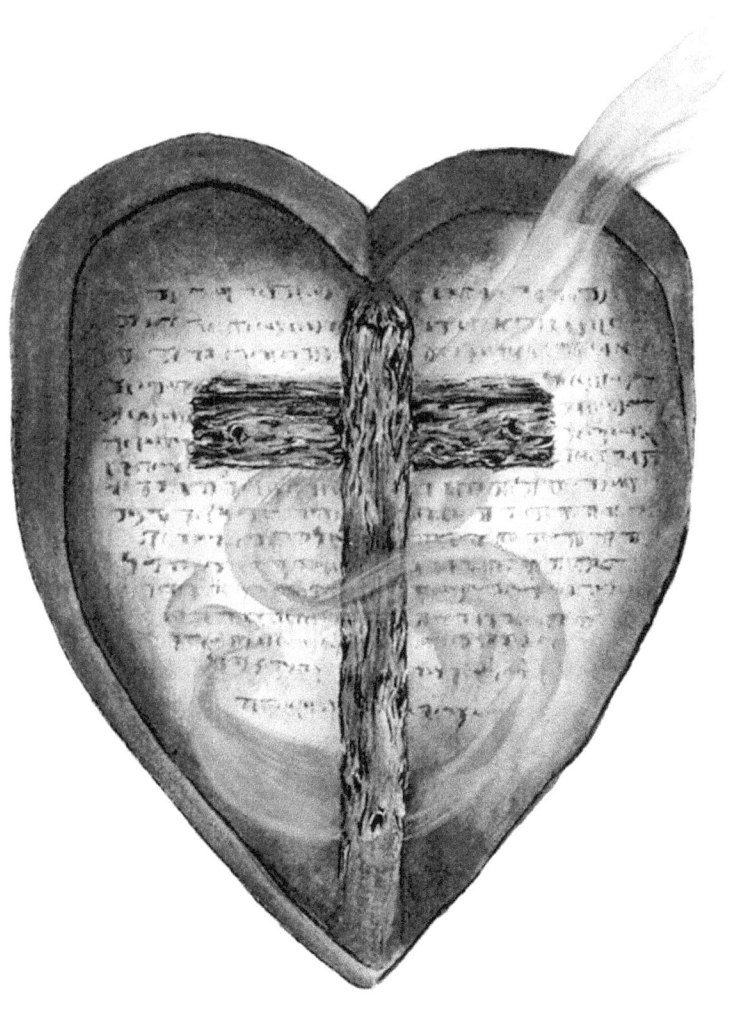

Read and Observe

1. Jeremiah 31:31-37; 32:37-44; 33:14-26
2. Ezekiel 11; 36:22-38
3. II Corinthians 3; Isaiah 43:7; Galatians 3-4; Hebrews 8-10

Read and Answer

1. Jeremiah 31:31-37
What wonderful promise does God make to the house of Israel and to the house of Judah while Judah is in Babylon?

What would this Covenant not be like?

What had His people done with that first Covenant?

In the Old Covenant where was God's Law written?

In this New Covenant where would God put His Law? What is the significance of the fact that God's Law would be written on their hearts instead of on tablets of stone?

How long would this New Covenant last?

In this New Covenant would God ever cast off His people?

Think back to why the people were sent to Babylon. Can you see why this New Covenant would bring hope?

Jeremiah 32:37-44
In this New Covenant, where would God bring His people?

Why would God give them one heart and one way in this New Covenant?

Would God ever turn away from doing them good in this New Covenant?

What would God do that would keep them from ever turning away from Him?

In the first Covenant, God took His people out of the land of Israel because they broke the Covenant. What would be different about this New Covenant regarding the land?

Jeremiah 33:14-26
In the days of the New Covenant what would God cause to spring forth?

What would He (the Righteous Branch of David) do?

Just so you don't miss it, Who is it that will execute justice and righteousness on the earth?

And whose descendant will He be?

How sure is this promise?

Can God's Covenant for the day and the night be broken? Can you be sure that day will follow night? Can you be sure that night will always follow day?

2. Ezekiel 11
Israel is now in exile because she sinned and sinned against the LORD. God made Jerusalem like a boiling pot and Israel was boiling! And all because she would not obey God! What is Ezekiel worried about in **verse 13**?

Although God removed Israel from the land and scattered her among other countries, what did He do for her?

What does He promise Ezekiel He will yet do?

    1.

    2.

    3.

When He brings them to Israel, what will they do?

What will God do to them?

    1.

    2.

    3.

    4.

Why?

When they obey God, what will they be?

What will God be to them?

Ezekiel 36:22-38
What will motivate God to act?

When He does act, what will be the result?

What will God prove?

List what God will do to Israel below. (Don't worry if you don't think you have everything. Just try to find the main things.)

What will God's Spirit cause Israel to do?

      1.

      2.

3. II Corinthians 3

From the text, fill in the chart with the contrasts between the Old and the New Covenant.

OLD COVENANT	NEW COVENANT
Written with ink	Written with the Spirit of the Living God
Written on tablets of stone	Written on tablets of human hearts
Of the letter	
Kills	
Ministry of death	
Came with Glory	
Glory faded	
Ministry of condemnation	
Compared with the New Covenant it had no Glory	
Fades away	
Sons of Israel were not allowed to watch the GLORY fade on Moses' face (They were not allowed to see the end of the Law → Jesus!)	
Their minds were hardened	
Veil remains unlifted over their heart	
Reads the Law of Moses	

What does it say will happen to us in the New Covenant in **verse 18**? Into what are we transformed?

Isaiah 43:7
What was it that God created us for? What did God want?

Galatians 3
How do you enter this New Covenant?

How do you stay in the New Covenant?

Who are the sons of Abraham?

How can you be blessed in Abraham?

If you are trying to follow the Law, what is true about you? What are you under?

Why?

How does a righteous man live?

Can you be under the Law and the New Covenant at the same time?

What is the blessing of Abraham?

What is the blessing that we receive?

How do we receive the blessing?

The promises were given to Abraham when God entered into Covenant with him way back in **Genesis**! Who else besides Abraham were the promises spoken to?

Did the Law invalidate the Covenant God made with Abraham?

On what was Abraham's inheritance based?

Why did God add the Law? ("Because of" can be translated "to define.")

Did the Law contradict the Covenant God made with Abraham?

Was the Law ever designed to give life?

What (or should I say "Who") had been promised to bring life since the time of Adam and Eve?

What did the Law do to everyone?

People under the Law (before faith) were kept in what?

What were they shut up to?

What has the Law become?

Why?

Once you believe in Christ Jesus so as to be saved, what happens to the Law?

What do you become?

In the New Covenant, is there a difference between a Jew and a Greek? Between a slave and a free man? Between a male and a female?

What are we in Christ Jesus?

If we belong to Christ, whose descendants are we?

What does that make us?

Galatians 4:1-6
What does Paul (the author of **Galatians**) compare us to before we are saved?

How does a child differ from a slave?

How long does the heir remain a child?

When was Jesus sent to earth?

What was He born under? What did He have to follow?

Why was Jesus sent?

Once you are saved through faith, what does God put into your heart?

What does the Spirit of His Son do?

Galatians 4:21-31
It seems reasonable to Paul that if you want to be under the Law you should listen to it. What does he point out that the Law says? Draw it out below.

The allegory he gives them is another set of contrasts between the Old Covenant/Law and the New Covenant/The Seed/Jesus Christ. Fill in the chart. I'll do the Law side for you.

Old Covenant Law	New Covenant The Seed—Jesus Christ
Abraham had a son by the bondwoman	
According to the flesh	
Proceeding from Mount Sinai	
Bears children who are enslaved	
Hagar	
Mount Sinai in Arabia	
Present Jerusalem	
In slavery with her children	
Children are numerous	
Not children of promise	
Born according to the flesh	
Persecutes him who is born according to the Spirit	
The bondwoman is to be cast out	
The son of the bondwoman will not be an heir	
Brethren (believers) are not children of the bondwoman	

Hebrews 8
I hope you like filling out charts because that's what we need to do again!

Old Covenant	New Covenant
Not the true Tabernacle	
Man pitched this Tabernacle	
Every high priest offers gifts and sacrifices	
Offers the gifts according to the Law	
Copy of the heavenly things	
Shadow of the heavenly things	
From the pattern of the real thing	
Ministry	
Covenant	
Promises	
First Covenant was not faultless	
Fault was with the people in the Covenant	
Covenant with the Fathers of Israel	
Israel did not keep this Covenant	
God did not care for them because they broke the Covenant	
Obsolete	
Growing old	
Ready to disappear	

List everything good about the New Covenant.

Hebrews 9:8-14
What is the Holy Spirit signifying while the outer Tabernacle is still standing?

During the time of the Tabernacle's existence, of what was it a symbol?

Can the gifts and sacrifices that are offered make the worshiper perfect in conscience?

Why not?

Where did Christ enter as a High Priest?

How did He enter? (Through what did He enter?)

What was His sacrifice?

Will He ever have to enter there again and present a sacrifice?

What did His sacrifice obtain?

What did the blood sacrifices from the Law do?

What more will Christ's blood do?

Hebrews 10:1
What does the Law have (concerning the good things to come)?

What does the New Covenant have (concerning the good things to come)?

What can the Law never do?

Why not?

What can the New Covenant do?

Why?

Hebrews 10:9-18
Jesus took away the first in order to establish the second. The first what? The second what?

What did that accomplish for us?

The priests of the Old Covenant had to work day in and day out. Why did Jesus sit down?

What has the offering of Jesus done?

What is this Covenant that God will make that is referred to here in **Hebrews 10:16**?

What will God do to their hearts in this New Covenant?

What will God do to their minds in this New Covenant?

What will God do to their sins and their lawless deeds?

Why are there no more sacrifices?

Read and Reason

1. Jeremiah 31:31-37; 32:37-44; 33:14-26
God not only gives Judah the hope of coming back to Jerusalem in 70 years, but He also promises to make a brand new Covenant with her and with the house of Israel. This New Covenant will not be like the Covenant He made with their fathers when He brought them out of Egypt. This Covenant will be better!

Even when the people wanted to obey God, they were not able to because of their heart condition. They still needed that heart transplant. God is now promising He will perform divine surgery on their hearts. In the New Covenant, God promises to give them a new heart—a heart of flesh. This is where He will write His Law—within them! He will be their God and they will be His people. He promises to give them one heart and one way. They will fear Him and follow His commands and will not turn away from Him. (Remember **Exodus 20:20** where God scared them to keep them from breaking Covenant with Him.) The New Covenant will be an everlasting Covenant—a Covenant in which He will not turn away from them, a Covenant in which He will do them good.

God promises He will gather the Israelites from the lands where He has scattered them and cause them to dwell safely back in Israel. He says that as surely as He took them out of the land, He will bring them back to it. He promises that Israel will *always* be a nation before Him. God is so emphatic about the surety of this promise that He compares its longevity to the fixed order of the sun and the moon. **As long as there is day and night, Israel will exist as a nation.**

Wow! If you had a choice between the Old Covenant and the New Covenant, which one would you take? Did you know that choice is placed before you now?

2. Ezekiel 11:1-20

During the days of Ezekiel, God showed him horrible things that would happen to Israel because she had broken Covenant with God. God told Ezekiel that Jerusalem would be the pot and the Israelites inside the walls would be like the food cooked in that pot.

Israel was going about her merry little way (sinning against God, ignoring Him and His Word), and God told Ezekiel to prophesy to her. The message was not encouraging! He said He would take the Israelites out of Jerusalem, kill them with the sword, and deliver them to captors. He said that by this Israel would know that *God* was the LORD. They had not obeyed God, but had mimicked the evil nations around them. Here it is again—Israel is following instead of leading.

Ezekiel is terrified and afraid that God is going to destroy Israel completely. God reassures him that although He scattered her among the nations, He still took care of her. God also promises Ezekiel that He will gather His people from among those nations and bring them back to Israel. Israel will ultimately possess the land promised to her since the days of Abraham.

But something big is going to have to take place to change the Israelites themselves! That big thing is the New Covenant! The New Covenant will give them a new spirit—a new attitude, new wants and desires. He will also give them one heart—they will no longer do what is right in their own eyes, they will follow God in unity. God will give them a heart of flesh, one that is sensitive to His touch, His Word. Then, and only then, will Israel obey God. Then, and only then, will they be God's people. Then, and only then, will He be their God.

Ezekiel 36:22-38

God again promises a New Covenant for Israel. However, He makes it clear that He is doing it for *His* Name's sake—not because of the people! His Name and reputation were tarnished when He had to send His people to other countries. He will vindicate the holiness of His great Name through a New Covenant! He will prove Himself holy in the sight of all the nations. They will all know that *God* is the LORD!

He promises to gather them back from all the nations where He has sent them and plant them once again in the land of Israel. (God is fulfilling this prophecy during our own generation!) When He is ready, He will sprinkle clean water on them and make them clean. He will cleanse them from all their filthiness and from all their idols.

His New Covenant promises that He will give them a new heart and put a new spirit within them. He will remove their heart of stone and give them a heart of flesh. In other words, God is going to change their wants and their desires. They will now want to obey God!

He will also give them the ability to obey Him by putting His Own Spirit within them. His Spirit will cause them to walk in His statutes and cause them to be careful to observe His ordinances.

He also promises they will live in the land that He gave to Abraham and the fathers of Israel. Then they will be His people and God will be their God. He will save them from all their uncleanness. He promises that they will no longer have famines because their trees and fields will produce great harvests. The land will be cultivated so richly that it will resemble the Garden of Eden.

In that day they will remember all their evil deeds and loathe themselves because of them. God says they are to be ashamed of their iniquities and their abominations. God will save them because of His Name—not because of Israel herself!

God will cleanse them from all their iniquities and cause the cities in Israel to be inhabited. The waste places will be rebuilt. The population of Israel will increase like a flock!

Then the nations and Israel will know that *God* is the Lord!

3. II Corinthians 3
Paul explains the benefits of the New Covenant to the Corinthian church. He compares the Corinthians to written letters that prove the New Covenant changes people. They are not written with ink, like the parchments that hold their Law, but with the Spirit of the Living God. They are not written on stones like the Law given to Moses, but on tablets of human hearts.

He then continues his epistle by contrasting the Old Covenant to the New Covenant. While the Old Covenant kills (because no one could keep it and was therefore cursed), the New Covenant gives life through the Holy Spirit.

Paul calls the Law the ministry of death or condemnation (because if you broke any of the laws you received the curse of death) and says it came with Glory. Then he reasons: if the ministry of death came with Glory it is obvious that the ministry of the Spirit—the ministry of righteousness —has even more Glory. In fact, it abounds in Glory. Actually, compared to the Glory of the New Covenant, the Old Covenant doesn't have *any* Glory! The Glory of the Old faded away, but the Glory of the New remains!

When a person looks to the Law, a veil is over his heart and he can't understand Truth, but when a person looks to Christ, his eyes will be opened and he will understand Truth. Once a person can understand Truth, he will study the Word of God. Once he understands and obeys the Word of God, he will be conformed to the image of Jesus Christ. Jesus Christ is the exact image and nature and representation of God the Father. He brings Glory to God because He shows Who God really is. When we are conformed into the image of Jesus, then we, too, show the world Who God really is! Hallelujah!!! Remember why God created man—to bring Glory to Himself!!! The New Covenant accomplishes the will of God. God's will is to bring Himself Glory!!! Glory to God in the Highest!!! Amen!!! Amen!!!

Galatians 3:1-16
To enter this wonderful New Covenant takes one thing only—faith in the Lord Jesus Christ. The Seed is the only way to receive Life! Not only does faith bring you to salvation, faith is the means by which we are perfected or completed.

It took faith (belief) in the Word of God for Abraham to be saved. It is those who have faith (belief) in the Word of God who are sons of Abraham and therefore blessed along with him. We receive the promise of the Spirit through faith!

As long as you are looking to the Law to save you or to sanctify you, you are cursed. You cannot be under the Old Covenant and the New Covenant at the same time!

The promises were spoken to Abraham and his Seed, Jesus. When we are in Christ, we are one with Him and receive what He receives. Jesus returned to the Father. The Father was satisfied with all that His Son had done and gave Jesus what He had promised to Him—The Spirit. Jesus then poured out His Spirit on all mankind that would believe.

Galatians 3:17-29
The Law was given 430 years after God's Covenant with Abraham (when He created the nation of Israel). It did not invalidate or contradict the promises of the Abrahamic Covenant. The inheritance offered in the Abrahamic Covenant was based on a promise. The Law was based on performance.

Paul then asks the question that he knows the Galatians are thinking. Why did God add the Law? Paul doesn't skip a beat and proceeds to answer their (his) question. The Law was added to define what transgressions were. Even before the Law, people sinned. Sometimes people were aware they were sinning directly against the Word of God; sometimes people sinned out of ignorance of God's ways. The Law was put in place so that no one could plead ignorance in his or her defense. God, through the Law, clearly defined what He expected of Israel.

The Law, Paul tells us, also benefited the people in another way—it kept people shut up and in custody until the New Covenant. Yes, the people were sinning and would continue to sin, but with the Law as their goal, they would sin less than without it. It would corral them in, keeping them away from the world's ways and keeping the world's ways away from them. In other words, although they would still be stained with the ways of the world, the stain wouldn't be as dark!

The Law was a tutor to lead people to Christ. The Law showed people that there was no other way to become righteous than by accepting the righteousness of Christ as their own. Once people find and receive Christ, they no longer need the Law. Now, the Spirit of Jesus lives in them and keeps them from sinning as a way of life.

And once people are saved through faith in Christ Jesus, they become sons of God. No longer is there a distinction between Jew and Gentile, male and female, or slave and free man. Every one is the same in Christ Jesus. And once you belong to Christ, you become a descendant of Abraham and heir of the promises!

Galatians 4:1-7
Paul continues his dialogue by using the example of an heir who is a child. Although a child will someday inherit his father's wealth, while he is a child he isn't treated any differently than his father's slaves. He is told what to do by guardians and managers. That's what the Law does for us until we are saved. It governs our walk in life until we have faith in Jesus. Then Jesus will govern our life.

Once we receive Jesus and become sons of God, His Spirit within us affirms that we are saved. We have a new relationship with God. No longer one of enmity, but one of parent and child. We are no longer slaves, but heirs!

Hebrews 8
The Covenant God made with Abraham was the *promise*. Jesus Christ is the *fulfillment*! The Law was given in the interim as a *picture* of salvation. Everything that was part of the Tabernacle and its rituals gave the Israelites a picture of the Truth of Jesus—if they would only have eyes to see! But it was only a copy and shadow of the real.

The New Covenant is so much better than the Old that it's hard to compare the two. The New Covenant has a much better Sanctuary and Tabernacle, a greater High Priest, namely Jesus, and a better ministry. The sacrifice Christ made was better than all the gifts and sacrifices ever offered in the Tabernacle put together!

The New Covenant even offered better promises than the Old Covenant. And most importantly, it offered a surefire way to obtain the promises. In the Old Covenant, you were responsible for keeping your side of the agreement. If you failed to keep your side you were cursed! But in the New Covenant, God is willing to keep not only His side, but your side for you!!!

The fault with the first Covenant was the people involved. They had wicked hearts and were incapable of keeping the Covenant. In the New Covenant, God guarantees that He will keep His promises, but He also gives you a new heart to replace your wicked heart and puts His Spirit within you, thereby guaranteeing that you will keep your side of the Covenant.

Here in **Hebrews**, the author is quoting Jeremiah's prophecy of the New Covenant. This Covenant is offered to any and all who would believe! Those who embrace all that Jesus is enter this Covenant!

When Jesus inaugurated the New Covenant, it superseded the Old Covenant.

Hebrews 9
The Tabernacle and its rituals were a symbol of the New Covenant to come—The Seed! While it was still standing, it was a symbol or message to the people that there was no access into the Holy

Place—no access to God. There was no access to God because the Old Covenant could never make a person truly clean and holy before God.

But the Tabernacle was not to last forever. It was only a sign for a time—a sign of the New Covenant to come, the Covenant that could and would make a person truly clean and holy before God. The Covenant that would give a person access to a Holy God!!!

When Christ entered the true Tabernacle as the High Priest for us with His Own perfect blood, God was satisfied and proclaimed that no other sacrifice would ever need to be made! Christ's blood didn't just cleanse our flesh, it cleansed our consciences from dead works to serve the Living God!

Hebrews 10
The author of **Hebrews** continues with his contrast of the New Covenant and the Law. He reminds them that the Law was only a shadow of the good things to come. Salvation in Jesus Christ *is* "those good things to come!"

Jesus came and performed the Father's will perfectly. The Father's will was that the New Covenant would be established so we could be sanctified!

Jesus is now sitting at the right hand of God because His work of atonement (redemption) is finished! Now the Holy Spirit dwells in each believer and causes him or her to remain faithful to God!!! There doesn't need to be any more offering because there is forgiveness for all of our sins!!!

Point of Depth

What should we do with the Law? Should we teach it to our children? Yes! By all means, Yes! We should bring up our children under the Law of God. They should be taught to follow the Law because it will show them their need of The Seed! The Law is a tutor that leads them to Christ. Galatians 3:24

Paul is very clear in Romans 2:17-29 that relying on the Law for salvation will never work! Many times, far too many times, people in the church rely on their own personal record of keeping the Law for the assurance of their salvation! They look at outward things, like baptism, church attendance, monetary giving, involvement in church activities, and "trying really hard" to do good things and feel a security in them. There is no security in *any* of those things.

Paul states the real rules: The one who is saved is the one whose heart has been circumcised by the Holy Spirit! And He will only circumcise the heart of the one who has faith in Jesus Christ the Lord!

Why was the Law given if it couldn't save you? Galatians 3 explains. The Law was given for two main reasons:

1. Before faith came (before the New Covenant), we were kept in custody under the Law (like a military guard), being shut up to the faith that was later to be revealed.

   Think of it this way—you are standing and surrounding you are ten military guards. Not one of them will let you get past so you can be free to go where you want. Each time you take a step towards freedom, you feel the painful tip of one of the guard's rifles in your flesh. You stop, turn to go another direction, and try again. Immediately, another guard is sticking his rifle right in your face. You try and try to escape, but there doesn't seem to be any way out!

   You are "kept in custody by the Law." You are shut up inside of the Law. You are being kept there until "faith" comes. You cannot escape in your own strength. You need Jesus Christ. You need to enter the New Covenant!

   By the way → one beneficial by-product of this captivity under the Law is that you are not free to run around with the world like you want to. You are kept from polluting yourself with the full potency of the world's stench.

2. The Law is our tutor to lead us to Christ so that we can be justified by faith!

   Keep picturing yourself inside of those ten military guards. The Law doesn't just keep you locked up forever. It wants to lead you to freedom—freedom in Christ! So it becomes our tutor, or child-conductor, to lead us to Christ.

   Let me explain what a tutor or child-conductor was in biblical times. It's different from how we think of a tutor nowadays. A tutor was hired in ancient times as someone who would be responsible for the well being of the child until he was taken to school. The child-conductor would escort the child to his teacher. Once the child-conductor, or tutor had delivered the child to the teacher, the tutor's job was finished and he went on his own way. Now, let's go back to our illustration.

   Picture the military guards (your tutors or escorts) in a tight circle around you. They are motioning you toward one point in the circle. They want to take you to the Teacher, and there is only one way to reach Him. They part and make a small opening in the circle.

   Now you see a small, narrow road leading out of the circle of the Law. Standing in the center of that road to freedom is none other than the Lord Jesus Christ! The military guards are happy to show you the *one* way out from under their dominion, out from under the Law! John 14:6 They point you to Jesus!

If you trust Jesus and try to escape through Him and to Him, you will find freedom—*Freedom in Christ!* If you trust in yourself or anything you can do to effect your freedom, you will still be held captive and condemned by the Law.

The Law won't let you out *any other way except through Jesus!* Jesus *is* the New Covenant! The Law keeps you shut up until you believe in Him. Your own works cannot bring you deliverance from the circle of the Law; only Jesus can effect your freedom!

Can you see now why you should put your children under the Law? The Law will help them to see the *way* to salvation, Jesus Christ! And it will keep them from looking and acting like the world! Not a bad deal!

POINT OF DEPTH

ABRAHAMIC COVENANT → The Promise of Salvation (Jesus, The Seed)
- God gives the Land of Canaan to Abraham and his descendants
- God promises to make Abraham into a nation
- God promises The Seed, Who will bless all mankind, will come through Abraham
- God promises this Covenant will be everlasting

God made an everlasting Covenant with Abraham. He promised that The Seed would come and bless all mankind. When we believe in The Seed, Jesus Christ, we are Abraham's offspring. We become heirs according to promise!

LAW / OLD COVENANT → The Picture of Salvation (Jesus, The Seed)
- Keep the Law and be blessed
- Break the Law and be cursed
- It is God's standard of Holiness
- Man could not keep the Law because of his heart condition
- Shows us our need of redemption **Galatians 3**
- Leads us *to* Christ **Galatians 3**

God gave the Jews the Law to keep them separate from the world until The Seed would come. Then Jesus, Himself, would keep them Holy unto Himself!

Everything in the Old Covenant was a picture of Jesus, Himself. Everything in the Tabernacle itself was a picture of Jesus! If only they would have had eyes to see…

Hebrews tells us the New Covenant promised in Jeremiah and Ezekiel is the Covenant of Christ Jesus! **II Corinthians 3; Galatians 3-4; Hebrews 8-10; Jeremiah 31:31-34; 32:37-41; Ezekiel 36:24-27**

NEW COVENANT → The Reality of Salvation! (Jesus, The Seed!)
    God takes out our evil heart
    God puts a new heart in us—one that is tender and responsive to Him
    God writes His laws on our new heart
    God puts a new spirit in us—one that seeks after Him
    God puts His Own Holy Spirit in us
    God's Holy Spirit causes us to walk in His ways and keep His laws
    God puts a fear of Himself inside of us so that we will not turn away from Him
    We have access to God through Jesus Christ
    We have Christ's righteousness applied to our account
    We are justified before God
    We are sanctified and made holy and blameless before Him
    Christ lives His life through us

The Old Covenant was a picture of the New Covenant!
Everything in the Tabernacle was a picture of Jesus!

Door	Jesus is the Door! Jesus is the Way!
Altar	Jesus is the Lamb that was slain!
Laver	Jesus is the Living Water! We are washed by the water of the Word. Jesus is the Word!
Table of Showbread	Jesus is the Bread of Life!
Candlestick	Jesus is the Light!
Altar of Incense	Jesus ever lives to intercede for us!
Holy of Holies	Jesus is God!

Have you entered this awesome Covenant where God keeps both sides?

How do you enter in? I am so glad you asked!

- God is Holy, set apart unto Himself. He cannot be with anything that isn't also set apart unto Him. Because God is Holy, He must judge all ungodliness.

- Man is not holy. Man is a sinner. He acts apart from God. So, because man is unholy, God *must* judge him! The judgment is death, separation from God!

- In order for God to be with man, and for man to be with God, one of two things must happen. Either God must become unholy, or man must become holy! God cannot change (Praise Him!!!) so God becoming unholy is definitely out of the question!!! The only solution seems to be for man to become holy, and yet man cannot become holy through his own efforts.

- No one seeks after God on their own so the sanctification process of the Holy Spirit is absolutely essential. The Spirit draws an individual, and if he truly believes the Truth, then he is saved. When an individual believes that he needs a Savior and recognizes that Savior as Jesus Christ, then he is able to enter in.

- God could not save us from His judgment without payment for the price of sin. That's because He is Holy. He couldn't just say we were innocent when we were guilty! It's just like a judge today. He can't declare someone innocent who is obviously guilty. At least he can't do that and still be a righteous judge—and God is a righteous judge!

- God's judgments are righteous and true. Each of us are obviously guilty and must pay for our crimes. The payment is death—separation eternally from God. If one paid his own debt he could never be with God because he would be... well... um... dead... (separated from Him eternally that is). So God sent Jesus to pay his debt for him. Once his debt had been paid, then God could declare him innocent so he could be with God.

- Once a person believes, truly believes, God puts His Holy Spirit, the Spirit of Jesus, inside of him. It is the Holy Spirit Who then causes that person to walk in a holy manner worthy of the LORD! Now, instead of the Law telling him what he could or could not do, Jesus Christ orders his steps through His Holy Spirit inside of him. And the steps He orders are just like the steps He took while He lived on this earth!

Do you recognize and accept that God is Holy and that you are not holy?
Have you bowed your knee to the One and Only God Who can make you holy?

Point of Depth

The wages of sin is death.
- ✓ You've worked for your wages.
- ✓ They are due you.
- ✓ You will receive them whether you want them or not.
- ✓ There's not a thing you can do about it.
- ✓ Jesus was willing to take your unwanted wages for you.

The free gift of God is eternal life.
- ✓ No matter how hard you work, you will never earn eternal life. You cannot work to receive this gift.
- ✓ You will never deserve it.
- ✓ Even though you want eternal life, you can't acquire it through your own efforts.
- ✓ There is not a single thing you can do to produce it.
- ✓ Jesus is willing to give eternal life to you.

Although you can't work for it or earn it, there are conditions to receiving eternal life.
- ✓ You must be given the faith by God to believe.
- ✓ You must confess and repent of the very fact that you exist as an unholy being.
- ✓ You must be willing to die to everything in that unholy existence and let God order your each and every step from that time forward. You will never have a right over your own life again because your life now belongs to Him!
- ✓ Although eternal life is the free gift of God → it costs everything!

Point of Depth

Jehovah-Mekoddishkem is the Hebrew name for God which means "I AM the LORD Who sanctifies you." Leviticus 20:8 God wanted the children of Israel to know that they were set apart from the world and that it was He Who set them apart!

God gave them a sign that would remind them that He was their God and they needed to be set apart unto Him. That sign was the Sabbath. For six days they were to work, but on the seventh day there was to be complete rest. The seventh day was God's! Exodus 31:12-17; Isaiah 58:13-14

Why was resting on the seventh day after six days of work to be this sign? Because it would remind them that He was their God—the God Who made the heavens and the earth—the God Who ceased from His labor on the seventh day and was refreshed. There is no other God like Him!

God is still Jehovah-Mekoddishkem to the church today. Yet, do we need to observe the Sabbath? Do we need this sign?

Let's remember what the sign was for. It was a sign for the Israelites that God was the One Who sanctified them. Are we sanctified today? Yes. Who is it that sanctifies us? It is still the LORD God Who sanctifies us. How does He sanctify us today? That's where things are a bit different for us as the church than they were for Israel. Hebrews 10:10, 14

It was external laws, commandments and statutes that set the nation of Israel apart from the world and unto God. They were under the Old Covenant which was a foreshadow of the New Covenant. We, in the church, are part of the New Covenant and have been told to throw out the Old Covenant! Galatians 4 If we throw out the Old Covenant, won't we have to throw out observing the Sabbath? The answer is "Yes" and the answer is "No!"

How can we fulfill the law of keeping the Sabbath while still throwing out the Law? We now walk according to the Spirit and not according to the Law. The Spirit will never break the Law of God, He will only enable us to fulfill it. Galatians 5:16-18

One year the highway by our ministry grounds underwent renovation. Normally to get to WORD Center Ministries you would simply follow and obey the road signs along the way → (the Law). However once the roadwork started, drivers were instructed to ignore the road signs and instead follow the instructions of the construction workers who were guiding the traffic flow → (the Holy Spirit).

Christ did not come to abolish the Law. He came to fulfill it! Matthew 5:17 In other words, there is a *new* way in which we are set apart from the world and unto God! It is no longer through the Law (road signs). It is now through the Spirit (construction workers)! It is the Spirit of God in us that sanctifies us, and He uses the Word of God to do it!

Trouble is, we are used to thinking that all God really wanted was for His people just to sit around on the Sabbath twiddling their thumbs. That is not so! Not only did He want the Israelites to spend the day meditating on His Word, He wanted the entire world, every living person, to notice that the Israelites were different than every other nation on the face of the earth! They were different because of their *God!!!* Being holy and resting on the Sabbath would point the world to *God!!!*

Today, when we are filled with the Holy Spirit and walk according to His instructions rather than listening to our flesh, we will walk in such a different way than the world that, of course, the world will notice! And the world will know we are different because of our *God!!!*

"But, I still don't see what resting has to do with it," you may say.

Resting means "to cease." We are to cease striving, to cease living by the strength of our own flesh. When we walk according to the Spirit we are walking in the strength of God instead of our own strength. Our own strength ceases and His strength uses us. We have been crucified with Christ, it is no longer we who live, but Christ Who lives in us. Galatians 2:20 We are dead to our flesh. It is Christ Who is living His life in us. We crucify our flesh and its desires and walk according to the will of God in the energy of the Holy Spirit!

We are to keep the Sabbath by resting from our own works and allowing the Holy Spirit (Jesus' Spirit) to work through us instead. We are resting because it is the power and strength of the Lord Jesus Christ that moves us, not our own! People will surely see His power instead of our own and be pointed to the God Who made heaven and earth and Who Himself rested on the seventh day! And it won't just be one day of the week—it will be every moment of every day.

HIStory Event 19
...GOD Brings Israel Back to The Land

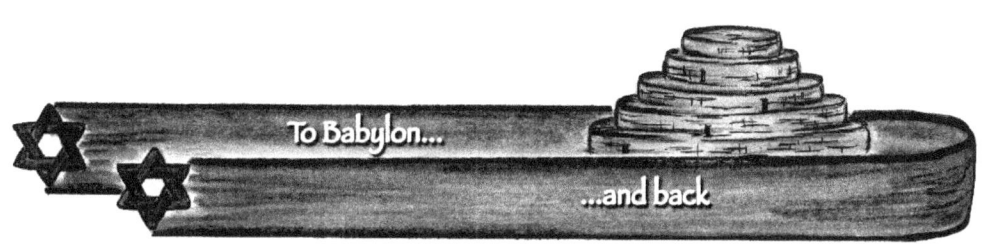

Read and Observe

1. Ezra, Nehemiah
2. Ezra 3:10-13; 5:2; 6:15
3. Isaiah 44:28; 45:1-13
4. II Chronicles 36:20-23; Ezra 1:1-8
5. Ezra 7
6. Nehemiah 1:11; 2:4-8; 4:7-9, 13-14; 6:8-16

Read and Answer

1. Ezra, Nehemiah
Read through both of these books before answering the questions below. Notice that the 70 years of exile in Babylon are over. God is bringing back a faithful remnant to rebuild His beloved city, Jerusalem.

2. Ezra 3:10-13
Zerubbabel brought back the first group from Babylon. When they had finished laying the foundation for the new Temple, there were two reactions. What were they?

1.

2.

Why did some of the people weep instead of rejoice?

Ezra 5:2
The foundation had been laid. Now what did they start to build?

Ezra 6:15
What was finally finished?

3. Isaiah 44:28; 45:1-13
What does God call Cyrus?

What will Cyrus do at God's command?

What will God do for Cyrus?

Could Cyrus have refused God?

This prophecy was made 175 years before Cyrus was even born. Who is in control of all things?

4. II Chronicles 36:20-23; Ezra 1:1-8
Why did Cyrus do what he did?

What caused him to do it?

Can God's plan be thwarted?

When Nebuchadnezzer took Israel captive, he also stole the furniture and utensils from God's house, His Temple. What did Cyrus do concerning those things?

5. Ezra 7
Ezra would bring back the second group of exiles from Babylon. He asked King Artaxerxes to help him accomplish the trip. Why did the king grant everything that Ezra requested?

Ezra's trip took him from where to where?

What had Ezra set his heart to do?

    1.

        2.

        3.

King Artaxerxes sent a decree with Ezra which helped him on his mission. Why did the king do that?

How did Ezra have the strength to do what he did?

6. Nehemiah 1:11
Nehemiah would bring the third and final remnant of God's people back to Jerusalem from Babylon. Nehemiah would go to King Artaxerxes and make a request just like Ezra had done. What did Nehemiah do that was of utmost importance before he went into the presence of the king?

Nehemiah 2:4-8
When Nehemiah was before the king, the king asked him what he needed. Before Nehemiah responded, what did he do?

Nehemiah 4:7-9, 13-14
Once Nehemiah was back in Jerusalem, there was opposition against him. What did he do?

When the people who were building the wall around Jerusalem became afraid because of the opposition, what did Nehemiah tell them?

Nehemiah 6:8-16
Opposition came in the form of lies and rumors. How did Nehemiah respond to this attack?

The wall was finally completed and all the enemies of Israel heard about it. What was their response?

Why did they lose their confidence?

READ AND REASON

1. Ezra, Nehemiah
It took three sieges on Jerusalem and three different caravans of captives to get everybody to Babylon. 605, 597, 586 BC. Now we see three different kings decreeing that three different remnants of freed exiles go back to Jerusalem and rebuild it. 537-536, 458, 445 BC.

2. Ezra 3:10-13; 5:2; 6:15
Zerrubabel led the first remnant back to Jerusalem from their captivity in Babylon. They completed rebuilding the Temple in 516 BC. The work on the Temple is described as sounding like thunder. That makes it seem like the Temple must have been magnificent—not so. Some of the people shouted with a great shout while the older people who had seen the former Temple wept aloud because it was nothing like the glory of the first Temple. They wept so loud that the people could not distinguish the difference between the shout of joy from some and the sound of weeping from others!

Ezra

Ezra begins by taking up where II Chronicles left off, in fact, the first three verses of Ezra are identical to the last two of II Chronicles. Ezra records the first and second returns of the remnant of Israel to the land of Judah. Under direction from King Cyrus they began rebuilding the Temple of God in Jerusalem, but opposition came and the work on the Temple stopped. So God sent Haggai and Zechariah to rebuke the people. God protected Israel from the opposition as they rebuilt the Temple.

POINT OF DEPTH

The people had gone into captivity in Babylon because of their sin—because they broke Covenant with God. He had been faithful to them. Along with taking them out of the land, He also brought them back to it. And yet, He did not want them to sin again. He gave them reminders.

They would never be able to look at the Temple without remembering the tears of the aged who had seen the former Temple. They realized how very much the present one lacked in

glory compared to its predecessor. If in remembering, they would also consider their sin which had caused it all—if they would only remember...

Zerubbabel had led the remnant back. Every time they talked about their return and the rebuilding of the Temple, they would mention Zerubbabel. The very act of speaking his name "Zerubbabel" would leave them without doubt as to what had happened to them. His name means "born in Babylon." Zerubbabel was born in Babylon because God had sent Judah there for breaking Covenant with Him by their sin. If they would only remember...

Haggai

After 70 years of exile in Babylon, Cyrus had sent God's people back to Jerusalem, at least the ones who wanted to go back. The people did not build God's house like Cyrus sent them back to do. They even took the money that Cyrus had given them to purchase wood for the Temple of God and instead used it to build their own homes! God's house lay desolate and the people lay idle. The funny thing was, things weren't going very well for them and yet they didn't even wonder why, so God connected the dots for them. "Consider your ways!", God roared at them! Obedience brings blessing and disobedience brings cursing.

Zechariah

Zechariah prophesied to Judah during the time of the first return from Babylon warning them to return <u>now</u> from their evil ways <u>before</u> God punished them completely as He was forced to do to their fathers. Because they were not completing the Temple, God gave Zechariah visions which promised a great future of prosperity for Israel if she obeyed Him completely. She did not, and will not, until her God comes and regenerates her. Zechariah prophesied about God's judgment on the nations, the worthless shepherd, His defense of Israel, and the future blessing for Israel. Zechariah provides us with specific information concerning That Day—The Day of The LORD.

ESTHER

The story of Esther takes place between the first and the second returns to Jerusalem. Esther was married to Haswererus, or Xerxes, the Persian king, and lived in Persia's capital city, Suza. Haman, the king's right hand man plots to wipe out all the Jews. Mordecai, her uncle, learns of Haman's intrigue and orders Esther to intercede with the king. Esther, however, is afraid and returns a message of "I can't!" to Uncle Mordecai, who reproves her with, "You must!" and tells her that if she remains silent, God will bring relief and deliverance from another place and she will perish. Esther finally responds correctly and assures him that she will do what needs to be done and adds a final seal to the deal with "If I perish, I perish!" God spared Israel because of the Covenant He made with them in **Genesis 12**. The custom of Purim was established at this time.

3. Isaiah 44:28; 45:1-13

Long before God ever sent Nebuchadnezzar to take Judah captive;
Long before the Temple and the city of Jerusalem were leveled to the ground;
Long before the nations of the Medes and the Persians even thought about forming an alliance;
175 long years before the ruler of the Medo-Persian empire was even born;
God decided what He would do:
> He decided to bring the Babylonians in to take Jerusalem captive.
> He decided to destroy the Temple and the city.
> He decided to cause the Medes and the Persians to form an alliance.
> He decided to enable the Medes and the Persians to conquer the world of that time.
> He decided to send them to take over Babylon.
> He decided to create a man and He decided to name him Cyrus.
> He decided Cyrus would be His shepherd over the people of Judah.
> He decided Cyrus would perform all His desire.
> He decided to order Cyrus to send His people home again.

4. II Chronicles 36:20-23; Ezra 1:1-8

In Cyrus' first year as king of Persia, the LORD stirred up his spirit to send Judah back home to Israel. He made a proclamation and put it in writing. *"Thus says Cyrus king of Persia, 'The LORD, the God of heaven, has given me all the kingdoms of the earth, and He has appointed me to build Him a house in Jerusalem, which is in Judah. Whoever there is among you of all His people, may the LORD his God be with him, and let him go up!'"*

God also caused him to send along articles of silver, gold, valuable goods, cattle, plus a freewill offering! And God made sure Cyrus sent back God's vessels from the Temple which had been sitting in the house of Nebuchadnezzar's gods! (The ones that the Babylonians had taken during the three sieges on Jerusalem and that Belshazzar had used to drink from the night he saw the handwriting on the wall.)

5. Ezra 7
Ezra, a scribe who was skilled in the Law of Moses, leads the second remnant of Jews back to Jerusalem from Babylon. King Artaxerxes, a Persian king, orders Ezra to adorn the house of God. He gives Ezra silver and gold and tells him to do whatever he wants to with it according to the will of Ezra's God. So, in 458 BC, Ezra heads back to Jerusalem with a remnant of 50,000 Jews.

I Chronicles

I Chronicles was not written until after Israel's captivity, between the first and the second return of Judah to the land. It holds a unique perspective on some of the same events covered in I and II Samuel. I Chronicles tells what had <u>already happened</u> rather than telling what <u>was happening</u>. The Jews go back to the land of Israel, and then the Chronicles are written.

I Chronicles gives the genealogies of Israel's ancestors going back as far as Adam. It then continues with the history of the kings of Israel through David.

The second half of I Chronicles shows David bringing the Ark of the Covenant to Jerusalem and how he desired to build a house for the Ark to dwell in. God says that instead, He will build a house (name) for David (Davidic Covenant) by promising to establish David's kingdom and throne forever (this is fulfilled through The Seed). God says that Solomon will build Him a Temple, so David makes preparations for his son to build it.

Though a lot of this information is found in I and II Samuel, I Chronicles goes deeper with additional details as it focuses on the Ark of the Covenant and the Temple, landmark items ever so important to the returning exiles of Judah.

II Chronicles

Like I Chronicles, II Chronicles was not written until after Israel's captivity. It covers, from a variant angle, some of the same events in I and II Kings.

II Chronicles begins with the reign of Solomon, continues through the time of captivity for Judah and the promise to return to the land, and deals with the kings of the southern tribes.

Continuing on from I Chronicles, the focus at the beginning of the book is Solomon building the Temple. Afterward it goes through the kings of Judah one by one revealing how they did not follow the "God of their fathers" and why God brought the calamity and judgment upon them that eventually took them out of the land of Judah. They are in dire need of The Seed.

Point of Depth

The king granted everything that Ezra requested because the hand of the LORD, his God, was on Ezra. Don't you just love to see the sovereignty of God over and over! He is no less sovereign today! Other than the inspired, inerrancy of the Word of God, there is probably no doctrine more important for us to understand and embrace in our everyday walk as Christians!

The good hand of the LORD was upon Ezra because he had set his heart to study the Law of the LORD, and to practice it, and to teach God's statutes and ordinances in Israel. Ezra 7:6-10

It's also important to see what Artaxerxes did. He gave Ezra gold and silver and told him to do with it whatever seemed good to him according to the will of his God. He even issued a decree to all the treasurers who were close to Jerusalem to give Ezra whatever he wanted!

Why would a Persian king do all this? Because God told him to! Artaxerxes told Ezra to do whatever God told him to do because he was afraid of the wrath of God coming against the Persian Empire! Ezra 7:23 King Darius had been afraid too, and had acted accordingly. Ezra 6:12

Ezra also knew why the king was doing this! He knew that God had put all those thoughts in the king's heart! Ezra 7:27-28

6. Nehemiah 1:11; 2:4-8; 4:7-9, 13-14; 6:8-16
The third remnant of Jews was led back to Jerusalem by Nehemiah to build the walls of the city in 445 BC. Nehemiah was the cupbearer of King Artaxerxes.

Nehemiah asked the king to send him back to rebuild the city and its gates. He asked for letters to direct the governors of the provinces along the way to let him pass through safely, along with a letter to Asaph, the keeper of the king's forest, to give him timber to make beams for the gates, for the wall, and for his own home. The king granted these to him because the good hand of God was on Nehemiah.

Nehemiah was confronted with enemies who tried to stop the work being done on the wall, but God frustrated the plans of those enemies! And it came about that all nations surrounding Israel lost their confidence because they recognized that the work on the wall had been accomplished with the help of the God of the Israelites!

The Arabs were trying to frighten Nehemiah so he would stop building, but instead, God frightened the Arabs! Do you see a recurring theme in the Bible? People need to fear the LORD and fear Him only!

Nehemiah

Nehemiah was the cupbearer to King Artaxerxes of Persia during the exile of Judah. When he heard that the walls of Jerusalem were broken down and its gates burned with fire, he wept and prayed before God. After confessing Israel's sins, he asked for "compassion before this man" as he went into the king and asked to go and rebuild the walls. God answered Nehemiah's prayer and he led the third group of exiles back to Jerusalem where they rebuilt the walls around the city despite overwhelming opposition. Ezra, who had led the second remnant of exiles back, read daily from The Book—the Law of God—during the Feast of Tabernacles. Nehemiah proclaimed the day as Holy to the LORD their God. The people turned to the LORD for a time, but then they continued to sin... and sin... and sin...

POINT OF DEPTH

Finally, the walls are rebuilt around the city. The Temple is in place, and it is time to worship the LORD in it! All the people gathered together in unity at the square which was in front of

the Water Gate. Ezra brought the Book of the Law of Moses forward. Remember, Ezra was a scribe who was skilled in the Law of Moses. He was on a wooden podium above the people and he would open the Book in the sight of all of them. When he opened it, all the people would stand up.

For seven glorious days, Ezra would stand on a wooden podium in front of the people, (all the men, women, and children who could listen with understanding) and read from the Law of Moses which the LORD had given to Israel. Nehemiah 8:4 Ezra, along with some Levites, would explain the Law to the people while the people remained standing. They would read from it, stopping here and there to explain it so it made sense to the people.

As someone with a teaching gift, I am inspired and blessed by the whole thing! Here is a masterful example of teaching! Reading → observing → translating → interpreting → applying!

He would read from early morning until midday, and all the people were attentive to the Book of the Law. They actually stood on their feet for a fourth of the day while listening to the reading of God's Word! I love it! It is so wonderful to think about!

Ezra would bless the LORD and all the people would answer, *"Amen, Amen!"* Then they would bow low and worship the LORD with their faces to the ground. When the people first heard the words of the Book, they wept because they realized their sin and the sin of their fathers. If only they had obeyed! Ezra told them to not be grieved for the joy of the LORD was their strength. Their reprimand was over. Now was the time to celebrate! Nehemiah 8:1-12

During the reading, they discovered that the LORD had written that they were to live in booths during the feast of the seventh month. So they went out to the hills of Jerusalem and gathered branches to make booths. The entire assembly of those who had returned from captivity made booths and lived in them. Nehemiah 8:13-18 The sons of Israel had not been following God's command regarding the Feast of Booths since the days of Joshua! (Remember the period right after Joshua? It was the dark period of the judges when every man did what was right in his own eyes.)

According to the ordinance they found written in God's Book, the Jews were to observe a solemn assembly on the 8th day. On the 24th day of the month, the sons of Israel assembled with fasting, in sackcloth and with dirt on their faces as they confessed their sins.

The descendants of Israel (Jacob) separated themselves from all foreigners, and stood and confessed their sins and the iniquities of their fathers. They stood again in their place for a fourth of the day while The Book was read to them. Then they confessed and worshiped the LORD their God for another quarter of the day! Nehemiah 9:1-3

Oh, LORD! May we begin to honor You today in the same way!

HIStory Event 20
...GOD Calls Israel Back to Himself...
Then He is Silent...

Malachi

Malachi is the last record of God speaking to His people in the Old Testament time period. God has loved and chosen Israel, but she has despised her God. Here, the <u>promise</u> of The Seed is simultaneously the <u>threat</u> of The Seed as God tells of Israel's coming judgment. Only God's Covenant with Israel has kept Him from destroying them earlier. Yet He pleads with His people to return to Him and commits to likewise return to them.

Finally, God talks more about the Day of The LORD—evildoers will be made like burning chaff and those who fear the Name of the LORD will be His! He will send Elijah the prophet before the coming of the great and terrible Day of the LORD, who will restore the hearts of the fathers and the children so that God will not smite their land with a curse.

It is a sad book because the people are sinning so greatly against Him— and yet it is a triumphant book because the last word ringing in their ears is The Promise of The Seed!

Read and Observe

1. **Malachi**

Read and Answer

1. **Malachi**
God accuses the priests of despising His Name. They have not honored or respected Him. What is the response of the priests?

What is God's answer to the priests?

God is not pleased with them and He says He will not accept an offering from them. Why won't He?

God describes what a priest should do and be in **chapter 2, verse 7**. List what God says.

    1.

    2.

    3.

Had this been true of the priests?

In **chapter 3**, who does God say He is going to send?

What is he going to do?

Who else is coming? (There are two different messengers talked about in **chapter 3, verse 1**.)

What will the Messenger of the Covenant do?

Who is this Messenger of the Covenant? Is He The Seed?

Read and Reason

1. Malachi
The people were obedient for a while after they came back from Babylon. But by **chapter 13** of **Nehemiah** the people are already abandoning The Book! They still had the same old heart—deceitfully wicked and impossible to cure! So God sends one last prophet with one last message to them. God sends Malachi.

The people have been back in the land for 100 years. Their spiritual condition was contaminated. The priesthood was defiled. They had diluted the Word of God to suit their own personal tastes.

The priests were divorcing their wives, and so were the people. The priests were marrying foreign women, and so were the people. They were bringing sick, blind, and lame sacrifices to God. They were not giving Him the best that He rightfully deserved and commanded! They were tired of serving God, and they robbed Him of His tithes and offerings! They said it was vain to serve the LORD!

God was angry! He said, *"I am a great King and My Name is to be feared among the nations! Should I put up with what you are doing?"*

God's message is fourfold in **Malachi**. He says, *"1) I love you. 2) I must judge you. 3) I'm going to send My Messenger and His messenger before Him. 4) I will take care of those who fear My Name."*

He was not coming as the King or Deliverer yet, but as the Savior for the heart condition of men. God would keep His Covenant. God doesn't change. God doesn't break Covenant. If the people wouldn't repent, He would have to judge again. God's message was simply, *"Return to Me, and I will return to you."* **Malachi 3:7**

God's last instruction in **Malachi** was to *"Remember the Law of Moses. Remember the statutes. Remember the ordinances. Remember My Word!"*

Jeremiah and Ezekiel had prophesied about the New Covenant that God would make with Israel. He would write His Law on their hearts, take out their evil heart, put a new heart inside of them and put a new spirit inside of them. He would also put His Spirit inside of them and cause them to walk after His ways and to keep His laws so that they *would not* turn away from Him! His Law would be on their hearts (their new healthy hearts that would seek after Him as a way of life!) so they would keep His Law!

Malachi ends with a promise of One Who is to come, One Who is to bring the New Covenant to them—the One Who is The Seed!

...GOD is silent for 400 years

Point of Depth

It was an Eastern custom for kings to send a messenger before them to remove every barrier—physical, political, and social. John the Baptist was the messenger of Jesus. He was sent to prepare the way for Jesus. He was sent to call the people to repentance therefore removing opposition to Jesus. Interesting, isn't it? People who are repentant aren't opposed to Jesus and His ways…

Point of Depth

One of the last things that God says before His 400 years of silence is that before the great and terrible Day of the LORD comes, He will send Elijah. Malachi 4:5-6

The Jews thought that John the Baptist might be Elijah the prophet, and they asked him if he was. He states, *"No. I am he that is the voice of one calling in the wilderness, the one Isaiah the prophet said would come."* John 1:19-23

John the Baptist was *not* Elijah, but one who was a forerunner before Christ in the spirit and power of Elijah. He was to turn the hearts of the fathers back to the children and change the attitude of the disobedient to the attitude of the righteous. He would make the people ready to receive the Lord. Luke 1:13-17

In Matthew 11:7-14, Jesus is talking about John the Baptist and tells the people that if they had believed, then John would have been Elijah. John is the fulfillment *if* they would have believed. But they didn't believe...

Point of Connection

Isaiah prophesied of John the Baptist. Isaiah 40:3 He also gave more prophecies concerning Jesus Christ than any other Old Testament prophet.

Isaiah was a prophet who was sent primarily to the Southern Kingdom before and during the Assyrian captivity of the Northern Kingdom. God told him that the people had ears but would not hear. He was told to deliver the message until the cities were devastated and had no inhabitants. Yet God preserved a holy remnant of the sons of Israel. Isaiah 6:9-13

It was to this remnant that John the Baptist was sent as a messenger of *The* Messenger. Isaiah prophesied about a voice of one calling in the wilderness. John the Baptist was sent to remove opposition to Jesus by calling the people to repentance. Matthew 3:1-3; John 1:19-23; Luke 1:13-17; Matthew 11:7-14

HIStory Event 21
...GOD Sends THE PROMISED SEED!!!

Mark

God sends His Son, The Seed, to take care of His people. Jesus is directed by the Father to perform works that show His divine power, and therefore His divinity; but He also came as the Servant of God, Who gave His life as a ransom for many.
Mark 10:45

The Gospel of Mark is filled with action. The Son of God, Jesus, performed deed after deed to show that He was truly God. His deeds served the nation of Israel to whom He was sent, but the people and His Own disciples hesitated (and even refused) to believe that He was The Seed that they had been waiting for all these centuries. Mark ends with Jesus sharply rebuking His Own disciples, and then commissioning them to preach to the world.

Luke

Luke is a marvelous account of the life of Jesus in chronological order. Luke portrays Jesus as the Son of Man. While Jesus was always fully God, He was always fully man and completely human at the exact same time.

The second half of Luke shows Jesus after three years of ministry "setting His face" to go up to Jerusalem for the last time. **Luke 9:51** Throughout His final ascension and even after His arrival at the Temple, Jesus was continuously teaching both His followers and the bystanders.

He foretold that the way of Salvation (the New Covenant) would be opened up to any Gentile who would believe. Why? Because, as He prophesied, Jerusalem and the Jews would reject Him as their Messiah (The Seed). Since they did not accept Him, their house would be left to them desolate. Therefore, Jesus endured many things at the hands of both Jews and Gentiles in His crucifixion, but "Was it not necessary for the Christ to suffer these things and to enter into His Glory?"
Luke 24:26

Matthew

From the first verse to the last words of the Gospel of Matthew, it is clear that he wanted to show the Jews that their Messiah, The Seed, The King of Heaven was Jesus. Matthew starts out with Jesus' genealogy, tracing it back to Abraham and David, the founding father and the greatest king of Israel, both of whom had received promises from God that The Seed would come through them. Since Jesus was a direct descendant of both of them He was shown to be an eligible candidate for the Promised One.

Matthew, more than any other gospel, uses the phrase "this was to fulfill what was written." Matthew uses Old Testament quotes all over the gospel that would bear his name to make sure there would be no doubt in the reader's mind.

The Jews had been waiting for The Seed for thousands of years. Matthew's job was to write a gospel to prove to the people that this Jesus of Nazareth was indeed the long-awaited Messiah—the King of Israel!

John

"In the beginning was the Word, and the Word was with God, and the Word was God. He was in the beginning with God. All things came into being through Him, and apart from Him nothing came into being that has come into being. In Him was Life, and the Life was the Light of men. The Light shines in the darkness, and the darkness did not comprehend it." **John 1:1–5**

Through the many discourses of Jesus recorded in John we see Jesus as the Light, the Way, the Truth, the Life, the Good Shepherd, and the True Bread and Wine. Jesus was fully God; but Jesus was also fully man. John wrote his gospel to prove beyond any shadow of doubt the Deity of Jesus of Nazareth so that you will believe, and by believing you might have life in His Name! **John 20:31**

Read and Observe

1. Luke 2:4-7; Matthew 1:1-17; John 1:1-36

Read and Answer

1. Luke 2:4-7
What family was Joseph from?

What family would The Seed come from?

Matthew 1:1-17
The genealogy of Jesus begins with whom?

What began with Abraham way back in **Genesis**?

Who else of importance is noted as being 14 generations after Abraham in the genealogy of Jesus?

What promise had God given to David?

What happened 14 generations after David?

Why did it happen?

Who was born 14 generations after the Israelites were sent into captivity?

Why were God's people sent into captivity?

What did Jeremiah promise them at that time regarding a New Covenant?

Who was that New Covenant?

John 1:1-36
Who was in the beginning with God?

Who was the Word?

What was in Him?

What was that Life?

When the Life came into a man, the man became a lamp (a holder for the Light). When the Light shone, how did the darkness react?

Who was the man who was sent from God to bear witness of the Light?

Why did John bear witness of the Light?

Was John the Light?

What did the True Light do?

The Seed had come to the world—the world that was made through Him—yet the world He had made did not know Him. Who specifically in the world did He come to?

Did His Own receive Him?

What about those who did receive Him?

What did the Word do when He became flesh?

What did we see in the Word?

What was given through Moses?

What was given through Jesus Christ?

In case you may have missed it, Who was The Word?

When John saw Jesus coming to him, what did he declare?

READ AND REASON

1. Luke 2:4-7; Matthew 1:1-17; John 1:1-36
After over 2,000 years of waiting and 400 years of silence, The Seed arrives!

If you haven't yet caught on to the theme of **HISTORY**, in just a few verses in **Matthew** you will see it encapsulated in the lineage of Jesus. Matthew starts off his gospel with the genealogy of Jesus. His genealogy begins with Abraham because the gospels deal with the Jews, and Abraham was the beginning of the Jews! Jesus is coming to take care of God's chosen people, the Israelites, so the record of His lineage must necessarily begin with the beginning of the Israelite nation → Abraham!

Matthew's gospel continues with the birth of Jesus, the flight to Egypt at the time Herod tried to murder Him and the subsequent return to Israel.

All four gospels record the preaching of John the Baptist in the wilderness when he declares to everyone who will listen, *"Repent! Prepare the way for the Lord to come!"*

POINT OF DEPTH

"Glory to God in the Highest, and on Earth → Peace, Good Will toward men!" Luke 2:14

Can't you just see Charlie Brown and his gang, holding hands around a "Charlie Brown" tree, and singing in perfect unity? My three boys watched it for many years—the annual Charlie Brown special. I remember watching it myself as a child year after year. It gave me such a warm fuzzy feeling when, after they had treated Charlie Brown so horribly, they realized the

"true" meaning of the "holiday" → *love*!!! They held hands and sang an inspiring and emotional rendition of "Silent Night, Holy Night." Ahhhh! Does it get any better than this?

All my life I have been influenced by the world. We all have. The world, even the church, persistently tells us that "man" is the center of things. When all is well with us, then all is well in the world, right?

When we hear the familiar passage in Luke 2:14, we tend to hear it as we want to hear it. We focus on what it means to "us." Then, when we watch our beloved "holy-day" specials, we further write the untruth of the world in our hearts and minds. Charlie Brown and his gang are missing the point! They are missing the truth! Are we, as well?

The angels proclaimed that peace and good will are "toward" men, not "between" men. The peace they proclaimed is not accurately pictured as a warm, fuzzy feeling between people. In fact, Jesus told His followers that He did not come to bring peace, but a sword. In other words, to follow Him did not bring a peaceful life with other people. To follow Jesus meant you would be enemies with the world.

> Remembering the birth of Jesus is not a time for everyone to hold hands
> and imagine a perfect world!
> The truth is → This is a wicked, wicked world!!!

What then, is this *"Peace"* that the angels proclaimed?

The world and God are enemies. James 4:4 All are born in sin, enemies of God. Romans 5:10 There is nothing anyone can do about it. You are helpless, absolutely impotent, to become a friend of God. Romans 5:6

It is *God* Who is offering *men* a way to be reconciled (to have peace) with *Him*! Jesus is The Way that God is offering! God is announcing through the angels that He is offering peace to men through His Son, Jesus. He is extending good will to men. He is extending His Son to men! If you take God up on His offer, if you truly believe in the Lord Jesus Christ (turn from *your* ways and walk in *His* ways), then you can be at peace with the God of the universe! *Wow!!!* What an offer!!!

> The angels proclaimed this fabulous offer to the earth.
> It would be received by those who would believe.
> We must still proclaim this offer.
> It is still available to those who will believe.

Now, the angels also pronounced that God in the Highest would receive Glory from this transaction of the birth of Christ. Exactly how would that happen? I am so glad you asked!

"Glory," from the Greek word "doxa," means "to seem." It means to give a correct estimate, or a correct opinion of something. To give Glory to God is to give others a correct opinion of Who He is. We need to show the world Who God is and what He is like by how we obey Him—by our deeds.

Man cannot Glorify God with *his own* deeds. Our deeds are filthy to Him. There is only one hope of Glorifying Him. Colossians 1:27 That way is to die to self and let the Spirit of Jesus Christ, Who is the perfect image and representation of the Father, *live in us instead*. Galatians 2:20; Hebrews 1:3 With God's Holy Spirit living in a person, He will conform the person into the image of His Son, Jesus → Who is the image of the Father. Romans 8:29 God's Own image alone is pleasing to Him. His Own image shows Who He really is which brings Glory to Him!

We can be holy, even as He is Holy. I Peter 1:15-16 We *must*, if we are to bring Glory to God in the Highest. And it's true that *we will* through His Son! It is His Spirit and His power that conforms us. I Peter 1:2 He actually changes us. It's a long process to be sure but His words are true. II Corinthians 4:16 We *will* be changed *if* the Spirit of Christ is in us. II Corinthians 3:18

Praise to God in the Highest Who has made a way! Man could not find a way. God brings Glory to Himself when the world, its principalities, and its powers see that God and God alone can make a human being pleasing to Him—when He places Himself inside of the human. Ephesians 3:8-10

God is Holy	→	So He cannot abide with anything unholy
Man is not holy	→	So he cannot abide with God
Man cannot make himself holy	→	So he remains God's enemy
God offers to make us holy	→	So we can stop being His enemy
He offers us peace with Himself	→	His offer is His Son, Jesus Christ
He is offering to put His Spirit inside of us	→	So we can bring Him Glory!

GLORY to God in the Highest!
How I wish I could talk to each one of you personally
and make sure you understand this precious, precious truth!
It is of NO VALUE WHATSOEVER, now or ever,
If we are <u>only</u> at peace with one another.
You need to be at peace with God!!!

POINT OF CONNECTION

Why did Herod try to kill Jesus? Matthew 2:13 Well, from the world's eyes it was because Herod worked for Rome. Rome ruled Israel. Jesus was predicted to be the Savior of Israel. Herod thought that meant Jesus would overtake Rome and set Israel free from Roman rule. So, the best way to stop that would be to kill Jesus. *But*, from God's eyes (true vision), it was because God had promised The Seed to set men free, not from Rome's rule, but from the rule of Satan!

It was Satan, *through Herod*, who tried to murder Jesus! Genesis 3:15; Revelation 12:4, 9 Herod was afraid of Jesus, all right, but he didn't even know half of the story, or should I say, "He didn't even know half of HIStory!"

HIStory Event 22
...GOD Anoints THE SEED!

Read and Observe

1. *Preaching:* Malachi 3:1; Mark 1:1-15; Luke 3:23; 8:1; Matthew 4:12-17, 23-25
2. *Teaching:* Luke 4:15; Mark 2:13; 4:1-2; Luke 11:1-13; Matthew 6:5-15; Luke 19:47; 20:1, 19, 39-40; Mark 4:1-34; Matthew 13; 15:10-20; Mark 6:34; 9:31-32; Luke 24:44-48
3. *Miracles:* John 2:1-11; Luke 9:12-17; Mark 6:35-44; Matthew 14:15-21; John 6:1-13; John 2:23; John 20:30-31
4. *Healing:* Luke 4:40-41; Mark 1:32-34; Matthew 8:16-17; 9:35-36; Mark 7:25-30; Matthew 15:21-31; 13:54-58; John 9:1-7; 1:4; Matthew 5:16; John 11:1-54
5. *Prayer:* Luke 9:18, 28, 22:31-32, 39-46; Mark 14:32-42; John 12:27-30; 17

Read and Answer

Point of Depth

Do you know what the word anoint means? It means "to smear." Interesting definition, isn't it? Unfortunately, the meaning of the word anoint has been abused and distorted by so many false teachers that it is almost impossible to use the word without its original intent being lost. Let me say up front—there is no "supernatural" anointing that hangs around in the air and adheres itself to things of this earth. Rather, the anointing unambiguously means that something is clearly seen as marked for whatever it is. As in, you put a post-it note on the pile you want someone to take—the post-it note anoints the pile. Almost too simple, isn't it? Man always wants to improve on God's purity—and always ends in corruption.

One year WORD Center Ministries needed to take down a lot of trees which were surrounding our ministry building. However, mixed in with the trees to be taken down were trees which we wanted to leave in place. What did we do? We anointed the ones that were to be left alone—we marked them with paint for identification purposes.

Next came a man on a bulldozer who could see each and every tree, and according to whether it was anointed or not, he knew if the tree was to be taken down or left alone. Sadly, that man on the bulldozer was not a righteous man and he bulldozed right through all the trees leaving much havoc and destruction in his path. He took down many trees that were not to be destroyed. It was heart-breaking looking at those beautiful trees lying splintered on the ground with a big red "x" on them. They were sacrificed for that man's carelessness.

I couldn't help but think of Jesus, everything He did... everything He said... everything about Him... His preaching, His teaching, His miracles, His healings, His prayer life—were like huge red marks declaring, "This is the One. He is My Son! I have sent Him! Listen to Him! Hear Him!" And yet the people paid no attention to His anointing and they cut Him down...

Even in His death, even today, the bloody red smear still shouts, "This is the Coming One! This is the Promised One! This is the Anointed One! This is the Messiah!" If people would only open their eyes to see Him, they would see His anointing and *know* He is the Christ!

As you study your way through this Event, be aware that everything you will see is part and parcel of the anointing God put on Jesus—God marked Jesus as the One He had promised to send way back in Genesis 3:15. The world could not miss this anointing—Jesus was clearly marked for all to see—His preaching, teaching, miracles, healing, and prayer life all marked Him out as the Messiah of God!

1. *Preaching:*
Malachi 3:1; Mark 1:1-15
God told us in **Malachi** that He was going to send His messenger and The Messenger of the Covenant. What do you see repeated here?

Who is identified as God's messenger?

What would he do?

What would he preach?

What did God's messenger say about The Messenger of the Covenant?

God's messenger baptized people who repented with water. What would The Messenger of the Covenant baptize with (here the Greek word for "with" can be translated: in, with, or by)?

Who is identified as the Messenger of the Covenant?

What did Jesus do when He came to God's messenger?

What did the voice from heaven say?

What happened immediately after that?

How many days did Satan tempt Jesus?

What were the angels doing?

Luke 3:23
How old was Jesus when He began His public ministry?

Luke 8:1
Where did Jesus proclaim and preach?

What was it that Jesus proclaimed and preached?

Who was with Him?

Matthew 4:12-17, 23-25
When did Jesus begin to preach?

What exactly did He say?

Where did He preach? (Take time to look at the map in the appendix. The Galilee area is in the northern portion of Israel around the Sea of Galilee.)

Let's look at this prophecy that is fulfilled by Jesus. Which prophet spoke forth this prophecy?

Where did he say a light would dawn?

Who were these people?

What did these people see?

How does it describe where these people were?

Mark 1:4
What did John the Baptist, the messenger of The Messenger, preach?

Mark 1:14-15
When did Jesus come into Galilee?

What did He do when He came into Galilee?

What was the Gospel of God? (What exactly was He saying?)

    1.

    2.

    3.

    4.

What was the right response to have for people who heard Him?

    1.

    2.

2. *Teaching:*
Luke 4:15
Where did Jesus begin teaching?

What was the reaction of His audiences?

Mark 2:13; 4:1-2
Was Jesus limited to teaching people in the synagogues?

Luke 11:1-13; Matthew 6:5-15
Jesus taught many things to those who would hear. What do the disciples ask Him to teach them how to do?

Luke 19:47; 20:1, 19, 39-40
While the majority of Jesus' audiences, the Jewish people, hung on every word He said, how was the reaction of the chief priests, scribes, elders, and the leading men among the Jews different?

Mark 4:1-34; Matthew 13; 15:10-20
What teaching method did Jesus often use when He was teaching the people?

Did even His disciples understand what He was teaching?

Who was it that could understand? What was needed?

Mark 6:34
On this occasion what prompted Jesus to teach? Remember to whom Jesus said He was sent—the lost sheep of the house of Israel. **Matthew 15:24**

Mark 9:31-32
What is Jesus' subject during this teaching session?

Did they understand what He was telling them?

Why didn't they ask Him to explain?

Luke 24:44-48
What had Jesus taught His disciples while He was in Galilee?

    1.

    2.

    3.

What was the right response of those who heard Him?

3. *Miracles:*
John 2:1-11
Jesus, His mother, and His disciples were attending a wedding in Cana of Galilee. What problem arose?

Who wanted to take care of the problem?

What did she do?

What was His answer to her?

What was her response?

What did Jesus tell the servants?

What happened to the water inside the water pots?

What happened when Jesus did this sign? What was seen?

What was the response of His disciples?

Luke 9:12-17; Mark 6:35-44; Matthew 14:15-21; John 6:1-13
One day, the twelve disciples came to Jesus with a problem. A huge crowd had been following them; it was turning dark, and no one had eaten. Jesus surprised them with His answer to the problem. What was it?

How many people were there?

How much food did they have at hand?

What did Jesus tell His disciples to tell the crowd to do?

When everyone was seated, what did Jesus do?

How much food was left over?

John 2:23
In Jerusalem during the Passover, what was Jesus doing?

What was the reaction of many?

What was "His Name"?

Why did they believe?

John 20:30-31
What did Jesus perform in the presence of the disciples?

Why did Jesus perform signs?

Why were some of these written down?

What did the signs enable a person to believe?

What would be the result of belief?

Where was that life found?

What has mankind needed ever since he disobeyed God in the Garden of Eden?

What would be the right response from those who saw the signs of Jesus or who heard about the signs of Jesus?

4. *Healing:*
Luke 4:40-41; Mark 1:32-34; Matthew 8:16-17
After teaching in the Capernaum synagogue and healing Peter's mother-in-law during the day, how did Jesus spend His evening?

Who came to see Him?

What kind of diseases did Jesus heal?

What did Jesus do with each person that was brought to Him?

What came out of many as He was healing them?

What did the demons say?

What did Jesus do?

Why?

What did Jesus fulfill by doing this?

Matthew 9:35-36
What kinds of diseases was Jesus healing?

What kinds of sicknesses was Jesus healing?

When Jesus saw the people who were distressed and dispirited, what did He feel?

Mark 7:25-30; Matthew 15:21-31
Who came to ask Jesus to heal her daughter? Was she a Jew?

Not only did she believe that Jesus *could* heal, she was insistent Jesus *should* heal her daughter! Who did Jesus say should be healed before her daughter?

Who are the "children"?

Who are the "dogs"?

What was the cause of her daughter's illness?

Did Jesus even have to speak to the demon? Who is in control?

Matthew 13:54-58
Where did Jesus *not* do many miracles?

Why not?

John 9:1-7
Who made this man blind?

Why was he made blind? (Why did God create man?)

Was it because of sin?

Was it because of demons?

What does light help people to do?

What was it that The Light of the world enabled men to see?

What do the works of God do?

John 1:4
What was in Jesus, the Christ?

What has man needed since he acted independently from God?

What did the life do for men? If they had His life, what else did they have?

Matthew 5:16
If a man lets the Light of Christ shine through him, what will other men see?

What will be the end result?

John 11:1-54
Jesus, upon hearing that His good friend Lazarus was sick, waited for two days until departing to go to him. What reason did He have to wait? Take your answer very carefully from the text.

What was it that Mary and Martha wanted Jesus to do for Lazarus?

What was it that Jesus wanted to do for God? (Remember why God created man.)

Why was Jesus glad that He let Lazarus die? How would His disciples benefit?

Jesus and His disciples then traveled to Bethany, about two miles from Jerusalem. Martha went to meet Him. By then Lazarus was dead, but what did Martha now want from Jesus?

What did Jesus answer her?

Did she believe?

What exactly did she say she believed?

     1.

     2.

     3.

Martha went to get Mary. When Mary and the other mourners found Jesus, how did He react?

When Jesus and the group following Him, which included Mary and Martha and the other mourners, finally arrived at the tomb, what was Jesus' reaction again?

What did Jesus command to be done?

What was their objection?

What did Jesus tell Martha she would see if she believed?

Why did Jesus pray to the Father out loud? What did it give them the opportunity to do?

What was the dead man's (Lazarus') response to Jesus' order of "Come forth"?

What was the response of many who saw this take place?

What was the response of the Pharisees when they heard of it?

What did the Pharisees say would happen if they let Jesus go on performing signs?

What was the right response of seeing Jesus do a sign?

5. *Prayer:*
Luke 9:18, 28
Was Jesus alone when He prayed?

Was He always alone when He prayed?

Luke 22:31-32, 39-46
On the basis of Jesus' prayers, up to Whom did He leave decisions? Who did Jesus acknowledge was in charge? To Whom did Jesus go to with His requests?

Mark 14:32-42
Why did Jesus feel the need to pray?

What did Jesus want?

What did Jesus want more than His Own desire?

John 12:27-30
Was Jesus alone when He prayed this time?

Why not? What was the purpose or request of His prayer?

John 17
The things that Jesus prayed for in this important prayer were revealed to us. List these things.

> **Verse 1**
>
> **Verse 5**
>
> **Verse 11**
>
> **Verse 15**
>
> **Verse 17**
>
> **Verse 24**

Who is the group Jesus is praying for according to **verse 20**? Does that include you?

According to **verse 21**, why does Jesus ask for believers to be sanctified in the truth?

Do you think Jesus would receive from the Father whatever He asked of Him?

John 17:11
Just to make sure you see this, for what did Jesus pray?

Why?

John 17:21
What was the purpose of all believers being one?

What is the right response to everything Jesus said or did?

READ AND REASON

1. *Preaching*
Malachi 3:1; Mark 1:1-15
The Gospel of Mark begins by repeating the prophecy of the Messiah and His messenger from Malachi. Malachi wrote about two messengers: The Messenger of God, and the messenger of The Messenger of God. The purpose of a messenger in those days was to go ahead of the actual person or persons and make everything ready for them—to remove any obstacles. A straight path was one without any hindrances in the way.

The messenger of The Messenger was a man called John the Baptist. His purpose was to prepare the way for The Seed, Jesus Christ. His job was to call the Jews to repentance, to call them to give up the self-rule of their lives and submit instead to the Word of God.

If peoples' hearts were repentant when Jesus appeared on the scene, they would receive His message. Jesus' message was "I am the way to God. I AM THE SEED—the Christ—the Messiah!" He was the One the world had been waiting for since Adam and Eve had been separated from God because of their disobedience and independence. They had died spiritually and they needed life. The Seed was coming Who would bring them Life!

After John the Baptist proclaimed Jesus to be the Lamb of God Who came to take away the sins of the world, he baptized Him. God then verified that Jesus was indeed His Son. He anointed Him. Jesus was then tempted in the wilderness by Satan. Jesus resisted him at every turn.

You know, I have heard the story of Satan tempting Jesus many times, but it wasn't until I went to Israel for the first time that I saw this wilderness and began to grasp the gravity of what had really happened.

In the United States when someone mentions a wilderness, I think of woods, timbers, and forests. That is not what a wilderness is in Israel. It is a wasteland, an uninhabitable desert with no shade or water. Nothing grows there—nothing! The nights are cold and miserable and the days are an intense test of survival because of the overpowering heat.

As our tour bus was passing through this unbelievable land, I thought of Jesus. Every single one of those forty days, even if He hadn't been fasting, would have been torturous. I prayed that our bus would not break down on the trip from Jericho to Jerusalem—I couldn't imagine being stranded there even for a couple of hours! I also saw the thousands and thousands of rocks scattered across the landscape. It wasn't hard to imagine loaves of bread—that's exactly what they looked like. Jesus would have known what Satan was going to use them for long before he actually did. He would have seen those stones day after day. He would have known…

The story I always heard in church also taught that Jesus was only tempted on the fortieth day. That's not true. He was tempted the entire forty days. He is so strong… He resisted Satan again and again for our sakes… Thank You Jesus…

After His forty days in the wilderness, Jesus then began His three-year public ministry proclaiming the Gospel of the kingdom to the Jews and proving that He was The Seed. He was there to visit them—to take care of them. He was their Messiah! Yet, in the end, they rejected Him…

Point of Depth

Why do you think Satan tempted Jesus? Why was it important to Satan that Jesus would sin? Think back to the reason Satan tried to kill Jesus when He was born. Think back to the reason that Jesus had to be born of a virgin. Satan used Herod to try to kill Jesus when He was born because Satan knew that Jesus was The Seed Who was promised to save those who would believe. Matthew 2:7-20

God is Holy and must pour out His wrath on all ungodliness and all unrighteousness. Man had sinned and was guilty. The payment required for man's sin was his life, and his life was in his blood. Leviticus 17:11 If Jesus was not born of a virgin, He would have sin-tainted blood in Him, and the purchase price for men would not be sufficient to satisfy God. Romans 3:23 Jesus could save all of mankind by offering His Own perfect blood from His perfect life as a propitiation (satisfactory offering) to God. Jesus could pay the debt that we owed to God so that we wouldn't have to pay it ourselves. Remember, the payment was our life! The payment was eternal separation from GOD! Romans 6:23

Satan gained power when Adam and Eve sinned. He wanted to keep that control! He didn't want to lose his battle with God and eventually be sent into an eternal lake of fire! If Jesus was able to pay the price that was owed to God, then Satan would lose the power he had gained and his destiny realized.

Since Satan wasn't successful in killing the Christ Child, he tried to get the Son of God to sin! If Jesus was to sin, then Satan would retain his power over the earth and over all those condemned to darkness. Satan needed to get Jesus to sin. He would tempt Him for forty days in the sweltering Judean wilderness. Jesus would not sin. Satan would lose…

Luke 3:23

There is so much we don't know. God ordained for Jesus to start His ministry when He was about thirty years old. We don't know much about His life before then. God chose not to inform us about Jesus' early years, but rather to focus on His three or so years of ministry. That is what we, too, should focus on. It's the main things that we are looking for. God has written down those main things in His Word and we can plainly see them!

God anointed Jesus as the Christ through Simeon and Anna the prophetess at the Temple in Jerusalem when He was only eight days old. Apart from the trip to Jerusalem when He was twelve years old, we don't see that public anointing again until He is an adult. Could Jesus have been anointed in between? God doesn't tell us. You see, those three years were the ones in which God would anoint His Son, Jesus, as the Christ. God marked Jesus out very carefully as The Seed He had sent to bring life to those whom He had called.

Luke 8:1; Mark 1:14-15; Matthew 4:12-17, 23-25

Jesus was sent to preach the Kingdom of God to the Jews. He was not sent to the Gentiles (all the other nations besides the Jews). While He was in their Jewish communities He would often teach in their synagogues, the place they would gather together as a people of one faith. They would listen to the Torah being read and listen as teachers commented and taught on the Scriptures.

What was the Gospel of God that Jesus was preaching in the synagogues? He told them that the waiting period for The Seed had ended. He told them to repent from sin—to be convinced that they were not to order their own lives, but rather they were to simply obey the orders of God. He told them to believe the good news was true—The Seed had finally arrived to bring Life!

The Jews were supposed to be a light to the surrounding nations of the world, but instead, they were sitting in complete darkness themselves. Darkness meant death, but the Light of The Seed meant Life!

POINT OF DEPTH

I often think the phrase "eternal life" has become cliché for believers in general. We emphasize the fact that we will live eternally, in other words, forever. But the fact is that everyone God has ever created will exist forever. The question is whether they will exist in eternal death (separation from God in the lake of fire) or in eternal life (communion and unity with God in the new Jerusalem.)

Think of it this way: It's Eternal _Life_ → not _Eternal_ Life. Salvation doesn't give us a life or existence that lasts for eternity, but rather salvation gives us an eternity of _Life_—existence <u>with</u> God, rather than an eternity of existence <u>apart</u> from Him.

2. *Teaching*
Luke 4:15
Jesus began teaching the Jews in the synagogues because that's where they gathered in each community. Usually the scribes and elders would stand up, read a scripture, and then explain it (either correctly or incorrectly). Jesus was neither a scribe nor an elder in their eyes, and yet they praised Him for how well He could teach. Their reaction was correct. If only they would have believed the truth that He spoke…

Mark 2:13; 4:1-2
Although Jesus began teaching in the synagogues, He didn't exclusively teach there. As His crowds grew, Jesus took advantage of open areas, such as the seashores or mountainsides.

I've sat under some pretty good teachers in my life… and I've sat under the other kind! I'm sure you have too. But can you imagine sitting under Jesus' teaching? Before we wistfully wish for something other than what we have, remember that the Spirit of Jesus, Himself, indwells each and every believer and that Spirit leads the believer into all truth. No matter what other teachers I am blessed or burdened with, I have one Teacher Who is all-sufficient—the Master Teacher, Jesus Christ of Nazareth!

Point of Depth

Jesus gave His disciples a format for prayer. He did not simply give them a liturgy of words. He told them to pray in this "way." One way to see the Disciples' Prayer (commonly referred to as Lord's Prayer) is to see it in segments. Luke 11:2-4; Matthew 6:9-15

Our Father Who is in Heaven,
- First of all, recognize that the One you pray to is God Himself. We go to Him because He is God; and God, after all, is the only One Who can effect changes!
- No one can come to the Father unless it is through the Son. In order for you to address God, He needs to be your Father. In order for Him to be your Father, you need to believe in His Son, The Seed.
- Recognize where His throne is. It's in Heaven, not on earth. He rules the entire universe from Heaven.

Hallowed be Your Name.
- Then, before you go any further, stop and praise Him for Who He is. His Name is Holy (hallowed). His Name is all that He is—His attributes, His character, His nature. So try speaking Truth about Who and What God is. Tell Him you know He is Holy, Awesome, Majestic, Righteous, True, Faithful, Eternal, Omnipotent (all-powerful), Omnipresent (present everywhere), and Omniscient (all-knowing)! Tell Him He is greater than anything you can even imagine—there is none like Him! Tell Him you know His Name to be Jehovah, the Great I AM, etc!!!

- As you begin to praise and worship Him in this way, the Holy Spirit will bring His attributes, character, and nature to your mind. Simply confess them as true.

Your Kingdom come.
- You have already recognized that God rules the universe from Heaven. Now ask Him to take up His sword and reign on earth. Ask Him to send Jesus soon. Tell Him that you want the whole world to know His power and His might! Tell Him you want the whole earth to bow before Him as King!

Your will be done, on earth as it is in Heaven.
- Ask for His will to be done on earth just like it is done in Heaven. How is that different? In Heaven His will is done without hesitation, without doubt, without grumbling, without thought to any personal will or desire, and *with* praise and thanksgiving in every thought, word, and deed. You can start the process by examining how your obedience would be described. Is it like the obedience of heavenly hosts?

Give us this day our daily bread.
- Ask Him for whatever you need for today. Don't ask Him for things in the future, as if you can take care of today yourself—you can't. Ask Him for each and every little or big thing you need. Then, as the day proceeds remember that He is your Provider and thank Him!

And forgive us our debts, as we also have forgiven our debtors.
- Ask Him to forgive you for any debt you owe to Him that you have not paid—for instance, complete, cheerful obedience each moment of your day.
- He tells us there is a condition to forgiveness. We must forgive others. So here is an opportunity to examine your relationships with others and see if there is anyone you need to forgive. If there is—do it!

And do not lead us into temptation, but deliver us from evil.
- Oh, how the day of a believer will be filled with attacks from the enemy! Ask Him to help you, to protect you, to spare you. Recognize that without Him, you would still be a slave to the tyrannical enemy called sin.

For Yours is the kingdom and the power and the Glory forever.
- What better way to say goodbye to God for the moment than to reiterate His eternal rule, His eternal power, and His eternal Glory.

Amen.
- I grew up thinking that saying "Amen" at the end of my prayers was like signing off! But that's not it at all. Amen is a word that means, "I agree it is true." If you have prayed according to His will honestly, then you can exuberantly declare "Amen!"

Luke 19:47; 20:1, 19, 39-40
Although the general public of Jews hailed Jesus, their leaders did not carry the same opinion of Him. They wanted to destroy Him, not let Him save them. They would often confront Him in front of the crowd, hoping to lower the people's estimation of Him. They wanted Him out of the way, because they wanted to lead the people their way! They were afraid of the people; and they were afraid the people would follow Jesus instead of them, because they realized that Jesus' ways were not like theirs at all! They wanted to rule, but Jesus demanded that God be Ruler over all.

Mark 4:1-34; Matthew 13; Matthew 15:10-20
Jesus used parables for a significant portion of His teachings. A parable is a story told to illustrate a particular truth. It has one central point—though it can be a very complex point that is hard to comprehend. Parables, rather than just simple children's stories, can actually be one of the hardest parts of Jesus' teaching to understand.

Sometimes Jesus would explain the parable later, sometimes He wouldn't. Sometimes Jesus would use a parable to explain a truth, sometimes He would use a parable to veil a truth. Many times He would tell a parable in response to a question or action from His audience. Always, always, always, the context is of major importance when listening to one of His parables—not only the environment of words surrounding a parable, but also the context of the environment of the culture of Jesus' day.

Mark 6:34
Jesus had come to take care of His people—to shepherd them. His compassion was infinite. If only they would submit to Him as their Shepherd…

Mark 9:31-32
One of the most important things that Jesus taught His disciples was information about His arrest, death, burial, and resurrection. **Luke 24:6-8** He kept showing them that He was The Seed. He kept proving to them that He was The Seed. But they didn't understand…

Even though they didn't understand everything, and were even afraid to ask Him to explain further, they benefited from His teaching. After His resurrection they remembered the things He taught them and then they understood—Jesus was The Seed that God had promised since the time of Adam and Eve. **John 2:22; 12:16; 16:4**

They needed to clearly understand because they had a tremendously hard task ahead of them. They were to be the apostles of the early church. They would be severely persecuted and they needed to know, understand, and believe for certain the central teaching of the Gospel. They needed to be able to proclaim the truth about The Seed to help others to believe! **I Corinthians 15:1-8**

POINT OF DEPTH

Matthew 5
Large crowds had followed Jesus from Galilee. He goes up on a mountain, His disciples come to Him, and He starts teaching what is commonly referred to as "The Beatitudes." They are called such because the word means blessed or blissful and Jesus repeatedly uses the phrase "blessed." The mountain in Galilee is now called Mount Beatitude.

Immediately after He delivers the Beatitudes, He tells them not to misunderstand what He is doing. He is *not* abolishing the Law or the Prophets; instead He has come to *fulfill* them. This explains the format of the rest of the chapter for us. He tells them that they have heard what the Law and the Prophets were teaching, but they didn't hear correctly. He does *not* change *any* of the Law or the Prophets, rather He *explains* the Law and the Prophets to them *correctly*.

Why had they heard wrongly? First of all, because not everyone had their own personal scroll from which to study like you and I do. So they depended upon the teaching, explanation, and commentary of their scribes, elders, and priests. If what their teachers told them was accurate —great! But many times it was not—it was only the personal opinion of that particular teacher.

Besides depending upon someone else for the message and its interpretation, an additional problem developed as the Jews were dispersed into Babylon and later into the entire world. In the lands of their dispersion, the Jews formed communities and appointed a teacher over them calling him Rabbi. Wherever they met was designated their synagogue. The problem was, not every man who became Rabbi really knew the Law and the Prophets correctly, and Torah scrolls were a very sparse commodity in Babylon! The Rabbis did the best they could, sometimes improvising or adding laws to fit a particular situation. Therefore, an entirely different set of laws was given to the people and not the original Law and Prophets. Whenever you add or take away from the Word you are in grave danger.

POINT OF DEPTH

I would like for you to consider two different occasions in the ministry of Jesus that I believe help explain each other. Let's go to John 13:1-17 first. This is immediately before the last Passover that Jesus participated in while on earth. He gets up and girds Himself with a towel after laying aside His garments. He pours water into a basin and begins to wash the feet of the disciples.

When Jesus gets to Peter, he is perplexed as to why Jesus would do this. Jesus answers Peter somewhat mysteriously by saying, "What I do you do not realize, but you will understand hereafter." Did Peter realize that Jesus was washing the feet of the disciples? Of course he did. Jesus told him that he would only understand the true meaning later. What was it that Peter and the others did not understand? What was Jesus showing them? Let's go on for now.

Peter wants nothing to do with the idea—the idea of Jesus washing his feet, that is. Jesus informs Peter that if he doesn't let Him wash his feet, he has no part with Jesus! Peter replies instantly, "Then wash every part of me—my hands, my feet, and my head!" Peter's enthusiastic response is still wrong because when he tells Jesus to go for it, Jesus informs him, "You've already bathed Peter, and you're completely clean. You only need your feet washed." Now remember, Peter understood perfectly that Jesus was washing his feet, but he didn't understand the point that Jesus was teaching while He was doing it. So we know that whatever Jesus meant by bathing and cleansing was not simply a literal bath nor was it physical cleanliness.

Jesus does give us a clue with His reply though. He states that not everyone there has taken a bath. The text explains to us that Jesus was referring to Judas when He said this. Everyone but Judas had taken a bath. Hmmm...

Okay, so far we know that Jesus was literally washing the disciples feet, but He wasn't *just* washing their feet. Whatever else it was that He was showing them, they didn't understand right then, but would later. We also know He was not referring to a literal bath and we can reason that the bath and cleanness implies salvation since Judas was the only one who wasn't clean. He was the only one who would not meet with the others in Heaven one day.

Now Jesus finishes washing their feet (which wasn't what He was *really* doing) and instructs them. He asked them if they understood what He had just done. Because their reply is not recorded for us, I have to wonder if there was no reply, instead each pair of eyes looking at another waiting for someone to speak up. Perhaps because Peter had misunderstood so far he kept his mouth closed.

Jesus answers for them and tells them they should wash each other's feet, the reason being no one was greater than another. And yet, He still couldn't be talking about literal feet washing. What was it that they were supposed to do for one another—and do it humbly?

Let's leave the passage in John for a moment and go to another passage that leaves us with another dilemma. Read Matthew 7:1-5. Jesus is teaching them from the mountain. He states emphatically, "Do not judge so that you will not be judged." Then He tells them why—they will be judged by their own standard.

But then, in seeming contradiction, He teaches them that they are to take specks out of each other's eyes. That would require a certain amount of discernment at least, if not actual judgment. He does clarify that they are to take the logs out of their own eyes first so they won't make a mess of things working on a brother's eye.

Notice the injunction in verse 5. It is not an option whether or not we take a speck out of a brother's eye—we are commanded to do it! There are so many people who read this passage with selective eyesight and come up with the conclusion that we are *not* to take the speck out of our brother's eye *because* we have a log in our own. The typical cliché is "I'm not perfect so

I wouldn't think of criticizing someone else!" But perhaps the honest truth is, "I don't *have* to exhort another believer because I have sin in my life *that I have not taken care of!*" Sadly, the log is left in the eye and the sin is left in the life. Jesus says to *take that log our of your eye* so you can see clearly <u>to</u> *take the speck out of your brother's eye!* In obeying a false cliché, people are actually disobeying a direct command of the Lord Jesus Christ!

"Don't judge!" has become the watchword of the modern day church. How wrong that is! The true watchword of the true church is the same as it has always been—"*Repent!*"

Now you are probably wondering, Jesus said specifically *not* to judge in verse 1 so how can that be? In verse 1 Jesus is referring to judging as in the case of a state fair, giving out ribbons to the good, better, and best of the exhibits. Our job is not to judge how good of a Christian someone is. We are not to line Christians up in our minds from left to right, bad to good, of course putting ourselves somewhere near the extreme right! But we are to exhort each believer to excel still more. You may not agree with me so far, but let's look at one more passage before we leave this subject.

Go to I Corinthians chapter 5. I think it may clear up both the John and the Matthew passages and even link them together for us. Paul, the author, is addressing a problem in the Corinthian church. Someone has had an immoral relationship with his father's wife and news has reached Paul! He is angry, but look who he is angry with! It's not with the man in sin, but rather, he is angry with the other believers in the church!

He tells them why—they have become arrogant and have not mourned and put the man who had done this deed out of the church. They are arrogant instead of humble because they don't deal with sin in the church. Paul then tells them to get this man out of the church and right away!

He tells them why—a little leaven will leaven the whole batch of dough. Leaven represents an individual in the church who has not repented of sin in his life, and the dough represents the whole of the church. If they don't get him out of their midst, then they too, will begin to sin as he has.

Plus, when someone looks at this man and understands that he calls himself a Christian they will get a distorted picture of what the body of Christ, the church, really is. The church is to be holy just as God is Holy. After all, the church hasn't kicked him out, so why would anyone peeking in think anything different? In other words, allowing sin to remain in the church presents the whole church as unholy. The church is to be conformed into the image of Jesus Christ, Who is the exact representation and nature of God, the Father. Remember why God created man—it was to bring Himself Glory—to show to the world Who He really is. When the church looks like it is sinful, it cannot bring Him any Glory!

Paul tells them that Christ is their Passover. They are to celebrate that Feast with the unleavened bread of sincerity and truth, not with old leaven (pre-salvation behavior) or the leaven of malice and wickedness (they are not to be cruel to this man) just lovingly and forcefully separate this man from the church.

In case they, or anyone else reading his letter, are still unsure as to what they are to do, he repeats a teaching he has given them before, but tries to clarify it. He says that he has previously instructed them to not even associate with immoral people. But he never meant unbelievers—Why! They would have to get on a spaceship and travel to another planet to get away from all unbelievers! What he previously told them was they were not to even associate with anyone who was immoral, covetous, an idolater, a reviler, a drunkard, or a swindler (or any such a one) *if* he called himself a believer!

In other words, there is a whole different set of rules governing our relationship and behavior toward unbelievers than with believers! How should believers behave toward unbelievers? Well, it's not a believer's place to correct an unbeliever's behavior. It's a believer's place to give an unbeliever the *Gospel*! The Holy Spirit will do the sanctifying! It's God's place to judge those outside the church. But we *are to judge those within the church!* Read verse 12. Paul says that it is not his place to judge those outside the church, but it *is* the place of Christians to judge those who are *within* the church!!! Can you see why? God's reputation is important to Him! Those in the church are the face of God to the world. He demands that we give the world a true picture of Who He is. We are to bring Him Glory!

His final exhortation is a command from the book of Deuteronomy that is given three times. Deuteronomy 13:5; 17:7, 12 We are still expected to obey that command!

Do you see the connection to the John passage? Jesus was teaching them to humble themselves enough to go to another believer and help them get the dirt from everyday life off of them. Remember it wasn't physical dirt that Jesus was referring to. And it wasn't a whole bath, just a foot wash. It probably will make more sense to us if we think of the culture at that time and how often they went barefoot. Even when they wore sandals, their feet were exposed to the dust of Israel. (I can personally attest to how dirty your feet get while walking the land of Israel!) The dirt from each day would be washed from their feet regularly. That's what we are supposed to do for one another. We shouldn't let a Christian walk around with dirt on his feet—with sin in his life. As dusty as the land of Israel is, so dreadfully sinful is the society in which we live. We are to humble ourselves enough to take the specks out of one another's eyes —to wash each other's feet!

Can you think of why humility is required to do this? The person with the speck in his eye (wrong belief) or the dirt on her feet (having sinned) will more likely receive the one trying to help them if he is humble instead of arrogant. When is the last time someone came to you to point out sin in your life? Have you ever received a phone call from someone asking you to meet with them because they "needed to talk to you"? If you are like me, your heart would skip a beat and you would wonder what you were in trouble for! Having a humble friend lovingly confront you would be the easiest way to bear the correction.

And yet, it is more than that. We need to be humble enough to risk the rejection of that so-called brother or sister. Think about it—when is the last time you went to someone to point out sin in his or her life? What would have kept you from doing it? The fear of man! The fear of losing a relationship or the fear of gaining a reputation! We are required to humble ourselves enough to be willing to do the unthinkable in the modern day church—to confront another believer who is in sin! It's true that I may lose the respect of those around me if they believe I am "judging" when they believe no one is supposed to "judge." But what is to be gained is of immeasurable value—protecting the reputation of Jehovah, the only True God, and being personally pleasing to Him through my obedience!

The true watchword of the church is still *"Repent!"* The question is, how often do we say it to one another?

POINT OF DEPTH

Luke 7:38 This little verse, which is only one part of a sentence, has much to say to us. One of its messages is simple and yet remarkable. Looking at two of its words—"began" and "kept"—provide us with great wisdom and advice. So many people start serving God, but quit when it brings them trials instead of pleasure. Others never even begin serving Him. They serve, instead, this world and its temporary pleasures. We need to begin serving God and we need to keep serving God. Begin and keep; start and continue—it's that basic. Simple, isn't it?

Luke 24:44-48
Jesus had taught the disciples that all the things written about Him in the Law of Moses, the Prophets, and the Psalms (the Old Testament) would be fulfilled. He was again proving that He was the Son of God, the Promised One, the Christ. After His resurrection, He opened their minds to understand all that He had taught them. He sums it all up in three declarations:
1. It is written that the Christ would suffer.
2. It is written that the Christ would rise again from the dead on the third day.
3. It is written that repentance for forgiveness of sins would be proclaimed in His Name to all the nations, beginning from Jerusalem.

He then pronounces them witnesses of all these things. They can proclaim with certainty that Jesus was the Christ—The Seed sent by God to bring life!

3. *Miracles*
Luke 9:12-17; Mark 6:35-44; Matthew 14:15-21; John 6:1-13
One day, the twelve disciples came to Jesus with a problem. A huge crowd had been following them, it was turning dark and no one had eaten. Jesus surprised them with His answer to the problem. He said, *"You feed them!"* There were over 5,000 people!

Later on in His ministry, another crowd of 4,000 plus would need to be fed. **Mark 8:1-10; Matthew 15:32-38** This time Jesus came to the disciples and gave them the opportunity to respond in faith, but they missed it. They had no idea where to get enough food to feed everybody.

So Jesus performed almost the exact same miracle, same restaurant, same menu. Would they understand this time?

I am impressed with the fact that both times Jesus had the crowd sit down before He started to feed them. And both times He looked up at the Father and then slowly broke off each piece of food that was to feed the multitude. Why did He have them sit down? Jesus created an outdoor podium, so to speak, by lowering His audience so they could see Him center stage! He wanted to make sure each and every person could witness the miracle The Seed would perform.

I believe, in the same way, He presents Himself clearly before us so that we will watch the work of God. Where is the stage? In earthly terms, it is all around us—His creation—the heavens and the earth. **Romans 1:19-20** In spiritual terms, it is when we look up and realize that He alone is God! **Matthew 5:3; Daniel 4:34-37** Jesus is clearly The Seed!

POINT OF DEPTH

Mark 4:35-41; Mark 6:47-51; Matthew 14:24-33; John 6:16-21
Jesus clearly showed His disciples that He was in command of everything—even the winds and the seas. He walked on top of the water, He let one of them walk on the water with Him, and twice He calmly stilled the storm, once by command and once without even speaking a word.

Peter was the one who was privileged to experience Jesus' majesty by walking on the water with Him. And Peter was the one who was privileged to experience Jesus' mercy as He saved him from sinking. How could we ever doubt His Deity? Jesus Christ is God! He is The Seed God sent to save us!

POINT OF DEPTH

Mark 6:1-6
This passage is amazing to me. Jesus traveled during His ministry to His Own personal part of the country, Nazareth, and taught in the synagogue there. Although people were astonished as they listened, they did not attribute Deity to Him, but rather humanity and they took offense and stumbled over Him. Jesus realized they did not honor Him—their unbelief was great—so great that Jesus wondered at it.

The word here for "wonder" is the exact same Greek word used for "marvel" in Luke 7:1-10 when Jesus was amazed and marveled at how great the faith of the centurion was. Jesus wondered/marveled at the lack of faith in His hometown. Jesus wondered/marveled at the great faith of one who was not even a Jew, but rather a Roman Gentile. Does Jesus wonder/marvel at your faith? What does He see?

POINT OF DEPTH

Matthew 17:24-27
Is there anything too small for Jesus to care about concerning mankind? Jesus paid a temple tax that rightfully He did not owe, and He performed a miracle by providing that money through a fish. But why did He do it? Because He didn't want to cause the collectors of the tax to stumble. How careful He was in what He did. How careful are we in our decisions? Do we take notice that our actions will affect others? Do we care enough?

John 2:1-11; John 2:23
When the wine at the wedding in Cana ran out, Jesus' mother knew Who to go to for help! Jesus responded to His mother with a Hebrew idiom not unlike one of our own in English, "What am I going to do with you?" He made it clear to her that this was not His idea, and yet He was moved enough by His mother's request to give her what she asked of Him.

The result was good. Everyone at the wedding party enjoyed the greatest wine ever known to mankind! His disciples believed in Him, but most importantly, His Glory was manifested. People clearly saw that He was the Son of God, Himself—The Seed!

Later that same result took place in Jerusalem as Jesus performed many signs during the Feast of Passover. Many believed in His Name!

POINT OF DEPTH

As Jesus preached, healed, performed miracles, and taught the Jews, news about Him spread through their land like wildfire. On many occasions Jesus warned those whom He had just healed or done a miracle for not to tell anyone else. At other times, He instructed them to tell everyone in the city, as in the case of the healed demoniac of the Gerasenes. Sometimes they listened, sometimes they didn't. He also rebuked demons who were shouting out Who He was. Why would He want His arrival kept a secret? Wasn't He here, after all, after many hundreds of years of waiting? Wouldn't He want everyone to know right away? Why the confusion? Luke 4:14, 41; 5:14-15; 7:17; 8:34, 39, 56; 9:36; Mark 1:28, 34; 3:11-12; 5:19-20; 7:36; 8:30; Matthew 4:24; 8:33-34

The explanation is found, as usual, in the Scriptures themselves. He was there for a purpose—to visit the Jews, to make them a light unto the rest of the nations. But God's plan was more intricate. Yes, God knew the Jews would reject Him, but He wouldn't reject them forever. He would set them aside for a while to purify them. In the meantime, He would offer any Gentile who would believe the opportunity to be a light to the rest of the world. God's intricate and wise plan included The Seed's death, burial, resurrection, appearance, and ascension to the Father (with a promise to return!) Jesus had not come at this time to be their Earthly King—He would be their Earthly King later. For now He was ordained to be the Heavenly King of all who would believe. John 6:14-15

Luke 9:20-22 and Matthew 16:20 show Jesus warning His disciples not to tell anyone Who He really was—the Christ of God! It then gives us the reason. The Son of Man *must* suffer many things and be rejected by the elders and chief priests and scribes, and be killed and be raised up on the third day. If the disciples revealed that He was truly the Christ of God, The Seed that had been promised, and the Jews believed them and accepted, rather than rejecting Jesus, God's plan would not run as planned. Mark 9:9, 30-31 and Matthew 17:9 show us the same thing. Jesus gives them orders not to tell anyone about what they had just witnessed (His transfiguration and God calling Him His Son) until *after* He was raised from the dead. Jesus was protecting God's plan.

Why not let every last one of the Jews know that Jesus was God's Christ and let them crown Him King? Because God's intricate plan also involved the Gentile world. In Matthew 12:14-21, Jesus warned the people not to tell Who He was and then it tells us why. It was to fulfill the plans revealed in a prophecy given in Isaiah 42:1-4. Jesus was sent only to the lost sheep of the House of Israel and yet it was prophesied that He was to proclaim justice and bring hope to the Gentiles. How could He do both? God's intricate plan was perfect.

The Jew's rejection of The Seed brought acceptance to the Gentiles—reconciliation to the world! Their transgression brought salvation to the Gentiles! Romans 11:11-12

But doesn't it seem unfair that Jesus sometimes hid the truth from the Jews? Oh no! They were cut off because of their unbelief. God didn't keep them from believing. They had the Scriptures which clearly told them how to identify the Messiah. They did not want to believe. They chose to not believe. God simply orchestrated events during the ministry of Jesus to assure that His wonderful plan of redemption for all mankind would be fulfilled! Romans 11:20

Point of Depth

Do you believe that Scripture is the best interpreter of Scripture? It is. In a very real sense, Scripture is actually the *only* interpreter of Scripture! It is the final word in any and every dispute over meaning.

Isaiah 53:4-6 is often quoted to prove that God has promised complete physical healing for every believer. Although I know that God heals each and every illness that He desires to, if that were true, why are there so many believers who are not healed physically? Is the answer that they do not have enough faith? Can the answer be that they are not claiming by faith what is rightfully theirs? The answer must come from Scripture, not from any experience.

Isaiah 53:4-6 is a prophecy concerning The Coming Seed and it is fulfilled by Jesus, The Seed. But let's let Scripture tell us *how* Jesus fulfills that prophecy. Read Matthew 8:16-17 below and then read Isaiah 53:4-6. Feel free to read the entire chapter to catch the context. Which verse is Jesus fulfilling?

Matthew 8:16-17
> 16 When evening came, they brought to Him many who were demon-possessed; and He cast out the spirits with a word, and healed all who were ill.
> 17 *This was* to fulfill what was spoken through Isaiah the prophet: "HE HIMSELF TOOK OUR INFIRMITIES AND CARRIED AWAY OUR DISEASES."

Isaiah 53:4-6
> 4 Surely our griefs He Himself bore,
> And our sorrows He carried;
> Yet we ourselves esteemed Him stricken,
> Smitten of God, and afflicted.
> 5 But He was pierced through for our transgressions,
> He was crushed for our iniquities;
> The chastening for our well-being *fell* upon Him,
> And by His scourging we are healed.
> 6 All of us like sheep have gone astray,
> Each of us has turned to his own way;
> But the LORD has caused the iniquity of us all
> To fall on Him.

Now read I Peter 2:20-25. Again read Isaiah 53:4-6. Which verse or verses from Isaiah are interpreted for us?

I Peter 2:20-25
> 20 For what credit is there if, when you sin and are harshly treated, you endure it with patience? But if when you do what is right and suffer *for it* you patiently endure it, this *finds* favor with God.
> 21 For you have been called for this purpose, since Christ also suffered for you, leaving you an example for you to follow in His steps,
> 22 WHO COMMITTED NO SIN, NOR WAS ANY DECEIT FOUND IN HIS MOUTH;
> 23 and while being reviled, He did not revile in return; while suffering, He uttered no threats, but kept entrusting *Himself* to Him who judges righteously;

> 24 and He Himself bore our sins in His body on the cross, so that we might die to sin and live to righteousness; for by His wounds you were healed.
> 25 For you were continually straying like sheep, but now you have returned to the Shepherd and Guardian of your souls.

Do you see that if we let Scripture speak instead of ourselves, it tells us that Matthew 8:16-17 fulfills only Isaiah 53:4? It is not referring to verses 5 and 6 anymore than it is referring to any other verse or chapter in Isaiah.

In the same way, I Peter 2:24-25 is very plainly interpreting Isaiah 53:5-6 for us. And there we see that, without a doubt, it is not referring to physical healing, but rather to our sin-sickness. We are healed from the disease of sin! He bore our sins in His body on the cross so that we might die to sin and live to righteousness. By His wounds we were healed of the sickness of sin. Pay close attention to the illustration of the sheep that are always straying but now have returned to the Shepherd. Returning is the result of being healed of sin. That is why The Seed was sent!

In no way does this imply that God does *not* heal physical illness. Of course He does! Yet, what it shows us is that we cannot hold God to a promise that He did not make. And by the way, the promise He did make is much greater than one of physical healing here on earth.

Neither does this imply that we will not ultimately be completely physically healed. That promise is most definitely made to us, but it will not be fulfilled until the redemption of our bodies. At this point in HISTORY, only believers' spirits have been redeemed. Romans 8:18-25; I Corinthians 15:12-58

4. *Healing*
John 9:1-7
Why would a man be born blind? Jesus' disciples thought it was because of sin, either this man's or his parents', but that was not the case. God purposely formed this man in his mother's womb without eyesight. Why would God do that? Jesus tells us here—that the works of God might be displayed in him! Everything God does is for His Glory! That is why He created each of us! This man was just one more proof that God was Creator and deserved to be thanked and honored as such! **Romans 1:21**

Matthew 13:54-58
The very people Jesus grew up with did not believe that He was the Son of God, their Messiah. There was no reason to do many miracles for these people who would not believe, so He did not.

John 11:1-54
This event is a wonderful example of how everything Jesus did pointed to Him as the Son of God. Jesus purposed to let Lazarus die because raising him from the dead was a sign that would point to the Glory of God, which would in turn Glorify Jesus—proving He was The Seed.

Even praying out loud was a sign. Jesus prayed out loud so that the crowd standing around might believe that God sent Him.

When Jesus asked Martha if she believed that He was The Seed sent from God to bring life, her beautiful confession showed that she understood what Jesus' signs pointed to. She said, "*Yes, Lord; I have believed that You are the Christ, the Son of God, even He who comes into the world.*"

Even the Pharisees understood the importance of Jesus' signs. They were afraid that if they let Him continue everyone would believe that He was the Promised One of God!

Mark 7:25-30; Matthew 15:21-31
Jesus was sent only to the lost sheep of the house of Israel. God created the nation of Israel to be a light to the Gentiles. Jesus was sent to take care of them—give them the life they needed to be that light. As the light, they would Glorify the God of Israel!

Point of Depth

Luke 4:38-39; 5:17-26; John 9:1-7
The connection between illness and sin is recurrent in the gospels. We must see the correlation between our own personal sin and sickness. Yet, we are also to know that personal sin, beyond inherent sin from Adam, is not necessarily always the reason someone is sick. The reason can be to bring God Glory as in the case of the blind man in John. How we react to situations in our life, pleasant or unpleasant, can bring God Glory or rob Him of it.

Luke 5:12-14; 8:26-39; 9:37-42; Mark 1:23-26, 32-34; Matthew 8:28-34; 12:22
We must also be willing to see the clear connection between illness and demonic possession or activity. Many people in the churches today like to attribute anything and everything to the presence and power of Satan and his demons, and yet many more are blind to see the reality of it at all. Demons are real—very real. Although we cannot teach doctrine from events, it is nevertheless extremely significant the number of times Jesus casts out demons in order to heal someone.

Luke 7:1-10; 18:35-43; Mark 10:46-52; Matthew 8:1-4; 9:27-31; 13:54-58; 17:14-21
Recognizing the important role that faith plays in the work of God, especially in our own spiritual or physical healing, is absolutely essential. The centurion had faith unlike anyone Jesus had seen in Israel. Jesus marveled at his faith. (Don't you want to have the kind of faith that Jesus will marvel at?)

On the other hand, how amazing is the record that Jesus did not do many miracles in His Own hometown because of the lack of faith of those living there. Jesus marveled at their unbelief, that is, their lack of faith.

Mark 7:32-37; 9:14-29; Matthew 8:5-13; 9:1-8
It is interesting to note that on occasion someone was granted a healing whose own faith is not mentioned, but rather the faith of his friends who brought him to Jesus. It makes me realize how important it is to pray for those I love.

Mark 8:22-26
Here is a perfect example of not being able to teach doctrine from events. Rather we need to gather our doctrine from clear, repeated teaching in the Bible. This record of healing is obscure because it mentions that the blind man was not healed immediately, but rather in a process. I have heard people reject a healing as coming from God simply for the reason that it was not immediate and full. Perhaps (just maybe) God is free to do whatever He wishes?

Also interesting, is that demons are not mentioned in this story. Neither is faith. Neither is compassion on Jesus' part. There is no "formula" for healing—there wasn't in Jesus' time and there isn't now. What I <u>can</u> see here is the <u>complete sovereignty of God</u>. He is in control absolutely and ultimately! He is God!

Luke 7:11-16; 13:10-17; Matthew 9:35-36; 14:14; 20:29-34
It feels good, something like the effect of medicine itself, that Jesus healed people simply because He had compassion on them. What love He has for us that He would notice us at all!

Point of Depth

Mark 3:1-6; Matthew 9:32-34; 12:9-14; John 5:2-16; 11:45-54
The Pharisees, scribes, high priests, and leaders of the Jews literally hounded Jesus throughout His ministry. They wanted to accuse Him of anything and everything so they could remove Him from the scene. The very Seed of Life that had come to save them, they regarded instead as poison.

Point of Depth

Mark 7:25-30; 6:54-56; Matthew 4:23-25; 14:34-36; 15:21-31; John 4:46-53
Jesus only went to the Jews, not the Gentiles. Jesus only went to the Jews because that is who He was sent to—the lost sheep of the House of Israel. Yes, Gentiles would soon play an important role in HISTORY, but remember, God chose the Jews to be the carriers of The Seed. They were to be the ones who would have the Light inside of them, shining forth the message of salvation to the rest of the world. It is only because of their rejection of The Seed that Gentiles were invited to come to The Seed.

5. *Prayer*
Mark 14:32-42
Jesus prayed to the Father about everything, even about the plan they made before the foundation of the earth—the plan of The Seed. Jesus was about to go through indescribable agony and horror, yet He was willing to do it to bring us life.

POINT OF DEPTH

Mark 14:32-42; Matthew 26:36-44
Jesus didn't just pray once and then forget about it. He prayed over and over again for the very same thing. That's because it was so important to Him. He was distressed and troubled. I wonder how many times we bother to plead with God for those things that we think are important to us. I wonder how many times we tell a friend or loved one about the things that are troubling us. I wonder to whom we go first and I wonder to whom we go the most.

POINT OF DEPTH

Luke 5:16; 6:11-12; 9:18, 28; Mark 1:35; 6:46; Matthew 14:22-23
I am so encouraged when I read about Jesus' life of prayer. He constantly went to places where He could be alone—just Himself and His Father. I love that! It's such an encouragement for me to make sure I spend time alone with my Father. We should pray corporately at church and with other believers as often as we can, but that should never take the place of private individual prayer time with God.

POINT OF DEPTH

Not only did Jesus many times slip away to pray alone, He also slipped away many times just for solitude—perhaps to quietly sit in God's presence. There are so many times that life, and even people you love, seem to crowd around until you feel you just can't breathe. Knowing that I can leave people, places, and things behind and sit in my Father's arms for as long and as often as I wish, knowing that He loves it too, is one of the greatest joys in life.

And yet, Jesus many times gave up His solitude because of the nature of His compassion. What an example He left us! There are times when it is right for me to leave everyone else, even when they want me to be with them, and spend the time instead alone with God and perhaps a close friend or two. And there are times when it is right for me to sacrifice that personal downtime and invest it in loving and caring for those around me. Luke 4:42; 9:10-11; Mark 1:35; 3:7-10; 6:31-32; 7:24; Matthew 14:13-14

Point of Depth

Luke 10:21; Matthew 11:25-26
Isn't it amazing to read about God, the Son praising God, the Father? If God, Himself, praised God, the Father, then how is it possible for us to remain silent?

Point of Depth

Luke 22:31-32, 39-46
Believers are so safe in the hands of God, their Father. Even though He may allow temptations to enter our lives, we can know that Jesus is there interceding for us, praying for us! And you can be certain that God, the Father listens and hears Jesus' prayers!

And yet, at the same time, we are to pray for ourselves. It is our responsibility. We must constantly ask God to help us not enter into temptation. And if we are believers, we can be just as certain that God, the Father listens and hears *our* prayers!

John 12:27-30
This is amazing. Jesus prayed out loud again in order to Glorify the Name of God. He told the crowd that the voice came, not for His sake, but for theirs. God spoke from Heaven supernaturally in order to anoint His Son as The Seed and to prove once more that Jesus was the One sent by God. If only they would believe…

Point of Depth

John 11:41-42; 12:27-28
Here Jesus prayed publicly. It was not for His sake, but for those listening. Their faith was built up and God received Glory by Jesus' decision to pray in front of them. Whenever we pray publicly, it would be wise for us to keep His example in mind.

I have so many times heard corporate prayer that comes across like a sermon or exhortation. It sometimes felt like the person praying was talking to me rather than to God. Although someone may learn something while I am praying publicly, the litmus test should be—is God receiving Glory or am I? If I am, then my prayer is out of line with God's will and is worthless. And yet, Jesus' example would urge us to talk to God in front of other people, because the very display of our faith can help build theirs. The best thing to do with a perfect example is to follow it!

John 17

Oh, I love this chapter! This chapter is often referred to as the High Priestly Prayer—Jesus, as the Great High Priest, was praying. The job of a priest was to build a bridge to God. Jesus most definitely was doing that here. He prayed not just that I could be with God, but that I would be one with Him—one, just like He is with God. Wow!!! I can't think of a greater request ever put before the Father on my behalf. Jesus prayed for that unity for one main reason. By now in **HIStory** you should know why—to bring Glory to God! Man thinks we are one when we don't judge one another and maintain peace at all costs. God says we are one when we obey Him!

He asked for wonderful things—that the Son (The Seed) would be glorified, that His disciples would be kept in His Name and from the evil one, that they would be sanctified in the Truth and last, but not least, that all believers would be with Jesus, where He is. Why did Jesus desire that those given to Him by the Father would be with Him? So that they would see the Glory that God gave Him! It's all about His Glory! It's not about us at all!

The most amazing thing happens in this prayer. Jesus mentions each believer by name. Where? In **verse 20**—Jesus prayed for me, specifically for me... oh, what tremendous love He has for those who will believe! If you are a believer, then He is praying for you, too, in this verse. Do you love Him? Oh, tell Him so! Right now!

Point of Depth

It's important to know that no one has access to God in prayer except through Jesus Christ. The only prayer God assures us He will hear from an unbeliever is the cry of a confessing, repentant sinner pleading for salvation.

Do you teach your children that they have unconditional access to God?
They don't until they are saved. No one does, not even little children.

But it is also important to contemplate to Whom we are to pray. We are to pray to God, the Father through God, the Son in the power of God, the Holy Spirit.

When our children are finally and truly saved, to Whom do we teach them to pray—God or Jesus?

While it is true that Jesus is our mediator to God, it is also true that Jesus, Himself, taught us to ask all things of the Father, not of Himself. He told us to ask the Father "in Jesus' Name." You see, knowing Jesus makes all the difference in our access to God, the Father. When we come to the Father because we are in Jesus and Jesus is in us, then, and only then, do we have access. Our entrance into the presence of God depends entirely on Who we know (and Who knows us), not who we are!

HIStory Event 23
...THE SEED Dies

Read and Observe

1. Luke 22:1-23, 70
2. Luke 23
3. Romans 5:6-21
4. I Corinthians 15:54-57; Revelation 20:14

Read and Answer

1. Luke 22:1-23
Who did Satan enter?

What did Judas do?

What did Jesus tell Peter and John to go and prepare?

What day was it?

What had to happen on this day?

What had John the Baptist called Jesus when he saw Jesus approach him at the Jordan?

What specifically did they eat and drink at the Passover that night?

When would Jesus eat His next Passover meal?

Jesus took a cup, gave thanks, and told His disciples to take it and share it among themselves. When would Jesus drink His next Passover wine?

Jesus took some of the bread that they were to eat. He thanked God for this bread. He broke off some of it and passed it to His disciples. What did He reveal to them about the bread as He gave it to them?

Repeating the process, Jesus then took a cup of the wine they were drinking. What did He declare that cup of wine to be?

Could this be the New Covenant that Jeremiah had promised during the time of the Babylonian captivity? **Jeremiah 31:31-32**

Then Jesus announces some bitter news. What is it?

Luke 22:70
What does Jesus confirm to the Sanhedrin (the leaders of the Jews)?

2. Luke 23
Read this chapter asking God to open your eyes to the horrible reality of what Jesus went through. He endured it all for everyone who would believe!

3. Romans 5:6-21
For whom did Christ die?

How did God demonstrate just how much He loved us?

Just so you won't miss it—at the exact time that Christ died for us, how are we described?

What did the blood of Jesus accomplish for us?

What will we be saved from once we are justified?

How did sin enter the world?

How did death enter the world?

Through whom?

What did death do once it entered the world?

Why?

From the transgression of one, what did death do?

What was the result of one transgression?

Where did sin reign?

4. I Corinthians 15:54-57
What happens to death?

What loses?

What was its sting?

Why is its sting gone?

What has God given us?

Revelation 20:14
What is the lake of fire?

What will be thrown into the lake of fire?

READ AND REASON

1. Luke 22:1-23
Passover was coming. In it the Jews of Jesus' generation would observe far more than their ancestors had ever perceived. They would not only see the clear picture of The Seed in their annual Passover ritual, but they would witness The Seed, Himself, in His flesh go through the agony of the slaughter before their very eyes.

Instead of listening to God as He spoke to them in the Passover, the leaders of the Jews were frantically trying to rid themselves of the nuisance of this Man. The people loved Him, therefore the chief priests and the scribes feared they might lose their control over the people.

Satan entered into Judas, who then went to the leaders and offered to hand Jesus over to them. They agreed to the loathsome deal.

The night of the Passover meal (remember Egypt) came. It was the first day of Unleavened Bread. When the time came Jesus and His apostles met together for the meal. He informs them that this will be His last Passover with them (they have been together for three years) until it is fulfilled in the Kingdom of God.

He announces that one of them will betray Him as He eats the Covenant meal with them. And yet at the same time, He tells them that God is in control. God has determined the life and death of Jesus of Nazareth from before the foundation of the earth. Still, Judas is responsible for his own actions and will be judged for them.

Luke 22:70
When Jesus is taken before the rulers, He professes very clearly to all that He is indeed the very Son of God!

2. Luke 23
After the crowd vehemently accuses Jesus, Pilate asks Jesus whether He is the King of the Jews, Jesus answers, "Yes." Rome was ruling over Israel at this point in time (remember the Pac-man illustration in **Event 17**) and yet Jesus was their true King. Pilate is not convinced of any guilt in Jesus, but because of the unrelenting insistence of the Jewish mob, he sends him to Herod, who *just happened* to be in town at the time.

After Herod hideously amuses himself with Jesus, he sends Him back to Pilate. At the Jews' vehement demand he pronounces the sentence of crucifixion for the Lord Jesus Christ. The crowd sneers and mocks the King of kings.

Jesus is brutally murdered on a cross. From the world's eyes, He is killed because He claimed to be God. If He truly was God, as He claimed to be, then the people should have acknowledged

Him as Lord and repented of their independence from Him. So they killed Him and got rid of that inconceivable scenario!

From God's eyes, Jesus is killed so He can offer His precious, sinless blood as the full and final payment that is due for all the sins of the world. Once Jesus pays God this great, imposing price, then individuals can be released from the debt of sin each one owes.

As Jesus nears death, He cries out to God the Father, trusting Him even to the end. God hid the sun from the land and covered it with darkness.

Then, while it is still the hour of God's grief, He rips the Temple veil in two, sending a message to the very same people who just savagely crucified His Son. His message to them was "I love you. I have made a way for you to come to Me." Only the love of God would do such a thing… Since Adam and Eve first rejected Him, through the day Adam's race murdered His Son, through this present age and past the horizon of eternity… He loves us…

3. Romans 5:6-12, 16-21

Christ didn't die for the "good people"; He died for the ungodly. Every one of us were born ungodly, unrighteous, sinners, and enemies of God. We were helpless to do anything about it! Though we really can't understand just how great the love of God is toward us, we can see it manifested in the timing of Christ's death. He didn't clean us up and make us righteous and *then* die for us. He did it while we were still sinners! Amazing Love!

The death of Christ accomplished a great deal for us. Having been God's enemy, we were reconciled to Him through His death. We became His friend. Death reigned before Christ died. But through The Seed, Jesus Christ, Life and Grace reign!

4. I Corinthians 15:54-57; Revelation 20:14

Because of the death of Christ, even death itself has been defeated! Death is no longer a fearful thing for believers! Christ has given us the victory!!! Death itself will soon be thrown into the lake of fire for all eternity!

POINT OF DEPTH

Even in the time of Jesus' greatest physical pain and torment, He was focused on His chosen, beloved people, the Jews. His great love for them knew no bounds. In His pain He saw their time of torment—Jacob's Distress, the Great Tribulation they would have to endure… The Day of the LORD would come. They would suffer. But He would save them… Luke 23:28-31

Point of Depth

Tetelestai!!! Tetelestai!!!
Jesus came to pay <u>our</u> Debt!!!
He Paid it in Full!!! It is Finished!!!

"Tetelestai" was a legal term that was printed across a certificate of debt when it was paid off. The certificate was then nailed to the doorpost of the debtor's home to show everyone that his debt was finished, paid in full!

We owed a debt we couldn't pay. Christ paid it for us!
Christ cried out, "Tetelestai!!!" just as He was ready to die!

God nailed the parchment of Christ's flesh to the cross to show everyone, Satan included, that your debt and mine had been paid in full! John 19:30; Colossians 2:13-14

Thank You, Thank You, Jesus!!!

HIStory Event 24
...THE SEED is Buried

Read and Observe

1. Matthew 27:54-66
2. Mark 15:40-47; Luke 23:50-56
3. John 19:31-42
4. John 12:32-33
5. I Corinthians 15:36, 54-57

Read and Answer

1. Matthew 27:54-66
Who buried Jesus?

What did Joseph do with Jesus' body?

What were the chief priests of the Jews and the Pharisees worrying about while Jesus was in the tomb?

What did Pilate tell them to do to alleviate their worries?

Did they do it?

2. Mark 15:40-47; Luke 23:50-56
Who asked for Jesus' body?

Why did he need courage to ask?

Was he a believer?

What did Joseph put against the entrance of Jesus' tomb?

3. **John 19:31-42**
Why did the Jews ask for Jesus' legs to be broken?

Did they break His legs?

Why not?

What did they do instead?

What came out?

Did anyone see it happen?

Why is John telling us about it?

Why did Joseph of Arimathea keep his devotion to Jesus a secret?

In what kind of a tomb did Joseph lay Jesus' body?

4. **John 12:32-33**
How was Jesus lifted up from the earth?

By dying, what would Jesus do?

5. **I Corinthians 15:36, 54-57**
Why did Jesus have to die?

What happens when something dies and is sown?

Did Jesus die?

Was He "sown"?

READ AND REASON

1. Matthew 27:54-66
When Jesus died, there were many who finally believed. Some said they believed out of fear. That sounds familiar doesn't it? The fear of the LORD can lead us to salvation!

Others had a different fear. The Jewish leaders were afraid that Jesus would somehow get out of the tomb, and they went to Pilate about it. They were afraid that people would follow Jesus, and they would lose their control. They would have had a much better end if they had been afraid of the LORD God Almighty instead of being afraid of losing their own selfish power.

2. Mark 15:40-47; Luke 23:50-56
Joseph of Arimathea had believed in Jesus, but had never fully and completely given Him his devotion. He had been afraid of men. After Jesus died, he summoned whatever courage he had and publicly aligned himself with the dead man, Jesus. How sad. How much greater it would have been if he had taken his stand beside Jesus while He was alive.

What about you? Have you taken your stand next to Jesus? Have you gone outside the camp and stood beside His cross, wrapping your arms around the legs of your Lord and Savior? Will you wait too long? Don't wait any longer. Go to Him. Embrace Him. Receive Him. He is Lord!!! He is The Seed!!!

3. John 19:31-42
The Jews needed the crucified men to be dead because they needed to take them off of their crosses before the Sabbath. So they asked Pilate to break their legs. However, when the soldiers came to Jesus' body they found He was already dead. Instead of breaking His legs, they pierced his side with a spear. Just think, they all thought they were making their own decisions, but God was orchestrating the symphony exactly as He had composed it. God said that not one bone of Jesus' body would be broken. **Psalm 34:20** God said they would pierce Him. **Isaiah 53:5** God stands over His Word to perform it! **Jeremiah 1:12**

4. John 12:32-33
Jesus said that if He died, He would draw all men (Gentiles as well as Jews) to Himself. Have you been drawn? Are you being drawn? Will you come?

5. I Corinthians 15:36, 54-57

I have been referring to Jesus as The Seed throughout this entire book. Here is a beautiful understanding of exactly what needed to happen to this Seed. He needed to die. Why? Because if He didn't die, He could not be resurrected to a new life, a life that would give life to others!

His death brought total and complete victory over death and sin! Hallelujah!!! Because of Him, we have the victory!!! Praise the LORD!!!

HIStory Event 25
...THE SEED Lives and is Seen!

Read and Observe

1. Luke 24
2. Acts 1:1-3
3. I Corinthians 15:1-8

Read and Answer

1. Luke 24
What had Jesus taught His disciples while He was in Galilee?

    1.

    2.

    3.

Two people who heard that Jesus had actually risen from death were on their way to Emmaus. They were talking about the events of the last few days. Jesus approaches them and begins talking to them. Did they recognize Jesus?

Why not?

Jesus asks them what they are talking about specifically. What do they tell Him?

Did the men truly believe what they had heard from the women?

What does Jesus say is wrong with them because they did not believe in all that the prophets had spoken?

    1.

    2.

What does Jesus tell them was necessary?

    1.

    2.

What does Jesus explain to them as they continued toward Emmaus?

Where does He begin with His explanation?

Who does Jesus say Moses, the Prophets, and the Psalms are talking about?

What did Jesus do so they would understand the Scriptures of Moses, the Prophets, and the Psalms?

> *Oh, Dearest Lord Jesus, will you open our minds*
> *so we will understand the Scriptures, as well!*

2. Acts 1:1-3
How long was Jesus on earth after He was raised from the dead?

To whom did Jesus present Himself alive?

Did He prove that He was indeed the Christ—The Seed?

Did Jesus teach the apostles after He was raised from the dead?

What did He teach them?

3. I Corinthians 15:1-8

Paul, the author of **I Corinthians**, gives us quite a bit of information about the Gospel. What does he say the Corinthians did with the Gospel he preached to them?

What does he say they are doing with it now?

What benefit did receiving the Gospel have for the Corinthians?

How can they know they are saved?

What was the Gospel that Paul preached?

    1.

    2.

    3.

    4.

Let's look more closely at the fourth point of the Gospel. Who witnessed that The Seed had come to Life?

    1.

    2.

    3.

4.

5.

6.

Read and Reason

1. Luke 24:13-35
On the first day of the week, after Jesus is resurrected from the dead, He talks to two men on their way to Emmaus. They are followers of Jesus but do not recognize Him now because their eyes were prevented from recognizing Him. They had been discussing all the happenings in Jerusalem that week concerning Jesus.

Jesus asks them what they are talking about. They respond, *"We're talking about the same thing that everybody is talking about. Aren't you?"* They proceed to share their grief over losing the "prophet, Jesus the Nazarene." They had been so sure He was going to set Israel free from Rome. (They had not studied the whole counsel of Scripture and they were confusing His second coming with His first!) Jesus answers them by telling them they are foolish men who are slow of heart because they did not believe in all that the prophets had spoken.

Now, think for a minute. What was it that they did not believe? Why, it was the Old Testament! It was the Word of God! The Seed had been written about over and over and over again in God's sure Word, yet they still would not believe what God had said!

So Jesus gives them the Gospel, right there on the road to Emmaus. Did He bring them some new and special teaching? No! He took them right back to the Word of God which had already been spoken. He told them all about Himself by showing them the Old Testament!

HIStory is all about Jesus! It's all about The Seed that God promised to send, Who would save those in the world who believed from having to pay the penalty for their own sin!

> Oh, dear friend, DON'T be foolish and slow of heart!
> You have heard the Gospel! You have heard all about The Seed!
> Believe Him! Believe in Him!
> Embrace the Truth so you will be saved!
> Enter the New Covenant of Jesus Christ!

2. Acts 1:1-3

After Jesus was given new life by God, the Father, He walked the earth once more for 40 days. During that time He appeared to the apostles many times and convinced them that He was truly resurrected. The Master Teacher used that time to continue performing the Father's will—teaching about the Kingdom of God.

3. I Corinthians 15:1-8

Paul preached and taught the Gospel. Paul lived and breathed the Gospel. That Gospel was the way of salvation for those who would believe. Here he summarizes God's Gospel into four main points:

1. Christ died for our sins according to the Scriptures.
2. Christ was buried.
3. Christ was raised on the third day according to the Scriptures.
4. Christ appeared to Cephas (Peter), the twelve, more than five hundred at once, James, all the apostles, and to Paul.

Point of Connection

I always wondered why Paul spent so much time listing all the people that had witnessed Jesus after He was raised from the dead. I guess I thought it was to prove that He really had risen. And although I'm sure that is true, I found through study of the Scriptures that there was much more importance to it than I had realized.

The Day of Atonement was a once a year ritual that took place during the years of the Tabernacle. Everything that took place and was written down for us in the Old Testament was given to us for our instruction. I Corinthians 10:11 In studying the Day of Atonement, I found the answer to why Paul listed individually all those people who had seen Jesus after His resurrection.

Leviticus tells us that on the Day of Atonement after the high priest had taken the blood from animals sacrificed into the Holy of Holies, Israel would wait expectantly outside the court for the high priest to appear. If he didn't come out of the Holy of Holies, they would know God had not accepted their offering and had killed the high priest. Besides the fact that the high priest was dead, they had another problem to deal with. The offering that was rejected had been their safeguard from the wrath of God for an entire year. Without it, God surely would have destroyed them because of the conditions of the Covenant that they had made with Him. You can almost hear the sigh of relief from the crowd on that day when the high priest came out and waved to all the people signaling that God had accepted their sacrifice. Atonement for their sins had been granted for one more year.

The Day of Atonement was only a picture of the time when true atonement, forgiveness, and cleansing would be made once for all sins and once for all time. The true "Day of Atonement" happened over 2,000 years ago, during the time that Jesus' body lay in the tomb. During that time, Jesus, Himself, entered into the True Holy of Holies in the heavenlies with the perfect offering—His Own blood. If God accepted that offering, then the entire world would have the opportunity to be saved from the wrath of God. If God did not accept His offering, then each person who ever lived or ever will live would be required to pay for his own sin with his own death—separation from God for all of eternity.

Can you see why it was so important for Jesus to be seen after He was raised from the dead? God was signaling to all peoples for all time that the sacrifice of Jesus had been accepted as the full, complete, and final payment for their sins. Can you see why Paul regarded the witnessing of the risen Lord Jesus such an important part of the Gospel? We can breathe a sigh of relief. Jesus has paid our debt for us! God is satisfied with His payment! Jesus was the propitiation for our sins!!! Tetelestai!!!

HIStory Event 26
...THE SEED Returns to GOD

Read and Observe

1. Luke 24:45-53; Acts 1:1-12

Read and Answer

1. Luke 24:45-53
What promise did Jesus say He would send to them?

Once they were clothed with that power, what did Jesus say that they were to proclaim to all the nations? Is that what you proclaim?

Acts 1:1-12
What did Jesus do until He was taken up to heaven?

Who did He teach?

Jesus gathered the apostles together one last time and gave them one last commandment. Where were they ordered to stay?

What were they to do in Jerusalem?

What had the Father promised? (Take your answer directly from the text.)

Had they been told about this promise before?

What did John the Baptist use to baptize people?

Would they receive a new baptism?

What would God use to baptize them with?

How soon would this happen?

What would happen to them when they were baptized by the Holy Spirit?

      1.

      2.

Where would they be Jesus' witnesses?

      1.

      2.

      3.

      4.

What happened to Jesus once He had ordered them to wait in Jerusalem for what had been promised?

Did the apostles see this happen?

While they were watching this unusual event, who joined them?

What information did the two men in white give to the apostles?

What did the apostles do after Jesus was gone?

READ AND REASON

1. Luke 24:45-53; Acts 1:1-12
Before Jesus left this earth, He gathered His apostles together one last time. I love what it says He did next—He opened their minds to understand the Scriptures. Although they knew the Scriptures, they didn't understand the Scriptures. Now, before He left them, He would tell them one last time what was going to happen. And this time they would understand it!

He reminded them that they had been witnesses of the things which were written about Jesus in the Law of Moses, the Prophets, and the Psalms—specifically that the Christ (The Seed) would suffer and rise again from the dead the third day and that repentance for forgiveness of sins would be proclaimed in His Name to all the nations!

They were about to become part of the fulfillment of those Scriptures. They were going to receive the power to witness to all the nations! He commissioned them to go into all the world and preach the Gospel, but they were not to leave the city of Jerusalem until they received that power. That power had been promised long ago—they would receive the Holy Spirit to dwell within them. Then they would have the power they needed!

After giving the apostles His command, He took them to Bethany. There He lifted up His hand and blessed the apostles. While He was blessing them, He was carried up into heaven and left them.

Two men in white clothing suddenly were standing beside the apostles. The men in white informed the apostles that Jesus would be back and that He would come back in the same way they had just seen Him go into heaven.

They worshiped and returned to Jerusalem with great joy, waiting for the promise of the Holy Spirit and continually praising God in the Temple!

ACTS

The book of Acts begins with the ascension of THE SEED—where the gospels end. It is an historical account of the birth of the Church. The Father gives His promise to Jesus—the Holy Spirit to be given to those who believe in THE SEED!

After Christ's ascension, His disciples (about 120 people) gather together to pray until the Day of Pentecost. When the Holy Spirit is poured out, a noise like a violent rushing wind is heard. When all the people who were gathered in Jerusalem at that time (the Day of Pentecost) heard the sound, they came to see what it was. This gave Peter the opportunity to give the Gospel—about 3,000 people were saved that day.

Peter continues leading with the help of the other apostles against much opposition from the Jewish leaders. They appoint seven men to help in the ministry of serving. Stephen, one of those servants, soon finds himself in the crosshairs of the Sanhedrin. Stephen testifies clearly that Jesus is the Christ and that the Jews have not recognized Him, just as Moses and Joseph were not recognized by their brethren on their first visitation. When Stephen declares that these men have sinned, they rush at him to stone him. Saul (later called Paul) was there and was in approval—he even looked after the cloaks of the men who were stoning Stephen.

But God had plans for Saul. Saul would be saved on the road to Damascus and become an apostle to the Gentiles. He would suffer much— much more than any other apostle recorded for us in the Bible.

After Paul's conversion, God shows Peter that Salvation should be preached to the Gentiles when He gives him a vision and takes him to Cornelius' home. He was a Gentile who would receive salvation along with his whole household.

Paul is then called to go into Asia Minor to preach Salvation to all who would listen, to the Jews first and then to the Gentiles. He made three missionary journeys before being taken into custody and tried over his belief in Jesus. He would go all the way to Rome, testifying to all on his way that Jesus was the long awaited SEED.

HIStory Event 27A
...The Nation of Israel – Set Aside and Purified Until THE SEED Returns

Israel has chosen her path. She chose to reject The Seed, her Messiah. There will be an incredibly high price to pay.

We will follow the path of Israel until the end. Then we will come back and follow the path of the church until the end. Don't worry! The end will be a grand and glorious finish for both of us!

Read and Observe

1. Daniel 9:26a; Luke 21:12-24; I Peter 1:1; James 1:1; Acts 8:1
2. Isaiah 11:11-14; Jeremiah 16:14-15; 30:3; 32:37-41; 46:27; Ezekiel 37:1-14, 21-28; Micah 4:1-8; Zephaniah 3:8-20
3. Daniel 9:27; 12:11; Matthew 24:15-16; Mark 13:14
4. Jeremiah 6:24-26; 30:1-11; Daniel 9:27; 12:11; Matthew 24:15-28; Mark 13:14-23; Zechariah 12:1-6; 14:1-2; II Thessalonians 2:8-10; Zechariah 13:8-9; Joel 3:9; Jeremiah 46:28; Daniel 7:19-25
5. **Hosea**—Read this beautiful story depicting the life of the wife of God—Israel!

Read and Answer

1. Daniel 9:26a; Luke 21:12-24; I Peter 1:1; James 1:1; Acts 8:1
A prophecy is given that Jerusalem will be destroyed once more. Many of God's people will fall by the sword. Where will the rest go?

Are the Jews still scattered around the world today?

2. Ezekiel 37:1-14
Who do the bones represent?

What do the graves represent?

The bones were dry without any breath in them. They were dead where they were. The Jews are scattered around the world in strange nations (their graves), and they have no hope because they are completely cut off from the land of Israel and the rest of the nation of Israel. They are in their graves. What does God prophesy that He will do?

Why will God open their graves?

What will God cause them to do?

> It is extraordinary that those of us living in this last century have seen the beginning of the fulfillment of this miraculous prophecy! Just imagine in what a time we are living! Israel has been coming back to her land from nations all around the globe. God is bringing His people home!

What will Israel know then?

What will God do when He has brought them all back?

When do the bones actually come to life? Is it when God opens their graves and they come out or is it *after* He has caused them to come back to Israel?

Ezekiel 37:21-28
Keeping in mind that God tore the kingdom of Israel in two shortly after Solomon's death and that there has been no record of the two kingdoms ever uniting again, what significant statement of prophecy do you see in **verse 22**?

What else will they no longer do?

What will God do for them?

Who will be king over them in Jerusalem?

For how long?

Will they finally obey the LORD?

Where will they live?

For how long?

Where will God live?

What will the rest of the world know?

Isaiah 11:11-14
What will God do here concerning Israel?

What will God do here concerning Judah?

How will Israel and Judah feel about one another? (Ephraim is another name for Israel.)

Micah 4:1-8
What will this time be like for Israel?

From where will the world be ruled?

Will there be peace or war?

Is there peace or war for Israel now?

Will Israel be afraid?

Is Israel afraid now?

Can this be fulfilled yet?

Zephaniah 3:8-20
What sort of people will God leave on Mount Zion?

What sort of people will He remove?

How will the world feel about God's people, the Jews, in those days? What will their reputation be like?

How does the world in general feel about God's people, the Jews, today? Has Zephaniah's prophecy been fulfilled yet?

3. Daniel 9:27; 12:11; Matthew 24:15-16; Mark 13:14
Yes, God is bringing His people back to the land of Israel. He will fulfill all His prophecies. What will be made with "the many" (Jews) when they are back in the land?

When they make this covenant with the prince who is to come (antichrist), will it be broken?

Who will break it?

When will he break it?

When the antichrist breaks the covenant that he has made with the Jews, will the sacrifices continue?

Once the sacrifices are discontinued, where is the abomination of desolation set up?

When the Jews see this abomination of desolation set up in the Holy Place, what are they to do?

Reason with me. Are there sacrifices in Jerusalem now?

Will there be sacrifices in Jerusalem in the future according to **Daniel 9:27**?

What is needed before the Jews can start making sacrifices again?

What then can you be assured is going to be built in Jerusalem in the future?

4. **Jeremiah 30:1-11**
Days are coming for Israel when God will restore her fortunes and bring her back to the land He gave her. Those days, however, bring a purifying for the Jews through tribulation. What will be heard in Israel in those days?

Why will men resemble women who are in childbirth?

What is the time of that great day called?

Will Jacob (Israel) be saved from that time?

How will the Jews be saved?

Who will save them?

Then whom will they serve?

What will God do to the nations where He has scattered all the Jews?

To what extent will God destroy Israel?

Although God will not destroy Israel completely, what will He do to her?

Daniel 9:27
God is indeed bringing His people back to Israel during our lifetimes. But when will this "Day of Jacob's Distress" begin?

Daniel 12:11
What is set up that determines the time that the Jews will no longer be able to sacrifice in their Temple?

How many days will there be after that time?

Matthew 24:15-28; Mark 13:14-23
When the abomination of desolation, about which Daniel prophesies, is seen standing in the Holy Place, then what are the Jews to do?

Why are they to flee to the mountains? What will happen?

How bad will this tribulation be?

During that time many false "christs" and false prophets will arise. For what purpose?

How can the Jews know that the reports of Christ's coming are false?

What will Christ's actual return be like?

Let's reason together for just a moment. God is even now at this present time bringing His people, Israel, back to the land He gave them. Eventually there will be a time of peace for Israel that will never end. And yet *after* He brings them back to the land and *before* the time of peace, there will be a time of distress. This time is called the Great Tribulation, or Jacob's Distress. God has just brought them home to their land—but when this time starts they are to flee from the land one last time.

It appears that *after* God brings His people back to His land, the antichrist makes a covenant with them. During the time of that covenant, the Jews will rebuild and start sacrificing at their Temple.

Yet in the middle of the covenant, which is supposed to last 7 years, the antichrist breaks the covenant and stops the sacrifices and defiles the Jews' Temple. This begins the 3 ½ year period known as the Great Tribulation. During this time there will be no peace for the Jews anywhere on the earth.

What (or Who) seems to be the reason for the end of the time of the Great Tribulation?

Zechariah 12:1-6
The antichrist will gather the nations of the earth to come against the Jews in their land, specifically Jerusalem. What will God do to those nations when they come against His City?

What will happen to all who try to get rid of Jerusalem?

What will happen to horses of war?

What does a firepot do to the wood that is placed in it?

What does a flaming torch do to sheaves?

Who is the firepot and the flaming torch?

Who are the pieces of wood and the sheaves?

Who wins?

Zechariah 14:1-2
Who will sovereignly bring the nations against Jerusalem?

Read and Reason

1. **Daniel 9:26a; Luke 21:12-24; I Peter 1:1; James 1:1; Acts 8:1**
The Jews are scattered from the land once again in 70 AD when Titus destroys Jerusalem. Their forced migration leads them to all corners of the world. I grew up hearing about Polish Jews and Russian Jews, but never once did I realize they were at all connected with Israel. Never once did I realize they were in those lands because they broke their Covenant with God.

2. **Isaiah 11:11-14; Jeremiah 16:14-15; 30:3; 32:37-41; 46:27; Ezekiel 37:1-14, 21-28; Micah 4:1-8; Zephaniah 3:8-20**
The Jews, both Northern and Southern Kingdoms, are gathered back to the land. This time, never to be dispersed again! This great and marvelous miracle is happening in my lifetime, it is happening in your lifetime! It is happening right now as you read this!

Unless you stop for a moment and contemplate the enormity of this miracle you will most likely miss the incredible blessing of realizing that you are personally witnessing an event much, much greater than the parting of the Red Sea!

Point of Connection

God isn't just bringing His beloved Jews back to the land He promised them—He is also getting the land ready to receive them! Let's go back to Deuteronomy 28:15, 23-24, 38-40, 63-66 and recall one of the curses for breaking the Covenant. God warned them repeatedly to obey Him. If they disobeyed He would have no choice but to curse them according to the Covenant.

One of the Covenant curses that came upon the people of Israel was that the land itself would be cursed. God would not send rain upon it, but He would send locusts! They would not be able to survive in their own land because it wouldn't produce anything. Then they would be scattered from the land. Jeremiah 44:21-23; Ezekiel 12:19-20; 14

Have you ever been to Israel? Have you ever seen pictures of Israel? What does the land look like? It has been mostly barren desert and rocky mountains for centuries. Recently, though, you will find great beauty in the land of Israel. Flowers of every kind bloom profusely year round. The crops of the fields are wide-ranging and abundant! Why the change? Because God is fulfilling His Word! He promised that before the end He would make Israel like the Garden of Eden! Isaiah 51:3; Ezekiel 36:33-36

Not only is God sending more and more rainfall each year, He is bringing the people of Israel back to farm it. The Israelis are known for their ingenious ways of irrigating. Who gave the Jews their wisdom and understanding for watering the dry land of Israel so productively? God did! Job 38:36; Proverbs 2:6

When I went to Israel the first time, our group crossed the Allenby Bridge from Israel into Jordan. What a contrast! Israel was green, lush, and inviting! Jordan was dry, barren, and hostile! How could there be such a difference between two parcels of land that sit next to one another? Easy! Jehovah, the Holy One of Israel, was fulfilling His Word to His people concerning their land! If you want to see for yourself, go online and look at an aerial photograph of the lands of Israel and Jordan—green versus brown.

3. Daniel 9:27; 12:11; Matthew 24:15-16; Mark 13:14

The Jews enter into a covenant with the antichrist. Israel will rebuild her Temple in Jerusalem. Watch the world news! We are living in the end days. There is no prophecy that needs to be fulfilled before the Jews enter into a seven-year covenant with a man who can guarantee peace for Jerusalem! The time is ripe! Just read any newspaper today—any day—and you will see just how necessary peace is for Israel! And you can understand why someone who could finally bring peace would be revered by the world at large!

4. Jeremiah 6:24-26; 30:1-11; Daniel 9:27; 12:11; Matthew 24:15-28; Mark 13:14-23; Zechariah 12:1-6; 14:1-2; II Thessalonians 2:8-10

The "beloved" antichrist will defile the Temple and proclaim himself to be God in the middle of Daniel's 70th week. He will break the covenant and begin to persecute the Jews. This begins the period known as the Great Tribulation, or Jacob's Distress. It will be worse than the Holocaust, as unimaginable as that seems!

Zechariah 13:8-9; Joel 3:9; Jeremiah 46:28; Daniel 7:19-25

Toward the end of the Tribulation, God gathers all the nations against Jerusalem to battle. The city will be captured, the houses plundered, the women ravished, and half of the city exiled. Horror will be the daily headline. Israel will pay for her disobedience as God punishes and purifies His chosen people.

POINT OF DEPTH

Matthew 24:15-22 and Mark 13:14-20 both tell us that once the antichrist breaks his covenant with the people of Israel and defiles the Holy of Holies in the Temple, the Jews in Judea must flee to the mountains if they are to survive the next 3 ½ years of great tribulation. And it will be a hard flight! They will not even have time to go back into their house to get a coat! They must flee the very moment they hear of the abomination of desolation standing in the Holy Place!

How will Israel survive in the mountains? She will have very little supplies, if any, because of the haste of her departure from Judea. Revelation 12:6, 12-14 God, Himself, will nourish Israel during those 3 ½ years. Her every need will be met by God.

Revelation 12 refers to the mountains as the wilderness. Many people suspect that the rocky, mountainous wilderness of Petra will be the sight where the Jews will flee from the antichrist. It's a very likely spot.

Petra was carved out of rock by the Naboteans centuries ago as a hidden refuge in the midst of mountains. The Naboteans were able to keep their independence from Rome by controlling its few entrances. The sanctuary of Petra is beautiful in its rough, raw magnificence.

Will this be the place that the Jews actually flee to at the beginning of the Great Tribulation period known as Jacob's Distress? No one knows for sure, but if I were you, I'd sure keep my eyes on this rocky wilderness in Jordan.

Point of Depth

There are three main characters that play out the evil side of the drama of the last days: the antichrist, the false prophet, and Babylon. All three of these characters are driven by the power of Satan, himself, also known as the dragon in Revelation and the serpent of old in Genesis. Revelation 12:9; Genesis 3

1. The antichrist is also called the man of lawlessness in II Thessalonians, the prince who is to come in Daniel, and the beast in Revelation.

2. The false prophet is also known as the "other" beast in Revelation.

3. Babylon is a most familiar character. We met her in Genesis 11 and have followed her maliciously evil career throughout the Bible. God's city is Jerusalem and Babylon is her challenger from antiquity.

Point of Connection

Speaking of Babylon, let's look a bit closer at her calling and destiny.

In Genesis 9:19 we are told that the whole earth was populated from the three sons of Noah. In other words, you and I are descendants of one of the three sons of Noah, and likewise, the people that established the land of Babylon are descendants of one of his three sons. We won't look at our own family tree, but we will look at Babylon's. Which son of Noah was the great-grandfather of Babylon?

Let's look at an incident that happened in Genesis 9 before we go any further because its connection is significant, as we will shortly see. Let me set the scene. After God created the heavens and the earth and man, His creation rebelled against Him. Sin entered the world and poisoned it thoroughly. Mankind was an ugly, distorted image of its Creator. God sent a flood to destroy everyone except the family of Noah. He spared Noah because of His promise to bring The Seed through Adam and Eve. The event in Genesis 9 takes place shortly after the flood had receded and Noah's family was back on dry land.

One night, drinking wine made from his vineyard, Noah greatly imbibed to the point of a drunken stupor. In his drunken state he uncovered himself inside his tent. Now, Ham went into his father's tent, saw his nakedness, and then proceeded to tell his two brothers, Shem and Japheth, all about it. When Noah woke up he discovered what had been done to him.

All right, now let's move forward a couple of chapters to Genesis 11:1-9. Here we see a plain in the land of Shinar (region of Babylon) chosen as a site to build a city. That city is the site of the infamous tower/ziggurat of Babel. (Recall the POD from Event 5.) Remember, the real reason God was angry and confused their language was because they were disobeying His direct command to scatter and fill the earth. Remember, too, that in Babylon we saw the beginning of idolatry, false religion, false worship, and the city that still exists today in the land of Iraq. Babylon is called the "Mother of harlots" because her pagan and idolatrous ways spread across the entire earth when God divided the people into nations.

Let's look closer at Babylon's architect, builder, and honored mayor. Genesis 10:1 begins the records of the generations of Noah's three sons: Shem, Ham, and Japheth. Now skip down to verses 6-10. Here we see Ham's offspring. The Bible tells us Ham had four sons: Cush, Mizraim, Put, and Canaan. Genesis 10:8 then tells us Cush had a son and called him Nimrod.

Nimrod became mighty among men and was a mighty hunter before (against) the LORD. Nimrod built himself an empire, the beginnings of which included Erech, Accad, Calneh, and *Babel!* All four cities were in the land of Shinar, present day Iraq. Nimrod enlarged his kingdom way beyond Shinar, but we are only interested in Babel for now.

What precisely do we know about Babel/Babylon so far?
- Babylon was built in defiance of God
- Babylon's residents did not worship God, but were idolaters
- All harlotry (adultery against God) came from Babylon
- Babylon's builder was the descendant of Ham, who was involved in the abuse of his father's drunken state

Now let's move forward to the book of Jeremiah. The nation of Israel had been formed, entered into a Covenant with God, broken that Covenant umpteen times, and was now in the position of being taken out of the land as a consequence. God had sent many prophets to warn the people to repent, but they would not.

The Northern Kingdom had already been taken into captivity by the Assyrians. Now God sends Jeremiah to Judah, the Southern Kingdom. Her time has run out—she is about to go into captivity. Jeremiah 4:18; 11:10-11; Ezra 5:12 In fact, God tells Jeremiah to not even pray for

Israel any longer. Jeremiah 7:16; 11:14; 14:11-12; 15:1 He has made up His mind and Israel will be taken captive by Babylon! Jeremiah 20:4-5

Why did God choose Babylon? For the same reason He chose the Assyrians to take the Northern Kingdom captive—because His people had adopted that nation's idolatrous ways! Since Israel was in Covenant with God, her actions were considered adultery—so God chose her *lover* to punish her. Assyria had been Israel's lover and Babylon had been Judah's. Ezekiel 23:1-23 Note verse 18. Do you see anything similar to the story of Noah and Ham? Yes! Israel uncovered her nakedness! Interesting, isn't it? Israel had committed adultery with Babylon—the city of rebellion against her God!

When God sends Babylon, many Jews are taken captive to the land of Shinar. Daniel the prophet and a group of nobles are deported in the first siege in 605 BC. Ezekiel (another prophet) along with 10,000 others are taken to Babylon in 597 BC. Finally, Jerusalem is destroyed in 586 BC at the hands of Nebuchadnezzar, king of Babylon. However, during this whole time Jeremiah has remained inside of Jerusalem speaking for God.

Jeremiah's message was progressive:
- Repent!
- If you don't repent, God will take you out of this Land!
- Since you won't repent, God is going to take you out of this Land!
- God is going to use Babylon to take you out of the Land!
- Don't fight against Babylon—or you won't live!
- Go to Babylon and live there—take your punishment!
- *Although you will be living in Babylon, don't learn her ways!*
- I will bring you back to this Land after 70 years!
- *I will punish Babylon, too!*
- I will make a New Covenant with you that won't let this happen again!

Let's look specifically at the two parts of Jeremiah's warning that I have marked above. First, the Israelites were not to learn the ways of the nations—they were not to do the things that Babylon did. What exactly did Babylon do? Well, remember her beginning was in direct defiance of God's command to scatter and fill the earth. Remember, too, she didn't just disobey God, she obeyed and worshiped false gods rather than Jehovah!

What exactly were the beliefs and the ways that the Israelites were not to follow? What did Babylon do that was so awful? Let's back up and look at her founding fathers again. Remember Nimrod, who built the city, was the great-grandson (or so) of Ham, Noah's son who had defiled his father by looking at his nakedness while Noah was dead drunk on the floor of his tent.

The book of Ezekiel is concerned with the same time frame and the same problem that Jeremiah is concerned with. Both prophets had a hardened and unrepentant audience—the Southern Kingdom. Ezekiel 8:14 (POD in Event 18) mentions a name that we see only once in the Bible—Tammuz. The women of Israel were weeping for him at the entrance of the gate of God's house. Who is Tammuz? He was believed to be the reincarnation of his father who was said to be Nimrod!

Nimrod was married to a woman named Simiramis (Smyrna). He was executed, probably by his Uncle Shem, as he proclaimed himself to be god. This left a queen without a king. She came up with a plan. She became pregnant (illegitimately) and then devised a great story—Tammuz, her baby, would not have an earthly father; he would be hailed as the god Nimrod, himself! How did Simiramis become pregnant? Why, through a sunbeam—of course! The story just gets better—if Tammuz was the reincarnation of Nimrod, then he also must be a god! And if Tammuz was a god (a sun-god of course, due to his conception by sunbeam) then Simiramis was the mother of god!

Tammuz (god) and Simiramis (goddess-mother of god) established a Babylonian festival in which the people worshiped the unconquered sun (Tammuz, of course). The date of December 25 was chosen because astronomers of those days determined that it was on that very day that the sun starts to come back to earth after having "died" on December 20, the shortest day of the year. The festival was called "Nativity of the Unconquered Sun." Through this festival Simiramis became known as the queen of heaven.

When God divided the earth and confused the language of the people in Babylon, the story was taken with them to their new lands. Therefore we see Simiramis still worshiped today under pseudo-titles. In Egypt, she is worshiped as Isis. The Greeks call her Aphrodite, while the Romans call her Diana. In Sumeria she was called Ishtar (the name of a famous gate still in existence today in Babylon), while in Canaan she was Asherah. The Phoenicians called her the Lady of the Lake and last, but certainly not least, the Italians worship Madonna and her Child. Uh-oh! Things are starting to take on an unpleasant twist. We are all too familiar with the Madonna of the Catholic faith who is worshiped!

The women of Israel who were weeping for Tammuz at the gate to God's house were participating in a similar Babylonian festival—the pagan Spring Equinox Festival or Festival of Oestre/Estre/Ishtar. The women would grieve over Tammuz' death (the sun god) for 40 days prior to the festival in hopes that he would come back to life, representing a renewal of nature. Because of Tammuz' "divine" birth, Simeramis became the goddess of fertility. Her symbol was—you guessed it—a rabbit! This Babylonian festival is where our modern world derives the word Easter.

Obviously many of the customs that Israel was not to learn and adopt while in Babylon were parts of these crazy festivals of Tammuz and Simiramis! Instead of obeying God, it seems that the people of Judah ignored Jeremiah's warning and obstinately pledged their allegiance to their queen! Jeremiah 44:16-19

Not only did God's people Israel adopt these Babylonian festivals before the birth of Christ, but also 300-400 years after the death and resurrection of Christ, most of their pagan customs were assimilated into the church because the majority didn't want to give them up! Constantine took this pagan religion and adapted it to Christianity with a very strong emphasis on the virgin birth and Mary's role in Christ's work here on earth. Mary became the new "queen of heaven"! Below I have listed some parts of the winter festival. Does anything sound familiar?

- Mistletoe – was considered a divine branch representing the reconciliation of man to the unconquered sun—kissing underneath it was recognition of that reconciliation.

- Candles were burnt in anticipation of the sun god returning to give another year of life to the earth.

- Chanting in the streets, going door to door, and wreaths put on doors were used during this time to keep away demons.

- Babylon's winter festival was known as the festival of drunkenness or the day of misrule (notice the interesting connection to Noah's drunkenness). Wild parties took place including debauchery and gift giving.

- The Yule log was burned for weeks before December 25 in memory of the death of Nimrod/Tammuz.

- On the evening of the 24th a tree was cut down and decorated to celebrate that the unconquered sun, seen through Nimrod/Tammuz, was returning to earth, thus bringing another year of life to the earth! Decorations included silver and gold balls symbolic of the planets and stars. The evergreen trees were worshiped as symbols of life, fertility, sexual potency, and reproduction. Nimrod/Tammuz received praise at this time! Jeremiah 10:1-5

Wild partying, gift giving, chanting in streets, wreaths, mistletoe, much greenery, and the beloved tree. Hmmm... that does sound rather familiar... it brings a whole new depth of meaning to the word "duped"!

God has always been very clear in His declaration that He will have no other gods beside Himself! He is a jealous God and He will not permit His people to love anyone else—even out of ignorance!

In reference to Babylon, God calls for His people to "Come out of her." Revelation 18:4 Is it possible many Christians are inside of Babylon and don't even know it? Is it possible that our holidays, instead of pleasing God, actually mock Him? Could it be that our actions rob Him of the Glory He created us for? Could we be offering God "false fire" (Leviticus 10:1-3) all the while thinking we are offering Him praise and a pure offering?

Have our traditions become our idols? Consider how you feel when you think about giving it up. Maybe you will discover whether it is an idol or not. Most people would say you were crazy if you didn't follow the traditions of our beloved "holy-days." But then, I wonder what God would say to you?

I think of when the disciples ate with unwashed hands and how the Pharisees accused them of sinning by not keeping the tradition of the elders. Jesus turned it around and reminded them that many of their traditions caused them to break the commandments of God. He told them that even though they may honor God with their lips in their traditions, their hearts were far away from Him. Matthew 15:1-9

> What about you?
> Do you honor God in word only, and not in action or deed?
> I pray you will honor Him because your heart is close to His.
> What will you do with what you know?
> As for me and my house, we have decided.

The second part of Jeremiah's prophecy, which we want to take note of, is that God declares He will punish Babylon for her deeds. God is not finished with Babylon. He prophesied through Jeremiah that He would punish her. He has a special plan laid out just for her! And she's not going to enjoy the end of it! Babylon, the city, will come to worldwide prominence once again. There will be a temple built in Babylon. Zechariah 5:5-11 Her idolatry will continue until then… but at that time… He will send destruction upon her in one day! Her idolatry will end! Jeremiah 50:45 Her destruction is laid out with exacting details in Revelation 17 and 18.

HIStory Event 27B
...The Church – THE SEED Sends His HOLY SPIRIT as Promised!

The Jews did not recognize the time of their visitation—the time when The Seed came to take care of them. Because the Jews rejected The Seed, He was made available to the rest of the world. The Jews rejected Jesus, so God birthed the church. The Gentile nations are given a Savior, Jesus Christ, *if* they will believe!

We will follow the path of the church until we come to that grand and glorious finish that God promises to all believers—Jew and Gentile!

READ AND OBSERVE

1. Ezekiel 36:27; 39:29; Isaiah 44:1-3; John 16:7; 14:16-17, 26; Acts 1-2; Joel 2:28-32; Hebrews 8:7-13; 9:15; 10
2. Jeremiah 4:3-4; 9:25-26; Romans 2:28-29; Colossians 2:11; Philippians 3:3; Romans 11; Ephesians 5:23-32
3. John 14:1-3; I Thessalonians 4:13-18; I Corinthians 15:51-53; Romans 11:25
4. II Corinthians 5:9-10; Romans 14:10
5. Revelation 19:6-8; John 3:25-29; Matthew 9:14-15

READ AND ANSWER

1. Ezekiel 36:27
What promise does God give concerning His Spirit?

What will His Spirit do?

What will someone be careful to do if God's Spirit is within him?

Ezekiel 39:29
How completely will God give His Spirit?

Isaiah 44:1-3
Upon whom will God pour out His Spirit and blessing?

John 16:7
Could Jesus give the Helper while He was still here on earth?

What did He promise to do if He went away?

John 14:16-17, 26
Who is this Helper?

How long would this Helper be with those who believed?

What would this Helper do?

Acts 1-2
As Jesus, The Seed, is leaving this earth, what does He tell His disciples to do?

    1.

    2.

He told them to wait for a promise—the promise He had told them about earlier. What was that promise? (What were they waiting for? What would happen to them?)

When they received the promise of the Holy Spirit, what would they have?

Power to do what?

Did they go back to Jerusalem and wait as Jesus commanded them to do?

What happened on the day of Pentecost (50 days after the Passover)?

What did they hear?

What did they see?

What controlled (filled) them?

What had they just received?

People from all over the city heard the sound and came to investigate. They were bewildered when they saw and heard what they did. Peter explained it to them. He said God was fulfilling a prophecy that He made through His prophet Joel. What part of Joel's prophecy was fulfilled that day? **Joel 2:28-32**

Then Peter gave a fabulous sermon. He preached on the promise of Jesus, The Seed! Who does Peter say planned the death of Christ?

When God raised Jesus from the dead, to what did He put an end?

After raising Jesus from the dead, God exalted Him to the right hand of God. Then Jesus received "Something" from the Father. What was "It"?

What did Jesus do with this "Promise"?

If people would repent, what would they receive?

For whom was the Promise?

Acts 2:33
Jesus received the Promise of the Holy Spirit after God had highly exalted Him. What did Jesus do with that Promise?

Hebrews 8:7-13
If the first Covenant, the one God made with Moses and Israel, had been able to impart righteousness, there would have been no need for The Seed to come. But there was a fault in the people. They had a heart condition that would not allow them to keep God's Law. So God promised He would make a New Covenant with them. This Covenant would not be like the one He made with Moses. What would it be like?

Where would God put His Laws in this New Covenant?

Where did God put His Laws in the first Covenant?

What became of the first Covenant?

Hebrews 9:15
What is the reason He, The Seed, is the mediator of this New Covenant?

Hebrews 10
Compared to the New Covenant, what was the Law?

Since the Old Covenant was only a shadow, of what was it a shadow?

Who is talking in **verses 5** through **7**?

What does Jesus, The Seed, do with the first in order to establish the second?

When we believe on the Lord Jesus Christ, The Seed, we enter Covenant with Him. What happens to us when we enter that Covenant?

2. Jeremiah 4:3-4
What had God told the men of Judah to do?

What would happen if they didn't?

Did they ever do this?

Jeremiah 9:25-26
What would happen to those who were not circumcised of heart?

Romans 2:28-29
Who are the true descendants of Abraham?

How is a Jew recognized?

Is true circumcision in the flesh?

What is true circumcision?

What is circumcised?

Who does the circumcising?

Colossians 2:11
In the New Testament every believer is circumcised in Him. How is this circumcision made?

What is cut away?

Philippians 3:3
Who are the true circumcision?

    1.

2.

3.

Romans 11:11-17
God chose Abram and made him into the nation of Israel. Many times God refers to Israel as an olive tree (or a vine). Why were some of the olive tree's branches broken off?

Who is the wild olive?

Romans 11:18-24
How is it that a Gentile can be grafted in? What does it take?

What are Gentiles grafted into?

What do they become?

Romans 11:25-27
What do you think "the fullness of the Gentiles has come in" means? What do you think they have come into?

What Covenant is referred to here?

Ephesians 5:23-32
What is Christ's relationship to the church?

What is His relationship to the "body"?

Are the body and the church referring to the same group of people?

What is the church's relationship to Christ?

How does Christ feel toward the church?

What did He do for her?

Why did He do this?

How does He sanctify her?

What will He do with her one day?

How will she look?

How are Christ's actions toward the church characterized?

    1.

    2.

Of what are believers a part?

The mystery is great, but in reference to Christ and the church, what will "two" become?

Romans 11:36
Where are all things from?

Who are all things through?

Who are all things to?

Do you remember why God made man in the first place? For *His Glory!!!*

3. John 14:1-3
Where has Jesus gone?

To do what?

What will He eventually do concerning believers?

Why?

I Thessalonians 4:13-18
Where are believers who have already died?

Believers will come with the Lord when He comes to get those of His church who have not already died. Where will the Lord come from?

How far will He descend?

When He descends, what two sounds will be heard?

      1.

      2.

Then what will happen to believers?

How long will the church be with Him?

I Corinthians 15:51-53
What will happen to the church when the last trumpet sounds?

What will happen to believers' bodies, as well as the bodies of all dead believers?

What will believers' perishable bodies put on?

What will believers' mortal bodies put on?

Romans 11:25
What happens before all of this will take place?

4. **II Corinthians 5:9-10**
Something is going to happen when believers go to be with Christ. That event should motivate believers to be pleasing to Him right now on earth. What is that event?

What will happen at the Judgment Seat?

Which deeds will be judged?

Romans 14:10
Who will stand before the Judgment Seat of God?

Should the fact that each believer will someday stand before the Judgment Seat of God make a difference in his or her life now? If so, what?

5. **Revelation 19:6-8**
After the rewards are handed out, or lost, at the Judgment Seat of Christ, a wonderful event will take place. What is it?

Who is the Lamb?

Who is His bride?

What will the bride wear?

Out of what material is it made?

Who gives her the garment she will wear?

Who will determine just how beautiful that garment will be?

John 3:25-29; Matthew 9:14-15
Who is the bridegroom?

Who is the bride?

READ AND REASON

1. **Ezekiel 36:27; 39:29; Isaiah 44:1-3; John 16:7; 14:16-17, 26; Acts 1-2; Joel 2:28-32; Hebrews 8:7-13; 9:15; 10**

Jesus told His disciples to wait in Jerusalem for what the Father had promised through His prophets. Jesus had also told them about the promise—the promise was that God would send His Holy Spirit to dwell inside of men who would believe in The Seed. The indwelling Holy Spirit would cause men to walk in God's ways and to keep His commandments so that God would not have to curse men!

This is the awesome Covenant of Grace! Present day believers have it so much better than those who entered the Old Covenant! God keeps His side of the Covenant, just like He did then, but now, praise our God, He keeps our side *for us*!!! God keeps both sides of the Covenant! What a God!!! What a Savior!!! This, my friend, is Salvation!!!

2. **Jeremiah 4:3-4; 9:25-26; Romans 2:28-29; Colossians 2:11; Philippians 3:3; Romans 11; Ephesians 5:23-32**

One of the main hindrances for the Jew to obey God was his heart; it was hard and unresponsive to Him, it was uncircumcised. God compared the hearts of the Israelites to hard, fallow, weedy ground. It's impossible to get that type of ground to produce good crops. Obedience was the crop God wanted to harvest. God warned that He would punish those with hard, uncircumcised hearts.

Fleshly circumcision was a sign of the Old Covenant, which in turn, was a picture of the New Covenant. Simply because a Jew was circumcised in the flesh did not make him a true Jew. A true Jew was one whose heart was circumcised by the Holy Spirit at the time of his conversion to Christ. Those who are truly circumcised put no confidence in their flesh because the power of the flesh has been removed. They now worship in the Spirit of God and Glory in Christ Jesus.

From this point in **HISTORY** (the beginning of the New Covenant) whoever would believe in The Seed would be indwelt by God's Holy Spirit. This group of people would be called the Church. There is a limited number that belongs to this group. Once Jesus comes in the clouds and catches His saints up to be with Him, there will be no more added to the church. Saints who believed before the church age are not part of the church. The Jewish believers from the time before the church are the wife of God. The Jews' relationship to God is depicted in the story of Hosea and Gomer. (Why don't you read the book of **Hosea**!) The Jewish believers during the church age become part of the bride of Christ.

The church has a definite purpose, similar to the purpose that the Jews had. The church is to be a light to the world of unbelievers showing them their need for a Savior, and leading them to the Savior. Believers have the Holy Spirit to cause them to walk in a manner worthy of God which brings Him Glory. The church is to show the world Who God really is! But it needs direction, correction, and encouragement along the way. So God wrote letters to believers in the different cities where they assembled—letters that have been handed down to us in the Bible. We don't know who wrote **Hebrews**, but God used Paul, Peter, James, Jude, and John as authors for the other epistles. His Own Holy Spirit chose each and every word that was written!

POINT OF DEPTH

Romans 11 is a very important passage for us to consider. In these last days, many have distorted the truth about the nation of Israel and God's dealings with her. We need to look to the Word of God and find the Truth He has spoken—then we will know what is true of Israel's future!

Some people say God is done with Israel, and in fact, some say He has replaced her—replaced her with the church or with America. This lie is an abominable smell in the nostrils of God. What does God say in Romans 11:1? God has not rejected His people!!! That is the truth—God has not, and never will reject His people, His precious people Israel! Paul even uses an emphatic phrase, "May it never be!" which literally means "It is impossible!!!" It is impossible, it could never happen that God would reject His people!

Twice in Deuteronomy 31 (as well as hundreds of times throughout His Book) God states His clear commitment to His people by declaring He will not fail or forsake them—instead He will be with them. Hebrews 13:5-6 broadens this promise to all believers even while exhorting them to be righteous when it states, *"I will never desert you, nor will I ever forsake you, so that we confidently say, 'The Lord is my helper, I will not be afraid. What will man do to me?'"*

The Timeline has split and we are following the path of the church, but I want to make sure you are fully aware that, although Israel is on the "back burner" so to speak right now, she has not been shelved and she never will be! She has simply been set aside and is being purified for her Husband—Israel is the wife of God, the apple of His eye, His special beloved treasure. God has plans for her and He will bring them all to pass—every single one!

Let's spend a little more time here in Romans 11 before moving on—it is such an important passage. Thoughtfully read through the chapter and then reason through a few thoughts with me.

Why does it seem to some (to whom Paul is writing) that God might have rejected His people? What is happening to their numbers? How many of the Jews seem to be faithful to their God (during the time Paul is writing)?

What does Paul show us? There are a few faithful, the remnant, and they are intact because of God's gracious choice of them! God, Himself, has kept faithful men for Himself! So when it seems that the Jews are few in number, we can still know that they are kept for God, by God—not because of anything they are doing—but because of what God is doing! Romans 9:11; 11:28

What does verse 7 say Israel is seeking? Look at Romans 10:1-3. Israel was seeking righteousness, but tried to establish their own rather than subjecting themselves to the righteousness of God. What was the result? Romans 11:7 says that, although Israel sought righteousness, she did not obtain it. Why? Because she sought to make herself righteous rather than relying on the righteousness of God for her salvation.

And yet, verse 7 goes on to tell us that some did obtain righteousness—who? And what happened to the rest, the ones who were not chosen? This should not have come as a surprise to them because it had been prophesied as Romans 11:8-10 shows us. Their law had become a snare and a trap to them, causing their own spiritual blindness.

So the first part of Romans 11 declares that God will not forsake His people even though they have become few in number because of their unrighteousness. Then in verse 11, Paul reiterates that their fall is neither a complete nor a permanent one, and that it actually is being used to accomplish another part of God's plan!

What change regarding the Gentiles became possible because of the stumbling (but not falling) of the Jews? In other words (technically speaking), if the Jews had not stumbled, would salvation have come to the Gentiles?

What is part of the result of the Gentiles being given salvation? How does that affect the Jews? Romans 11:11 What is the purpose of making the Jews jealous of the Gentiles' salvation? You see, even in that, God is not finished with His people—He is purposely making them jealous, stoking a desire in them to come to Him! He is not finished with His people, oh, no!!! May it never be!!!

Let's just keep walking through this chapter—it has so much to show us! Look at verse 12. It says the Jews' transgression or failure (unrighteousness) is riches for the world. What does that mean? It means that because the Jews did not subject themselves to the righteousness of God (and instead tried to produce their own) the world (Gentiles, nations) were given riches—the riches of salvation. So what was a bad thing still turned out a good product—Jew's failure (bad) offered the Gentiles salvation (good).

Now Paul shows us a contrast. He says that if the "bad" that the Jews did resulted in producing a "good" for the Gentiles, then how much more "good" will be accomplished when the Jews finally do subject themselves to the righteousness of God!!! You see, here is another promise that God is not done with His people! He is predicting their salvation! Hallelujah! Every last chosen Jew will be saved!

Paul goes on to say almost the same thing in the next few verses. He says he is speaking to those who are Gentiles so that the Jews will see his ministry and out of jealousy become believers. He describes their rejection of the salvation as bringing reconciliation to the world (the Gentiles) and he exalts their future acceptance of God's salvation (His way) as life from the dead! Paul is completely committed to the fact that the Jews will be saved! He believes every word he writes!

Paul takes time to caution the Gentiles to be humbled by the situation, rather than puffed up; he reminds them that the Jews are before the Gentiles. The Gentile branches are supported by the root—it is not the other way around. *And* he forewarns them that since God did not spare His people, the Jews, because of their unbelief, He will not spare the Gentiles either.

Verse 24 is another declaration of promise that the Jews will still be part of God's plan in the end. They will be grafted back into their own olive tree, just as if they had never been broken off. It is true.

Paul now turns a corner in Romans 11 and gives his readers some extremely important information about a mystery. Why does he give them this information? What does he tell them has happened to Israel? What is a partial hardening? How long will this partial hardening continue?

Jesus says in Luke 19:42 as He approached Jerusalem and wept over it, *"If you had known in this day, even you, the things which made for peace! But now they have been hidden from your eyes."* This is the hardening... the Truth has been hidden from those who would not see it... Jesus was the Coming Messiah Israel had waited for throughout the centuries, but when He came they would not receive Him. So God partially hardened His people Israel and gave His invitation for salvation to the Gentiles.

But it was only a partial hardening, as John 1:12 shows us. Those who would receive Jesus would be given the right to become children of God. To whom would be given that right? To those who believe in the Name of Jesus!

It also was a temporary hardening—once the last Gentile is saved, then all of Israel will be saved! Israel! Look up! Your time draws nigh! Soon your Deliverer will come in power and majesty and He will draw you to Himself and you will be saved! He will remove ungodliness from you and take away your sins!

How do we know this will happen? Because He said so! There is nothing more sure than the Word of God! He promises a Covenant, the most solemn binding agreement that can be made, to assure His people of His intentions! The Jews, although enemies of Christians because of the Gospel, were the beloved of God because of the Covenant God made with their fathers. The gifts and calling of that earlier Covenant (Abrahamic) were, and are, irrevocable!

The Gentile believers (Paul's audience) were once disobedient to God, but were shown mercy because of the Jews' disobedience. In other words, because the Jews rejected Jesus, the Gentiles were offered Jesus in mercy. And in like manner, because the Gentiles were shown mercy because of the Jews' disobedience, so would the Jews be shown mercy once again. Only in the economy of God could this take place—because of *disobedience* there was mercy for the Gentiles and mercy for the Jews! Glory to God! He shut up everyone in disobedience so that He could show mercy to all!!!

Oh, the depth of the riches both of the wisdom and knowledge of God!
There is oh, such rich depth in the wisdom of God in how He saves His people.
There is oh, such rich depth in the knowledge of God in how He saves His people.
Both Jew and Gentile.

How unsearchable are His judgments and unfathomable His ways!
His ways cannot be searched—they are too far beyond the horizon!
His ways cannot be fathomed—they are too great beyond any measure!
His judgments and His ways of salvation are His alone!
We dare not tread to examine or question!

For who has known the mind of the Lord, or who became His counselor?
The answer is an absurdity!
No one has known the mind of the Lord!
How preposterous, illogical, and senseless to ever conceive of counseling the Lord!

Or who has first given to Him that it might be paid back to him again!
Does the Lord owe anyone anything at all!

May it never be!!!

For from Him and through Him and to Him are all things!
God alone is the source of all things, including the salvation of His chosen ones!
He chooses, He calls, He saves!
He will lose not one!
He alone is God!
And we are His alone!

To Him be the Glory forever! Amen!
...and amen and amen and amen...

Galatians; I & II Thessalonians; I & II Corinthians

The **Galatians** had received Paul's gospel, but they had decided to listen to false teachers and believed them instead. Now they believed that faith in Jesus Christ wasn't sufficient for Salvation. They were believing that they needed to follow all the customs and practices of the Old Law—adding them to the New Covenant. Therefore Paul vehemently rebuked them, telling them that they now have the Spirit; the Law and their flesh could never perfect them—only the Spirit of God.

Paul preached in Thessaloniki, but he was only there a few weeks. After Paul's departure, the time passed and he could bear it no longer—he had to know how they were doing. He sent his first letter with much concern, loving exhortation, and reaffirmation of doctrine. Later, Paul heard reports of **Thessalonians** who thought that the Day of the Lord had come—they even thought that maybe Paul was the one who announced its coming. So Paul sent a second letter to let them know that the Day of the Lord had not come. For their protection, Paul reminded them about what would proceed the Day of the Lord and His coming.

In Corinth were many problems. There were iniquities, divisions, and quarrels over spiritual gifts, resurrection, marriage, and even who got baptized by which apostle! Paul's letter was a mixture of stern rebuke and loving correction. What spurred Paul's second letter to the **Corinthians** was gossip and slander. Certain men had come in to tear down Paul's apostleship and his teaching. He had to make sure the Corinthians stayed faithful and pure to Christ—they were Christ's bride.

ROMANS; COLOSSIANS; EPHESIANS; PHILIPPIANS

Romans is aptly called the Constitution of the Faith. No other epistle more clearly lays out the Gospel—God's sovereignty over, and your responsibility in, salvation.

Colossians shows the all-sufficiency of Jesus Christ. Nothing else is needed. No extra doctrine, no commandments of men, no extra-biblical knowledge or wisdom. For in Christ, Himself, are hidden all the treasures of wisdom and knowledge.

Ephesians stresses the unity of the body of Christ. All were sinners, whether Jew or Gentile, but now we have been reconciled to God—by grace we have been saved!

Philippians is an encouraging letter. Paul is in jail for His faith and chooses to use his own imprisonment to remind those in Philippi that, no matter what situation they are in, they are to persevere—for the joy of the Lord is their strength!

POINT OF DEPTH

If someone gave you a lawnmower for a gift, what would you assume they had in mind? It would be pretty obvious that a mowing job needed to be done and they wanted you to do it! God has given the believers in His Church "lawnmowers" and other pieces of equipment—they are called spiritual gifts and they most definitely have a purpose—to do a job that He wants done! I Corinthians 12-14, Romans 12:1-13, Ephesians 4:1-16, and I Peter 4:10-11 together give us basically all the information we need in order to build a foundation of truth on the subject of Spiritual Gifts.

So many Christians I meet are confused about what spiritual gifts are—in fact they usually don't even know what gift they have been given. Now, what if someone expected me to mow a lawn and had given me a lawnmower to do it with, but I didn't do it because I was confused? Perhaps I might try to do it by hand, an inefficient and clumsy process, or maybe I'd try to get someone else to do it for me, possibly taking that person away from some important task of his own. Either way, the original plan is thwarted. That's why God clearly tells us we are not to be unaware about spiritual gifts. We are responsible to study what the Bible says about spiritual gifts for ourselves in order to be faithful stewards of those gifts. I Corinthians 12:1

The gifts are given for the good of all the brethren for the equipping of the saints for the work of service to the building up of the body of Christ. In other words, God doesn't give us a lawnmower to polish and show off; He gives us a lawnmower to mow the lawn and keep the weeds down, which provides an area for someone to easily walk to his destination. The body is supposed to grow—the bigger it becomes the more work it can do. The gifts are given to serve one another in the body, whereas the body's job is to reach the world and Glorify God through Jesus Christ. I Corinthians 12:7; Ephesians 4:11-12, 14-16; I Peter 4:10-11

The Bible tells us that it is the Holy Spirit Who, according to His will, gives each believer at least one gift at the time of his conversion. I Corinthians 12:7, 11; I Peter 4:10-11 The Lord Jesus Christ then gives a ministry to that person and God, the Father, produces effects from that ministry. Although there are a variety of gifts, ministries, and effects given (sometimes more than one) each believer can be assured of at least one gift to use in one ministry that will produce at least one effect for the Kingdom of God—guaranteed! I Corinthians 12:4-6 Although every believer receives at least one gift there is no one gift that every single member of the body has. I Corinthians 12:29-30

The analogy of a body is used to refer to the church of Jesus Christ when the Bible teaches about spiritual gifts. When we are saved we are placed or positioned, according to God's choice, in the body as a working body part—some as eyes, some as fingers, some as feet, etc. The fingers are expected to do finger things, the eyes are to do jobs that require sight, and the feet are responsible to do the walking. Each part is necessary, useful, and responsible for its own specific tasks. There is no room for jealousy, division, competition, or self-sufficiency. All the gifts are important and are to be used to care for one another. I Corinthians 12:12-27; Romans 12:4-5; Ephesians 4:15-16

Although each gift is important and necessary, God has appointed an order to the gifts: first apostles, second prophets, third teachers, then miracles, then gifts of healings, helps, administrations, and tongues. I Corinthians 12:28 Why this order? Well, what do you notice about the first three gifts? They are all three speaking gifts. I Peter 4:11 We are to earnestly desire that God place believers with speaking gifts in our own church because ultimately the preaching of the Gospel is the most important job of the body! I Corinthians 12:31

We are also told clearly to use the gifts we are given and to stay in the sphere of our gifting. In other words—if you are a foot, then do foot jobs and not hand jobs. If you are a teacher, then teach! If you are a giver, then give! Don't try to be a mouth if you are an ear! You'll be doing someone else's job, and you'll probably be doing it in the flesh, rather than in the Spirit. Romans 12:6-8; I Peter 4:10-11

Spiritual gifts are supernatural abilities given by God to serve the body of Christ. They are not skills you have obtained or natural gifts you were born with. God gave you natural abilities when He formed your physical body. God gave you a new spiritual ability when He created you as a new creature. A listing of the spiritual gifts from I Corinthians, Romans, Ephesians, and I Peter are:

    1. Word of wisdom
    2. Word of knowledge

3. Faith
4. Gifts of healings
5. Effecting of miracles
6. Prophecy
7. Distinguishings of spirits
8. Various kinds of tongues
9. Interpretation of tongues
10. Apostles
11. Teachers
12. Helps
13. Administrations
14. Service
15. Exhortation
16. Giving
17. Leading
18. Mercy
19. Evangelist
20. Pastor/teacher

If you are a believer, you have at least one of these gifts, maybe more. How long will you have it or them? As long as you are here on earth. How long will the gifts last? Are they for today? The gifts are given until we all attain to the unity of the faith and of the knowledge of the Son of God to a mature man—to the measure of the stature which belongs to the fullness of Christ. And that won't be achieved until Christ comes again to take the church from this earth to be with Him forever. The gifts will be around in one form or another until then. Ephesians 4:8-11; I Peter 4:10-11

Point of Depth

Steak and Cauliflower

Why does the world have to hate Christians? It's simple—it is because we smell like cauliflower!

Jesus said that the world (unbelievers) would hate His followers because they hated Him. John 15:19-25 Why did the world hate Jesus? As light, He exposed the sin in them. John 1:4-5 They hated the sin they saw in themselves, but refused to surrender to Him, so they hated Him! With Him around, they couldn't forget what they were truly like. They weren't able to hide their sin from Him or themselves!

The world didn't like the "smell" of Jesus. They liked the smell of the world. Let's say the world smells like steak on an open grill. I can almost catch a whiff of it right now. It smells good! The world likes its own smell. It loves those people and things that smell like steak.

Jesus did *not* smell like the world. They thought He smelled more like cauliflower! And they hated the smell of cauliflower! So, when we become Christians, "little Christs," we become like Jesus. We are conformed into the image of Jesus more and more daily. Romans 8:29; 12:2 So guess what we smell like? That's right! Cauliflower! That's why the world hates us. It's not just because we claim the name of Jesus, but because we are so like Him that we smell like Him. Because we are like Jesus, we will be light to the world. We will remind the world of Jesus, and we will remind the world of their sin! Sinners hate that!

POINT OF DEPTH

A Moth or a Cockroach?

Jesus is the life. Jesus is the light of men. John 1:4-13; Psalm 119:105; Proverbs 6:23
When the light shines in the darkness, the darkness can't stand it!

Have you ever been asleep in the middle of the night and suddenly someone shone a flashlight right in your eyes? If you have, you know that your immediate reaction would not be a pleasant one! The light would hurt your eyes. You would try to cover your eyes to get away from the light!

On the other hand, have you ever been alone at night somewhere when the lights went out unexpectedly? You would have a very positive reaction to someone at that moment if they had a flashlight! The light would show you where you were and where everything else was. It would light your path so you could move. It would make you feel safe!

Let me use the illustration of moths and cockroaches to explain the difference between those who reject the claims of Jesus and will not receive Him and those who believe in His Name and become children of God!

Cockroaches are everywhere when the lights are out, but click that light on and—zoom! They scurry back into their holes where they feel comfortable in their darkness. Moths, on the other hand, are drawn to the light. They want to be near it.

Are you a moth or a cockroach?

3. John 14:1-3; I Thessalonians 4:13-18; I Corinthians 15:51-53; Romans 11:25
When the last appointed Gentile comes to belief in Jesus, the church will be complete. At that time, Jesus will gather His bride, the church, to Himself. The term that has been coined for this event is the "Rapture." He will come in a cloud as far as our sky, then He will catch us up to be with Him all together. The entire event will only take as long as a "twinkle of an eye."

4. II Corinthians 5:9-10; Romans 14:10

Once we, the church, are with Jesus, He will hand out rewards. We will stand individually before the Judgment Seat of Christ. This is *not* a judgment that decides whether we are saved or not! If we are part of the church (because we have believed), then we *are* saved!

This judgment is according to our deeds whether deserving of a reward or worthless. For every bad and worthless deed we did once we believed, we will not receive recompense—no reward—because it is not worth a reward! For every deed that we did in the power of His Holy Spirit, Who indwelt us, we will receive recompense.

I used to be in a 4-H Club. They would have a fair every summer when club members were honored for their quality of work. The baked goods brought were examined very carefully and the best were given ribbons. Even among the ribbons, there were degrees of honor. For instance, a red ribbon was much more desirable than a white ribbon.

There is a beautiful difference in the rewards given to the church. When we are given our rewards, it will simply reflect how mightily He controlled us during our walk on earth so all the honor and all the Glory will go to Him!

5. Revelation 19:6-8; John 3:25-29; Matthew 9:14-15

Jesus, the Lamb, is the church's bridegroom. We will be united, one with Him, for all of eternity. How it speaks of the greatness of God that He would choose even me… to be the bride of His Son.

POINT OF DEPTH

Jewish weddings and marriage customs in biblical times can give us a stunning picture of what is going to happen to us, as the church.

In today's marriages, who usually chooses the bride? The groom does. In biblical times that was not the case; the father of the groom chose the bride. Jesus is the church's bridegroom, and God is His Father. If you are a believer, God chose you in Christ before the foundation of the world. Ephesians 1:4 God, the Father, chose those that would come into the church. God, the Father, chose the bride for His Son, Jesus Christ. Think about the gravity of this as a Christian —you have been chosen to be the bride of the Son of the Creator. *Wow!*

When the father chose the bride, a binding wedding agreement took place. Two cups of wine were sipped while the bride and bridegroom's arms were intertwined with one another. The obvious picture was two becoming one!

The closest thing we have to this agreement would be an engagement. The groom gives the bride an engagement ring after she accepts his proposal. Our engagements, however, are not

entirely binding. Either party of the engagement can break it. In biblical times, however, to be betrothed, or engaged, was almost as serious as the covenant agreement of marriage. To be released from it would require a bill of divorcement; one had to be divorced legally from a betrothal.

Paul betrothed the church at Corinth to Christ as a pure virgin. In the context of a wedding, Paul is saying that the marriage has not yet been consummated, and in the meantime, they need to be completely devoted to Christ. He was afraid they might slip away and have an affair with the world. II Corinthians 11:2-15

You, as a Christian, are betrothed to Christ right now! But you have a time period in which you are waiting for your bridegroom to come and get you. It is during this time period that false teachers, false apostles, and dark angels disguised as angels of light will come in and teach and preach false doctrine and a false gospel to get you to turn away from your devotion to Christ.

As Christians, the world and its ways are "under the ban" to us. We belong to Christ! There is a lot of temptation during our wait. If we are friends of the world, we are adulteresses. James 4:4 The word points to the feminine gender. That is because in God's eyes, whether we are male or female, we are the bride (feminine gender) of Christ, our bridegroom (masculine gender). If a believer becomes friends with the world we are adulteresses, whether we are a man or a woman!

Paul said here that it was he who betrothed the Corinthians to Christ. This made complete sense to the Jews of that day. Many times, after the father would choose the bride for his son, he would send a trusted servant to go and offer his agreement of marriage. That was Paul's job; Paul was the Master's servant! He came and offered those in Corinth an agreement and they accepted!

Usually there were witnesses present to make the agreement binding. We follow this practice in present day wedding ceremonies. States require witnesses to sign marriage certificates. But, do you realize what the invited guests are at a wedding? They are witnesses of the binding agreement that the couple enters into. Do you realize that <u>every time</u> you go to a wedding it makes you a witness before God?

That means that when you hear that the couple is having marital problems, possibly one is thinking of leaving, you don't have the option to hide your head in the sand! You are a witness and you are obligated to hold that couple accountable to the vows they took before God in your presence! It doesn't even matter if they are believers or not. Marriage is an institution for believers and unbelievers. It is a sign of what God's family relationship is like. It is a picture of what God offers us. When you go to a wedding, remember, you are a witness before the LORD and you have a responsibility!

Promises were made at the betrothal. We make promises at the wedding ceremony itself. Perhaps we don't think our commitment becomes serious until the wedding. Just like many so-called Christians don't think their time here on earth is all that serious. They don't consider their actions as being adultery against Jesus. The Jews realized their commitment was serious beginning with the betrothal!

There was a token given at the betrothal. We still do that today by giving a ring as a token of our intention to eventually wed. These tokens weren't always given to the bride. Sometimes they were from family to family.

Usually there was at least one year between the betrothal and the wedding. The reason was that both the bride and the bridegroom had preparations to make.

- The bride had to prepare herself for her bridegroom. She worked on her hair, her skin, her nails, and her skills. She accumulated her dowry from her relatives. And she worked on her wedding garment with her family. She would sew it and prepare it so that when the bridegroom came to get her, she would be ready! And guess what? She didn't know when he would come!

    Do we know when our bridegroom will come to get us, and how do we prepare our wedding garment? How can we, as the bride, ready ourselves for His coming? Revelation 19:7-8 He has told us what to do. It has been given to us to clothe ourselves in righteous acts. As saints, holy ones, those set apart unto Christ, we are to do the will of the Father, which will result in our being clothed in fine linen, bright and clean. The fine linen is woven of righteous deeds.

    When we consider that our wedding garment will be made out of our righteous deeds and that all of our worthless deeds will be burned, we gain insight into what God means when He warns us to not be found naked!

- The bridegroom prepared a place for his bride in his father's house. John 14:2-3 Since he would be adding to the family that would dwell in the home, he would build an addition onto his father's existing home. There he and his bride would dwell as part of the father's family. The son was the one who would construct the addition, not the father. Yet, the father would oversee the work, and it was he who would determine when it was time for the son to go get his bride. When the bride came home to be part of the father's house, she was his child, as well.

    Even Jesus doesn't know the time or hour when He will return to get us. Matthew 24:36; Mark 13:32 Only His Father does. God will tell Jesus when to come and get us. In the meantime, Jesus is preparing a mansion for us in His Father's house!

At the father's appointed time, he would send his son to the home of the bride. The bridegroom and his attendants or friends would go to the house of the bride where she and her attendants were waiting. We still have attendants in present day wedding ceremonies. The bride and her wedding garment needed to be ready because she didn't know when her bridegroom was coming. It usually took place near midnight. This is why the virgins in the parable needed lamps! The virgins in the parable were the attendants of the bride.

The bridegroom would not knock on the door. He would stand outside of the bride's yard. Guess how she would know he was out there? He announced with a trumpet that he was there! He was calling her to come and be with him! When she heard the trumpet, she and her attendants ran out to meet him outside of her home. Are you beginning to see the wonderful ceremony that you and I will be a part of? Jesus is going to come in the clouds with the voice of the archangel and the sound of the trumpet and call us to meet Him in the air! And we will be raised up and meet Him there! I Thessalonians 4:13-18

Once the groom called his bride to be with him, the festivities would continue with the wedding procession. The groom would take all the guests to his home through the streets of the city. On the way home, people joined in the celebration and there was jubilation and instruments and shouts and dancing in the streets. The procession literally became a parade.

The bride and groom would be placed under a canopy where that most important part of the ceremony would take place—the joining of the couple! When does that take place for the church? Where will our "canopy" be? Jesus will take us with Him in the cloud back to heaven to the Father's mansion. Most likely, our actual wedding to Jesus will take place there!

After the wedding ceremony, guests were invited to the marriage supper, or feast. It usually lasted three to seven days, becoming more jubilant and vibrant as the days went on. The marriage supper was the bringing home of an already accredited bride to her husband with whom she had entered into covenant. Blessed are those who are invited to the marriage supper of the Lamb! Revelation 19:9

Philemon; I Timothy; Titus; II Timothy

Onesimus was a slave. He had run away from his Christian master, **Philemon**, but now was with Paul and had come to belief in the Lord himself. Paul sent him back with a letter telling his master, Philemon, to treat Onesimus as a brother.

Paul wrote to **Timothy** and **Titus** directing them how to organize, stabilize, and guide the churches in the cities where he left them, Ephesus and Crete respectively.

At the end of his life, Paul wrote to **Timothy** and urged him to keep the faith. Paul was passing on his apostleship to Timothy because Paul would soon be executed for his faith in the Lord Jesus Christ.

JAMES; I & II PETER; HEBREWS; JUDE; I, II, & III JOHN

James wrote to exhort his brethren. In fact, out of 108 verses, 54 are imperative. He starts by telling them to "consider it all joy" when they "encounter various trials" because the "testing of their faith produces endurance." **James 1:2-3** James goes on to show that if they really are Christians then they will perform deeds that line up with their profession of faith. It is not enough to simply say they are a Christian and move on with life. Why! To not act like a Christian while claiming to be one would be like a man who said, "Go in peace, be warm and be filled," to someone who needed clothing and food, BUT didn't give him the very clothes and sustenance he needed to live! Ergo, that man would be a hypocrite. Thus, the conclusion that James comes to is that "Faith without works is dead!" **James 2:15-17**

Peter wrote two epistles with different thrusts. The first was to instruct and encourage the Jewish believers from Israel who had been scattered abroad by persecution that they keep their behavior excellent among the Gentiles. His second letter was to warn of the bumper-crop of false prophets and teachers that had arisen among them and would continue to multiply until Christ returned.

No one knows who wrote **Hebrews**, so its title is derived from its recipients. This letter was sent to Jews that had believed in Jesus, but after persecution from Jews, Gentiles, and the Roman authority were considering forsaking Christ to escape the torment. Therefore, the author shows how Jesus, Who is the New Covenant, is far greater than angels, Moses, high priests, the Tabernacle, and the Old Covenant. These things were merely a foreshadow of THE SEED. They were not the finality; they were the fountainhead—the promises and pictures of the New Covenant!

Jude's purpose and theme can be summed up in **verse 3**. He exhorts Christians to contend earnestly for the faith, because evil men have crept into the church.

John wrote three epistles with the corresponding theme of, "if we love Him we will keep His commandments." John was very glad to hear of his brethren walking in the truth, "just as we have received commandment to do from the Father." **II John 4**

HISTORY EVENT 28
...THE SEED Returns in Glory!!!

Now let's put **HIStory** of the Jews and **HIStory** of the Church together. Why? Because that's what God does! First, let's remember where we left off with each of them (**Events 27A - Jews and 27B - Church**).

> (**Event 27A - Jews**) The Jews have been going through a horrible time of punishment and purification known as the Great Tribulation. It has lasted 3 ½ years and only one-third of them have survived. They have been crying out to their God for deliverance. Rejoice, O Israel! Your Deliverer is on His way!

> (**Event 27B - Church**) The Church, on the other hand, has been caught up from the face of the earth to be with Jesus. Rewards have been handed out to each individual believer according to the deeds done after he became a believer. The engagement to Jesus has been consummated by marriage. The salvation of Gentile believers has been completed and they are about to witness the salvation of the Jews!

READ AND OBSERVE

1. Matthew 24:29-31; Revelation 19:11-21; Romans 11; Revelation 1:7; Zechariah 12:9-14; 13:8-9
2. Isaiah 11:1-4; 34:5-6; II Thessalonians 2:8; Zechariah 14:2-5
3. Zechariah 12-14; Joel 3:12-17; Matthew 25:31-46

READ AND ANSWER

1. Matthew 24:29-31
What will happen in the heavens after the tribulation of those days?

Then what sign will appear in the sky?

When God refers to the tribes of the earth, He is referring to Israel. What will the Jews see?

What will the Son of Man do?

Revelation 19:11-21
Who is this One Who comes on a white horse?

What is He called?

What does He do?

What does He look like?

What else is His Name called?

Who is following Him?

What is coming from His mouth?

What will He do with it?

What will be His relationship to the nations?

What is written on His robe and on His thigh?

What happens next? Who is invited to what?

What will they eat?

What was assembled to make war with Him?

Who wins?

What happens to the beast and the false prophet?

What happens to all the rest who were fighting against the LORD?

Romans 11:25-27
What needs to happen before all of Israel will be saved?

Who will come?

What will He do for them?

> God will fulfill the promise of the New Covenant that He made through Jeremiah while the Jews were living in captivity in Babylon. This New Covenant was offered to the Jews when Christ came the first time. They did not receive Him and therefore could not enter this Covenant. The New Covenant was then offered to the Gentiles. What we see here is that when all the Gentiles who are going to enter this Covenant have done so, then God will send His Son once more. This time He will save all of Israel who have survived the purification process of the Great Tribulation! Amazing! Read all of Romans 11 to appreciate what He has done for both groups!

Revelation 1:7
When Jesus comes with the clouds, who will see Him?

Who are those who pierced Him?

Who are the tribes?

How will they react to Jesus' coming?

Zechariah 12:9-14
In the Day of the LORD, God will destroy all the nations that come against Jerusalem. What, however, will He do differently with Israel? What will He pour out on them?

What will be their reaction?

How great will be that mourning?

Zechariah 13:8-9
During the Great Tribulation, how many of the Jews living at that time will perish?

What will happen to the other one-third?

What will they do?

Will God hear them? Will He answer them?

What will He declare?

What will they declare?

2. Isaiah 11:1-4
To Whom are **verses 1** and **2** referring to? (Remember God identified the line of David as the one to bring The Seed! Hint: David was the son of Jesse!)

What will He do to the wicked?

Isaiah 34:5-6
What will the sword of the Lord do? (Remember Who it is that will have the sword in His mouth.)

II Thessalonians 2:8
The lawless one referred to here is the antichrist (the prince who is to come prophesied in **Daniel**). What will happen to him?

Who will slay him?

Zechariah 14:2-5
What will God do personally to those nations that have come against Jerusalem during the time of the Great Tribulation?

What will happen when Jesus, The Seed, finally stands on the Mount of Olives just outside of Jerusalem?

Who will be with Him?

3. **Joel 3:12-17**
God will bring all the nations of the earth to the valley of Jehoshaphat. What will He do to them there?

For whom will He be a refuge?

What will His people know for certain?

How is Jerusalem described at that time?

Matthew 25:31-46
When Christ comes triumphantly in all His Glory, where will He sit?

What will He do from there?

Where will He put the sheep?

Where will He put the goats?

What will He say to those on His right?

Why?

What will He say to those on His left?

Why?

Who are these brothers of Jesus? Could they be the Jews who have just gone through the Great Tribulation? Could these people be the ones that helped the Jews during their time of distress? It seems they were. Since Jesus told them to enter into the Kingdom that had been prepared for them and also called them righteous, we know that they were believers. The way to be saved will never change. It always has been, and always will be, faith in Jesus Christ. Obviously, the help these people gave to the Jews (Jesus' brothers) flowed from that faith.

Read and Reason

1. Matthew 24:29-31; Revelation 19:11-21; Romans 11; Revelation 1:7; Zechariah 12:9-14; 13:8-9
After the rapture, after the Judgment Seat of Christ, and after the marriage of the Lamb, Jesus will come again to judge the entire world. His eyes will be a flame of fire and He will have many crowns upon His head. Believers will come with Him. All His armies, including the church, will be on horses behind our Faithful and True Lord of lords and King of kings, Who will judge and wage war in righteousness!

When He arrives He will put an end to the Great Tribulation during which two-thirds of Israel will have perished. But, one-third will have survived the purifying, refining fire of the Tribulation. The Day of His Coming will be a unique day—the sun will be darkened, the moon will not give its light, and the stars will fall from the sky. The powers of the heavens will be shaken. The whole world will see heaven opened up and realize that the Son of God has come to earth!

On the day of Christ's return, every Israelite that is still alive will be saved! All the Jews on earth will see Jesus coming in the clouds in all His Glory. God will pour out a spirit of supplication and grace upon them. Their eyes will be opened, and they will look on The Seed, Jesus, the One they pierced. Then Israel will mourn because her opened eyes will see that Jesus of Nazareth was, and is, her long-awaited Messiah. The Jews will mourn and repent. Then God will cleanse them from their sin and save all of them in *one* day! God will go in to His wife as a husband once again!

When teaching on the passage of **Zechariah 12:9-10**, I use an illustration of one of my own sons. I don't enjoy using this illustration, but it definitely helps us understand what God is saying.

Imagine I hear a sound in the middle of the night and I think it is an intruder. Imagine, too, that I have a gun and I walk out into the living room tensely. I see a shadow and I am sure I am in danger, so I shoot… but when I turn on the lights I see my own son lying dead on the floor! In horror, I weep and mourn over him.

That is exactly what the Jews have done. Jesus came to His Own, but they killed Him. When Jesus comes again in Glory, He will pour out His Spirit on them and their eyes will be opened. They will see Jesus and realize that He was The Seed. Jesus was the Messiah! They will mourn over Him as for an only son…

2. Isaiah 11:1-4; 34:5-6; II Thessalonians 2:8; Zechariah 14:2-5

After opening Israel's eyes, Jesus will slay the antichrist and his followers. All the wicked will be destroyed before Him! The beast and the kings of the earth will actually stand to make war against Him. They won't be standing long. Christ will bring the antichrist to an end. The beast and the false prophet will be seized and thrown alive into the lake of fire for all eternity. God will call the birds of the sky to assemble for the great supper of God—the flesh of all those slain.

Jesus will descend and return to the earth in Bozrah of Edom. (Remember back to the **POD** in **Event 27A** regarding Petra? Well, guess where Bozrah is? Edom is present day Jordan!) He will save Israel and advance northward through Judah and on to Jerusalem.

When Jesus gets to Jerusalem He will stand on the Mount of Olives and it will be split down the middle from east to west. The whole topography of Jerusalem will change in that one terrible and awesome day.

3. Zechariah 12-14; Joel 3:12-17; Matthew 25:31-46

God will bring all the nations to the valley of Jehoshaphat where He will sit on His glorious throne and judge them. Their judgment will be His decision and it will be a righteous and true decision! He will separate the sheep (righteous) from the goats (unrighteous). The sheep on His right side will inherit the Kingdom prepared for them from the foundation of the world. The goats on His left side will be sent into the lake of fire for all of eternity.

Revelation

The last book of the New Testament and of the Bible was written by the apostle John on the island of Patmos; he was on the island as a prisoner because of the Word of God and the Testimony of Jesus. John tells of a series of visions that he has on the Lord's day. Going from one scene to the next, these visions make up the Revelation of Jesus Christ (not the revelation "about" Jesus, but the revelation which belongs to Jesus; He is the One who reveals these things).

It begins with seven messages for the seven churches that are in Asia (Asia Minor). After commending, encouraging, but mostly rebuking the seven churches in the first three chapters, John is then taken up in the Spirit to the heavenly throne room and sees with his own eyes the things which must soon take place. A scroll with seven seals is slowly opened before John's eyes by the Lion of Judah, the Root of David, The Seed, the One Who has overcome—Jesus. First, the Lamb opens the seven seals one by one, the seventh of which contains the trumpets. The trumpets are blown one by one, the seventh of which is the seven bowls of the wrath of God. When the last bowl is poured out on the earth the wrath of God is finished.

There is a plethora of events that take place rapidly: Babylon, the arch-nemesis of Jerusalem will be judged and destroyed, the marriage supper of the Lamb and His spotless bride will take place. Jesus Christ, The Seed returns in all His Glory and annihilates those assembled to make war against Him. He will seize the false prophet and the beast (antichrist) and throw them alive into the lake of fire. Satan will be held captive in the abyss for 1,000 years. The martyrs from the Tribulation will come to life and reign with Christ for those 1,000 years, after which Satan will be released and deceive the nations to attack Jerusalem again. God will devour them all with fire and the devil will be thrown into the lake of fire to be tormented day and night forever and ever! God will judge the rest of the dead (unbelievers) at His great white throne; heaven and earth flee away; the sea and death and Hades give up their dead for judgment and all are thrown into the now vastly inhabited lake of fire.

Then John saw a new heaven, a new earth, and in all its Glorious contrast to the old—the new Jerusalem with those whose names are written in the Lamb's book of life.

HIStory Event 29
...THE SEED Reigns!

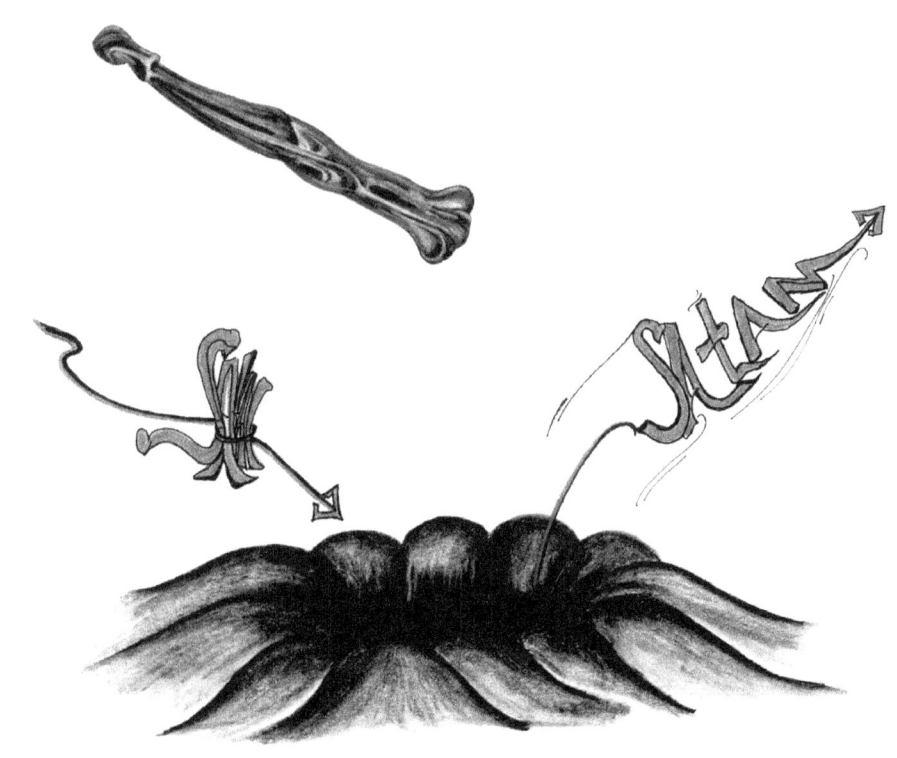

Read and Observe

1. Revelation 20:1-3, 7
2. Isaiah 2:1-4; Revelation 20:4-6; 2:26-27; 5:9-10
3. Zechariah 14:16-21

Read and Answer

1. Revelation 20:1-3, 7
When Christ comes and defeats the nations that are gathered against Jerusalem, He will throw the beast and the false prophet into the lake of fire. That is not where Satan goes, at least not yet! What happens to Satan at this time?

Who binds him?

How long will he be bound in the abyss?

What isn't he allowed to do during those 1,000 years?

What happens to him at the end of the 1,000 years?

2. Isaiah 2:1-4
Where will be the most important place on earth?

Who will come there?

What will they learn there?

What will come from there?

What is another name for Jerusalem?

What are swords and spears used for?

What are plowshares and pruning hooks used for?

Why will there no longer be a need for swords and spears?

For how long?

Revelation 20:4-6
Judgment (authority to judge) will be given to certain people. Who are they?

With whom will they reign?

Revelation 2:26-27
Who else will reign with Christ?

Who will they rule?

How will Christ rule?

Revelation 5:9-10
What did Christ's blood purchase for God?

What did He make them into?

Where will they reign?

3. Zechariah 14:16-21
What will the nations, which once had gathered against Jerusalem, do?

What Feast will be celebrated?

Who is this King?

What will happen if a family or a nation does not travel to Jerusalem and worship King Jesus during His reign in Jerusalem?

What will be inscribed on the bells of the horses in Jerusalem?

How will the cooking pots in the LORD'S house be like the bowls before the altar?

What will be Holy to the LORD?

Will absolutely everything be Holy to the LORD?

I must ask you this now—are you... Holy to the LORD?

READ AND REASON

1. Revelation 20:1-3, 7
Satan is bound for 1,000 years by an angel. It doesn't take hundreds of God's angels to bind Satan. It doesn't even take the strongest angel God can find. It just takes "*an*" angel! God is in control of all. He is the LORD of hosts! Jehovah Sabaoth! The LORD Who fights our battles!

2. Isaiah 2:1-4; Revelation 20:4-6; 2:26-27; 5:9-10
Jesus rules over the entire earth with a rod of iron for 1,000 years. His saints and holy ones will rule with Him during this Millennial Reign. During Christ's Millennial Reign over the earth, many people will go to Jerusalem. His law will go forth from Zion. The nations will not be at war with one another ever again.

3. **Zechariah 14:16-21**

All the nations of the earth will celebrate the Feast of Booths annually in Jerusalem where they will worship the King—King Jesus, the LORD of hosts. If any family or nation decides foolishly to stay home rather than traveling to Jerusalem to worship the King, their land will receive no rain whatsoever.

In an incredible picture of holiness to the LORD, every single item will have one purpose and one purpose only—that of the LORD's use. *All things* will be *only* for the LORD's use—nothing will be used for any other thing. Do you see it? No one will use anything for themselves—everything will be rotating around the LORD alone—because we will all be focusing on His Glory and worshiping Him!!! No other purpose!!! He is worthy!!!

HIStory Event 30
...The Last Rebellion Against GOD

Read and Observe

1. Revelation 20:7-9
2. Revelation 20:10

Read and Answer

1. Revelation 20:7-9
What will happen when the 1,000 years are completed?

When he comes out what will he do?

How many will be deceived and follow him?

Where will they gather?

What is the name of this "beloved city"?

What will happen to them before they are even able to wage war against Jerusalem?

2. Revelation 20:10
What happens to the devil when the others are devoured by fire from heaven?

Who will be with him?

What will happen to them day and night forever and ever?

Read and Reason

1. Revelation 20:7-9

At the end of the 1,000 years, Satan is released for a short time. He quickly deceives nations in all four corners of the earth! This is amazing to me! People have been living on earth and have seen the Glory of Jesus Christ, the Lord, yet because the depravity of man is so acute, Satan will be able to deceive them into thinking they actually have a chance to wage battle against the Son of God and win! How completely foolish! How utterly blind they are!

So Satan gathers the nations to battle in the war of Gog and Magog. There are so many of them that the Bible describes their number as being like the sand of the seashore! Satan brings them up to the broad plain of the earth and surrounds the camp of the saints and Jerusalem.

However, God has no intention of wasting any time on these ridiculous men. He consumes them with fire from heaven and simply devours them. There is no war, just defeat for Satan and his minions and victory for God and His saints!

2. Revelation 20:10

Satan is then thrown into the lake of fire and brimstone to be tormented day and night forever and ever. The beast (the antichrist) and the false prophet already dwell there as permanent residents. The unholy trinity (Satan, the antichrist, and the false prophet) is united once again and the goats are their roommates!

394

HIStory Event 31
...GOD's Great White Throne Judgment and the Lake of Fire

Read and Observe

1. **Revelation 20:11-15**
2. **II Peter 3:7, 10-11; Psalm 102:25-26; Matthew 24:35; Hebrews 1:10-12; Revelation 20:11; 21:1**

Read and Answer

1. **Revelation 20:11-15**
What does John the prophet see?

Who is on the throne?

What did earth and heaven do in His presence?

Where did they go?

Who was standing before the throne?

What was opened?

Then what was opened?

What was that book called?

What happened to the spiritually dead who were standing before the throne?

What was written in some of the books?

What did they wish was written in the book of life?

If anyone's name was not found in the book of life, they were spiritually dead. Where were they thrown?

What else was thrown into the lake of fire?

What is another name for the lake of fire?

2. II Peter 3:7, 10-11
God promised mankind that He would not destroy the earth with water ever again after the flood of Noah's time. But He didn't say He wouldn't destroy it by fire! When will the earth be destroyed by fire?

What else happens to ungodly men during this time period?

How will the Day of the LORD come?

What will happen to the heavens and the earth during that time?

Psalm 102:25-26
What will be the end for the heavens?

Matthew 24:35
What will happen to both heaven and earth?

Hebrews 1:10-12
Who created the earth and the heavens?

Who will destroy the earth and the heavens?

What will happen to the earth and heavens?

    1.

    2.

    3.

    4.

What will happen to the LORD?

Revelation 20:11
During the Day of the LORD, when the LORD judges the spiritually dead, what will happen to earth and heaven?

Where will they go?

Revelation 21:1
What happened to the first heaven and the first earth?

READ AND REASON

1. Revelation 20:11-15
God will judge the dead at the Great White Throne Judgment. These spiritually dead are judged according to their deeds which have been written down in one of God's books. This Judgment determines the severity of punishment for them. Then, once their address in the lake of fire is appointed, they will be thrown into the second death. Whew!!! It's done! Just think of it! Evil men, gone forever!!!

2. II Peter 3:7, 10-11; Psalm 102:25-26; Matthew 24:35; Hebrews 1:10-12; Revelation 20:11; 21:1
During the Day of the LORD (a period of time starting with the Great Tribulation and extending through the end of our universe) God will destroy the earth! The heavens will pass away with a

roar and the elements will be destroyed with intense heat, and the earth and its works will be burned up!

And yet, quite the opposite will be true of the LORD! The earth and the heavens will perish, but God will remain! The earth and the heavens will become old and withered and changed, but God will always be the same! The earth and the heavens will be destroyed, but the years of the LORD will never come to an end!!!

POINT OF CONNECTION

Read Genesis 9:8-17. God promised Noah and all his descendants after him (that includes you and me) and all flesh and even every living creature of the earth that He would *not* destroy the earth again by flood. However, He didn't say He wouldn't destroy the earth again. He promises us later on in His Word that He will destroy the earth once more, not by water this time, but by fire. II Peter 3:10

God is faithful to His Word. He has not destroyed the earth again by flood. God is faithful to His Word. He will destroy the earth by fire! You can count on it!!! Hebrews 12:26-27

HIStory Event 32
...Beyond the Horizon of Eternity GOD Exists Forever in His Glorious Glory!!!

Read and Observe

1. Revelation 21-22

Read and Answer

1. Revelation 21-22
According to John's vision, what would exist after God judged the spiritually dead and after the heavens and the earth perished?

Was there a sea on this new earth?

What did he see coming down from heaven?

Where would God now dwell?

Who will He be among?

What will He do for them?

What will be no more?

Why?

Who will inherit these wonderful things?

Where will the cowardly, the unbelieving, the abominable, murderers, immoral persons, sorcerers, idolaters, and all liars go?

What is that existence called?

When the angel tells John he is going to show him the bride, the wife of the Lamb, what does he show him?

Where will the church, the bride of Christ, live for all of eternity?

Where is this city?

Who else lives in this city with the church? (Hint: The church is Jesus' wife and she will live with Him. God has a wife too. Think about where she'll live.)

Describe the new Jerusalem.

Will there be a Temple in it?

Who is the new Jerusalem's Temple?

Will there be a sun or a moon?

Why not?

    1.

    2.

Think for a moment. The new Jerusalem is on a great and high mountain on the new earth which comes down out of the new heaven. This city is where God, Himself, and the Lamb, Jesus Christ, live with their wives. The Glory of God is shining in the city as well as the light of Christ. They illuminate the city so brightly there is no need for a sun or a moon. Their brilliant light illumines the entire earth as well. Who is walking on the new earth in the overflow of Jerusalem's light?

Who will bring their glory into Jerusalem from the earth?

Will there be nighttime?

Will anything unclean ever come into the new Jerusalem?

Will anyone who practices abomination and lying ever come into the new Jerusalem?

Who will be in the new Jerusalem?

The throne of God is in the new Jerusalem. What comes from the throne of God?

Where does the river flow?

What is on either side of this river of the water of life?

Do you remember reading about this tree of life? Where did it used to grow?

Does this tree bear fruit?

What kind?

How often?

What are the leaves of the tree for?

Where are the nations?

How long will God and the Lamb reign?

In light of what will happen, what does God urge all readers of the Bible to do?

Besides heeding the words of the Bible, what else are we commanded to do?

When The Seed returns, He will return quickly. What will He bring with Him?

How will the handing out of rewards be determined?

Who is this God?

    1.

    2.

    3.

Who enters by the gates into the city?

Who is outside?

What is the Spirit saying?

What is the bride saying?

What should the one who hears say to others?

Who is the one who is being invited to come?

READ AND REASON

1. Revelation 21-22

When God destroys this present earth and its heavens with fire, He will show us a new heaven and a new earth. It will be qualitatively new, something never seen before. This is our future, O believers in the Lord Jesus Christ!

The nation of Israel will live forever with her husband, God, in the new Jerusalem. The church, as well, will live forever with Christ in that wonderful city which will come down from heaven from God, made ready as a bride adorned for her husband.

God will dwell with man. He will wipe away every tear from every eye. There will no longer be any death or mourning or crying or pain.

POINT OF DEPTH

Before we go any further, I want you to do something for me, and for yourself! Stop right now and think about where you will spend all of eternity. (I am assuming you are a Christian.) Picture all the details in your mind. Write it down or verbalize it to someone else. You may be surprised at how that picture is supposed to look once we observe what God has said in His Word.

I am going to ask you some questions to help you visualize your thoughts. Answer each one in your mind before going to the next question.
1. Will you be living in heaven or on earth?
2. What will your feet be touching?
3. What will you do with your time each day?
4. Will you live in a house with your family?
5. Will there be houses?
6. Will there be clouds around you?

Now, think with me for a moment. Where is this new Jerusalem?
- It's on a great and high mountain that will be on the new earth. It is not *in* heaven. It comes down *from* heaven to earth.

Answer this: Where will Jesus and God live forever and ever?
- They will live in this new Jerusalem on the new earth.

One more question. Where will the saints live forever and ever?
- We will live in the city of the new Jerusalem with God and Jesus forever and ever.

Do you see it? How many times have you thought about living for all of eternity in heaven? I know I have. It's what I was taught all through many years of Sunday School. But will I live in heaven, or will I live on the new earth, in the new Jerusalem with my Bridegroom, Jesus Christ?

If I live in heaven for all of eternity, I won't be with Jesus, because He will be living in the new Jerusalem on the new earth! We will rule and reign together with Him from there. We will serve Him day and night, contrary to the popular opinion that we will be lazing around on clouds sipping lemonade!

And what about your house? Have you hoped that your mansion would be close to a dear friend's mansion? Remember what we learned from the Jewish wedding customs. Our Father has a mansion which is being prepared for us to live in. Granted, we may have our own separate "apartment," but we will not live isolated from Him or from the rest of the church or from Israel. We are all going to live in His mansion as one big holy family!

Are you disappointed? Don't be! This is what He has planned for those He has loved so dearly throughout the ages. This is where He will dwell forever and ever with those that are so very precious to Him! I'm excited! I can't wait! Eternity is going to be great!

I want to give you some measurement statistics that will help you to understand how grand the actual city will be. These have been taken from various sources.

The city seems to be laid out as a square. Its length, width, and height are equal, each measuring 1,500 miles, which seems to indicate a cube. Fifteen hundred miles equals 7,920,000 feet. That is enormous. Just to give you an idea, from north to south, it would cover the area from the Great Lakes to the Gulf of Mexico. From east to west, it would spread from the Pacific coast to the Mississippi River. The highest you've probably been is in an airplane which can fly at a height of around 37,000 feet. 37,000 feet is only 7 miles. The new Jerusalem will be 214 times higher.

Now, let's contemplate the size of the new Jerusalem in regards to living space. If the city were a mammoth apartment building, there would need to be 528,000 stories! Each floor would have a 15-foot ceiling! That's 2,250,000 square miles of footage on each floor! (Can you imagine the cost of carpeting!!!) There would be 1,188,000,000,000 square miles in the whole thing! Wow, oh wow!!! That's quite a place!!!

There have been over 100 billion people that have lived and died since Adam's life. If *all* the people that ever lived were to inhabit this place, *each* person would have almost 12 square miles! But, all the people that ever lived will *not* inhabit this place. Jesus said there would be few who would. Can you just imagine?

The city, the new Jerusalem, sits on a great and high mountain. There is no Temple in the city because the Lord God the Almighty is its Temple!

There will be no sun and moon because the Glory of God illumines the city, and the Lamb is its lamp. All the light in the city comes from God and Jesus. In fact, all the light on the earth comes from God and Jesus. The nations on the earth will be able to see where they are walking because of the light from Jerusalem. That is a lot of light! And the light is endlessly shining. There isn't even going to be nighttime.

Just stop and savor this fabulous thought! There is no need for a sun or a moon to shine on the earth because God is there *in all His Blazing Glory*! The Light is not coming from the sun, or the stars, or the moon. There are none! Yet, there is Light because there *is* God!

What happens inside of Jerusalem? We don't know everything. God hasn't chosen to reveal everything. But we do know this: the kings of the nations on the new earth will come into the city and bring their glory and honor into it.

Why are the kings coming to Jerusalem? And who are their nations? Well, the nations are not the "unrighteous" because they have all been thrown into the lake of fire. The nations also are not the bride of Christ, the church, because the bride *is* the city of new Jerusalem. The bride and the nations are two different groups. It follows that the righteous people that come out of the 1,000 year reign make up the kings and the nations.

We only know about one street in Jerusalem. Revelation 22:2 talks about *the* street of the city, singular, not plural. That sounds logical; after all, we only know about one mansion, the Father's! So why would we need more than one street?

Let's look at what else is on this street. First of all, in the center of everything, we have the throne of God and of the Lamb. There is a river of the water of life, clear as crystal, coming from the throne of God and of the Lamb right in the middle of the street.

On either side of the street is the Tree of Life. We only know about one Tree of Life and somehow, miraculously, it is on both sides of the street! Amazing! It bears twelve kinds or crops of fruit monthly. Either it has twelve different types of fruit that it bears or it replenishes itself twelve times a year. Interesting!

And here's another really interesting part. The leaves of the Tree of Life are for the healing of the nations. Do the kings receive leaves when they come into the city for their nations at home? Or perhaps, since we never read of the sheep that enter the Millennial Reign ever receiving a new, eternal body, yet they are to live in the everlasting Kingdom prepared for them since the foundation of the earth, maybe they will use these leaves to heal themselves so they can live forever? Matthew 25:34

Here is where God ends His Bible.
Therefore, here is where I, too, must end.

I have faithfully tried to tell HIS STORY,
HIS ETERNALLY GLORIOUS STORY—
at least the part of HIS STORY that He has revealed to us.

But HIS STORY will continue
forever and ever and ever and ever,
way "Beyond the Horizon"
of our minds' ability to compute time…

GOD WILL EXIST FOREVER IN HIS GLORIOUS GLORY!!!

I pray you will believe in THE SEED and repent
before the sands of time run out—
before Jesus comes again. By then it will be too late.
The offer for His Life (THE SEED) is available now—
but that offer won't last forever…

(Compare hourglasses on front and back covers.)

HIStory

**From Event to Event
The Bible is One Story—**

Appendix

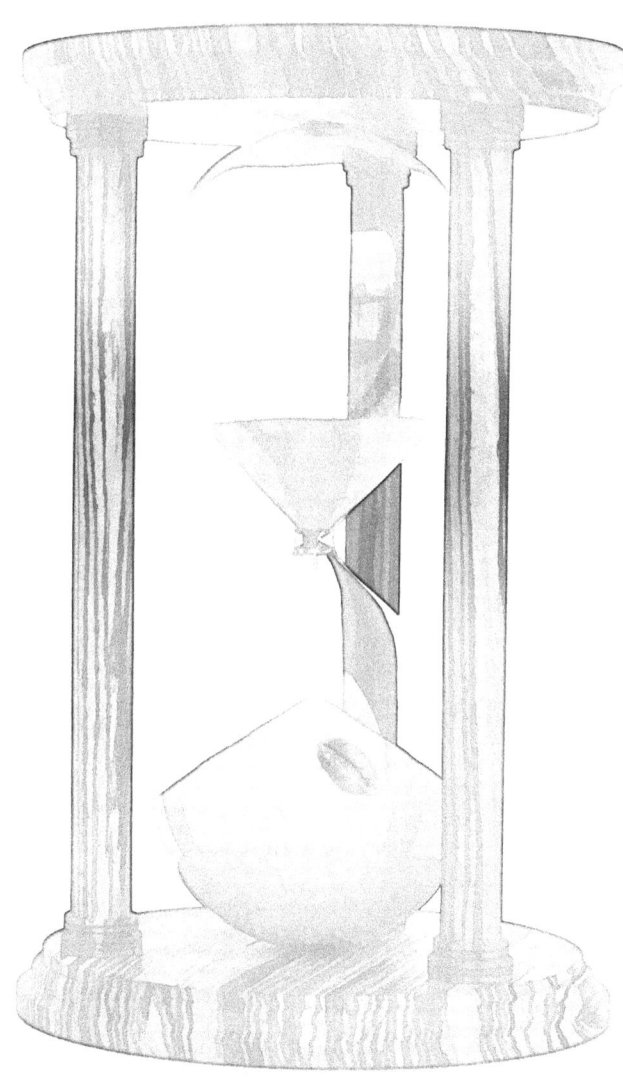

WORDCenterMinistries.org

HIStory

Lesson Plan for Eleven Week Course

WEEK 1
Event 1 …Before the Beginning GOD Exists in His Glorious Glory!!!
Event 2 …In the Beginning GOD Creates so His Glory will be Seen!
Event 3 …Man Sins and Dies Spiritually – GOD Promises THE SEED to Bring Spiritual Life!

WEEK 2
Event 4 …GOD Destroys the Distorted Image of His Glory
Event 5 …GOD Creates and Scatters the Nations
Event 6 …GOD Creates the Nation of Israel

WEEK 3
Event 7 …GOD Sends His Nation, Israel, to a Foreign Land
Event 8 …GOD Delivers Israel
Event 9 …GOD Gives His Law to Israel

WEEK 4
Event 10 …GOD Brings the Nation of Israel into The Land
Event 11 …GOD Sends Judges to Rule Over Israel
Event 12 …Israel Rejects GOD as her King

WEEK 5
Event 13 …GOD Splits the Kingdom of Israel in Two
Event 14 …GOD Sends Prophets to the Northern Kingdom of Israel (Israel)
Event 15 …GOD Sends Assyria to Take the Northern Kingdom into Captivity

WEEK 6
Event 16 …GOD Sends Prophets to the Southern Kingdom of Israel (Judah)
Event 17 …GOD Sends Babylon to Take the Southern Kingdom into Captivity

WEEK 7
Event 18 …GOD Promises a New Covenant…THE SEED!
Event 19 …GOD Brings Israel Back to The Land
Event 20 …GOD Calls Israel Back to Himself…Then He is Silent…

WEEK 8
Event 21 …GOD Sends THE PROMISED SEED!!!
Event 22 …GOD Anoints THE SEED!

WEEK 9
Event 23 …THE SEED Dies
Event 24 …THE SEED is Buried
Event 25 …THE SEED Lives and is Seen!
Event 26 …THE SEED Returns to GOD

WEEK 10
Event 27A …The Nation of Israel – Set Aside and Purified Until THE SEED Returns
Event 27B …The Church – THE SEED Sends His HOLY SPIRIT as Promised
Event 28 …THE SEED Returns in Glory!!!

WEEK 11
Event 29 …THE SEED Reigns!
Event 30 …The Last Rebellion Against GOD
Event 31 …GOD's Great White Throne Judgment and the Lake of Fire
Event 32 …Beyond the Horizon of Eternity GOD Exists Forever in His Glorious Glory!!!

HIStory

LESSON PLAN FOR NINE MONTH COURSE

MONTH 1
Event 1 …Before the Beginning GOD Exists in His Glorious Glory!!!
Event 2 …In the Beginning GOD Creates so His Glory will be Seen!
Event 3 …Man Sins and Dies Spiritually – GOD Promises THE SEED to Bring Spiritual Life!
Event 4 …GOD Destroys the Distorted Image of His Glory

MONTH 2
Event 5 …GOD Creates and Scatters the Nations
Event 6 …GOD Creates the Nation of Israel
Event 7 …GOD Sends His Nation, Israel, to a Foreign Land
Event 8 …GOD Delivers Israel

MONTH 3
Event 9 …GOD Gives His Law to Israel
Event 10 …GOD Brings the Nation of Israel into The Land
Event 11 …GOD Sends Judges to Rule Over Israel

MONTH 4
Event 12 …Israel Rejects GOD as her King
Event 13 …GOD Splits the Kingdom of Israel in Two
Event 14 …GOD Sends Prophets to the Northern Kingdom of Israel (Israel)
Event 15 …GOD Sends Assyria to Take the Northern Kingdom into Captivity
Event 16 …GOD Sends Prophets to the Southern Kingdom of Israel (Judah)

MONTH 5
Event 17 …GOD Sends Babylon to Take the Southern Kingdom into Captivity
Event 18 …GOD Promises a New Covenant…THE SEED!
Event 19 …GOD Brings Israel Back to The Land
Event 20 …GOD Calls Israel Back to Himself…Then He is Silent…

MONTH 6
Event 21 …GOD Sends THE PROMISED SEED!!!
Event 22 …GOD Anoints THE SEED!

MONTH 7
Event 23 …THE SEED Dies
Event 24 …THE SEED is Buried
Event 25 …THE SEED Lives and is Seen!
Event 26 …THE SEED Returns to GOD

MONTH 8
Event 27A …The Nation of Israel – Set Aside and Purified Until THE SEED Returns
Event 27B …The Church – THE SEED Sends His HOLY SPIRIT as Promised

MONTH 9
Event 28 …THE SEED Returns in Glory!!!
Event 29 …THE SEED Reigns!
Event 30 …The Last Rebellion Against GOD
Event 31 …GOD's Great White Throne Judgment and the Lake of Fire
Event 32 …Beyond the Horizon of Eternity GOD Exists Forever in His Glorious Glory!!!

Event 2 ...In the Beginning God Creates so HIS Glory will be Seen!

Quiz

A. For how many days did God create?
   Six

B. On what day did God make man?
   Six

C. On what day did God make light?
   One

D. Out of what did God make the earth?
   Water (II Peter 3:5)

E. Who did God tell not to eat from the Tree of the Knowledge of Good & Evil?
   Adam. Eve was not even alive yet! (Although we know she was told eventually either by Adam or God)

F. What was it that God named "night"?
   Darkness

G. On what day did God create the waters?
   Before any of the days of creation

H. What did God do to the waters?
   Separated them

I. What was it that God named "earth"?
   Dry land

J. Where did the trees and the vegetation on the earth come from?
   From the ground/dry land

K. What did God call the expanse?
   Heaven

L. What was the expanse for? What did it do?
   Separated the waters above the expanse from the waters below the expanse

M. What did God tell the sea monsters to do?
   Be fruitful and multiply and fill the waters of the seas

N. What is the key repeated word in **Genesis 1** and **2**?
   GOD

O. Name five things over which man was to rule.
   1. **Fish of the sea**

2. **Birds of the sky**
   3. **Cattle**
   4. **All the earth**
   5. **Every creeping thing that creeps on the earth**

P. What did God say was "very good"?
   All that He had made (This comment was not directed only at man.)

Q. What did God give man to eat?
   1. **Every plant yielding seed that was on the surface of all the earth**
   2. **Every tree which had fruit yielding seed**

R. Did God create the heavens and the earth? Or did He make them? Was it a process?
   God created the heavens and the earth *and* God made them. It was a process.

S. Which did God make first—Adam or the Garden of Eden?
   Adam. God planted the Garden of Eden after He made man and then placed Adam there. Eve was not alive yet.

T. Why did God make Eve?
   Because it was not good for Adam to be alone; there was not a suitable helper for him

U. Did God create the animals or make them?
   God made the animals (out of the dry land)

V. Who named all the fish?
   The Bible doesn't tell us

W. Why are there weeds?
   Because of Adam's sin, God cursed the ground and caused weeds to grow

X. How did Adam become like God when he sinned?
   He knew the difference between good and evil. God did not want man to be like Him in this area because God wanted man to be dependent upon Him.

Y. Why did God send Adam out from the Garden of Eden?
   So he wouldn't eat from the Tree of Life and live forever in the condition that he was in (a state of death—separation from God because of his sin)

Event 3 ...Man Sins and Dies Spiritually – GOD Promises THE SEED to Bring Spiritual Life!

Sketch of Genesis 3:15

"And I will put enmity
between you and the woman,

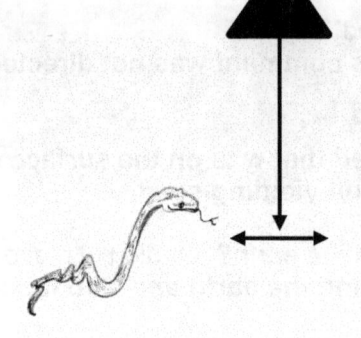

And (enmity) between your seed and her Seed;

He (her Seed) shall bruise you
on the head,

And you shall bruise Him on the heel."

f

When you put them all together you have a picture of **Genesis 3:15** ready to be used to explain this Truth to someone!

Event 6 …GOD Creates The Nation of Israel

Map of Middle East

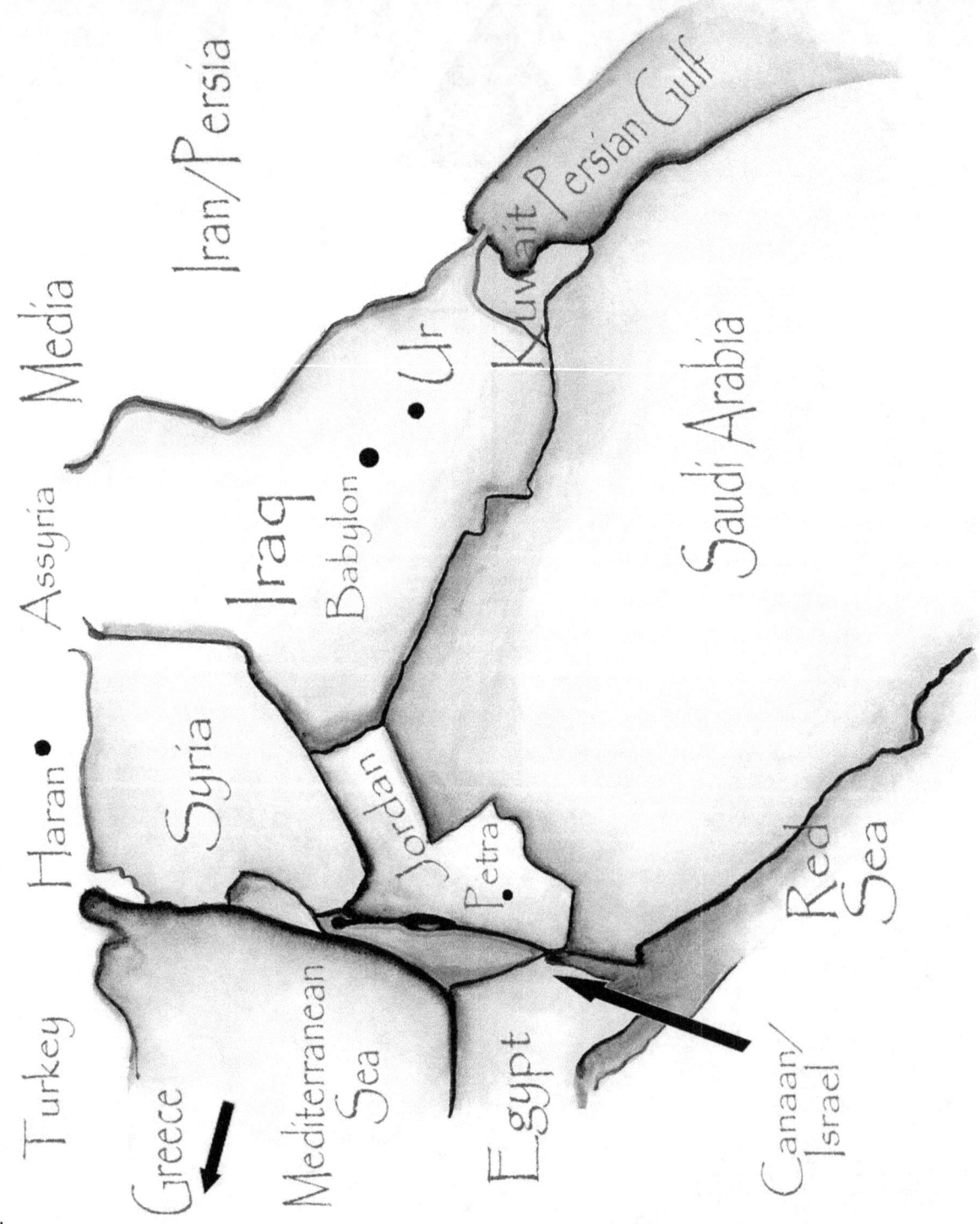

h

Event 22 …GOD Anoints THE SEED!

Map of the Land of Israel

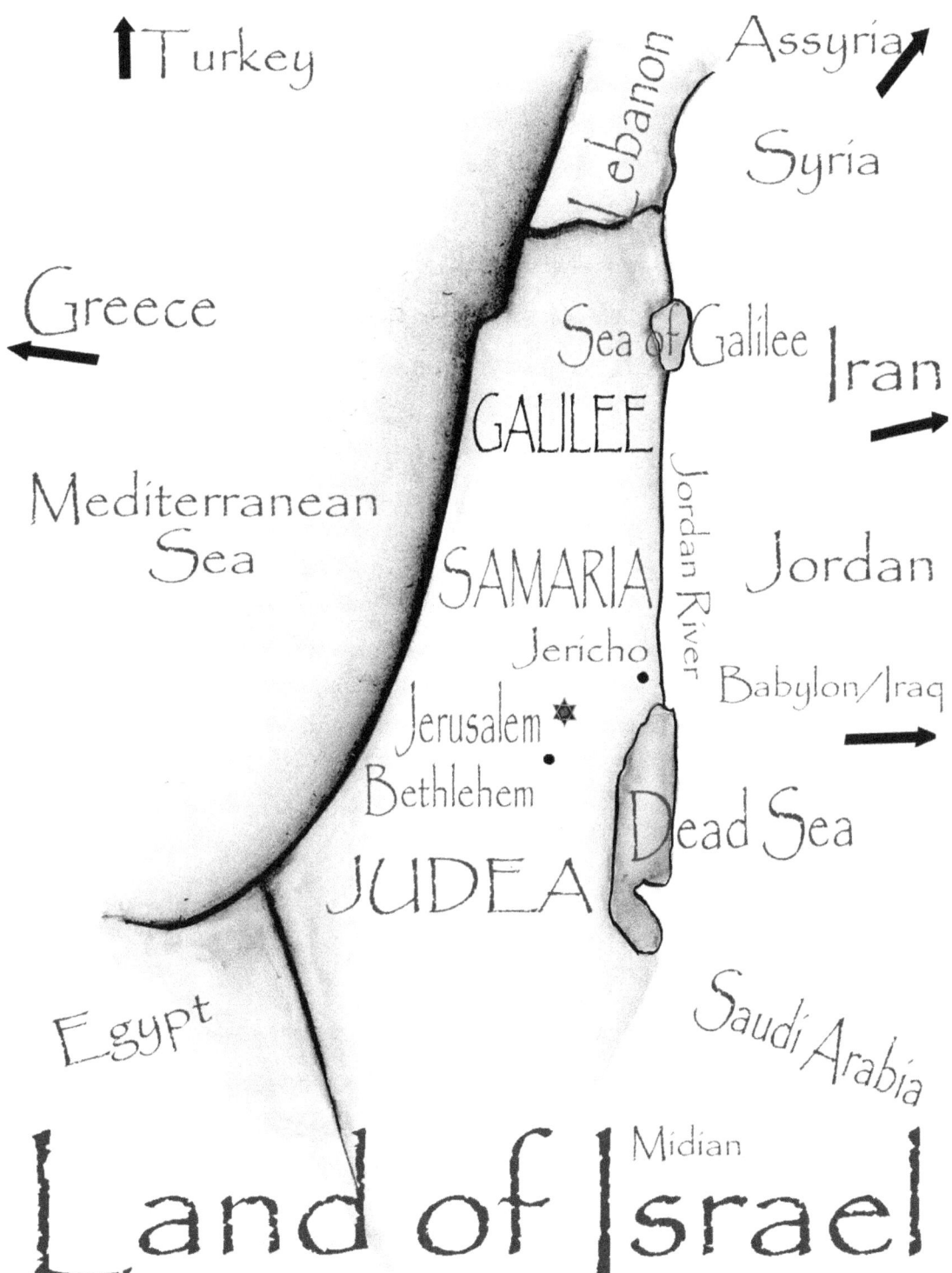

HISTORY for me...

When my oldest son was only 10 or so he asked me, "Did Jesus raise Himself from the dead or did God raise Jesus from the dead?" I assumed Jesus raised Himself from the dead. After all–if God raised Jesus, then what would that prove? God could have raised anybody, right? When I looked it up in the Bible and saw that it was God Who raised Jesus, I didn't understand...

- I realized that I had believed for most of my life that Jesus brought Himself back to life. I thought bringing Himself back to life somehow proved He was God. No one else could do that, I figured.

- I even thought that Jesus dying for our sins was the ultimate sacrifice → i.e. the ultimate sacrifice Jesus could make for me to prove He loved the world (like giving up something).

- I thought Jesus died for me (again, proving that He loved me). But—*Jesus died <u>instead</u> of me!!!*

- I didn't understand it was a sacrifice—a (blood) offering to God!

- I knew He paid for our sins → but I didn't understand *Who* He was paying...or *why!*

I grew up inside the church; I was very active in all of its programs and functions. I dedicated my life to full-time Christian service when I was in junior high school. My husband and I became full-time missionaries during the 90's. Everyone who knew us thought we were some of the "best Christians" around. How wrong they were! We lived righteously—according to the world. We were set apart to the Christian lifestyle. But there was something unaccountably missing. God's Spirit was not living inside of us—we were not saved. We, of course, didn't know that. Everyone assured us that we were Christians, and in fact, looked to us for direction and leadership for their own "Christian" lifestyle.

It wasn't until 1993, after 30 years of trying my best to please God, that I finally met Him. I met Him *after* I had been a full-time missionary for years! You may be wondering how that could possibly be. Others have wondered, too. I wondered myself. And yet the Bible is clear that many who think they are saved are not! Many will say to Him, "Lord, Lord" and He will respond, "I never knew you!" How horrific and tragic!

Please take the time to examine yourself and make sure you are in the faith. It could make the difference between life and death. You may be where I was—if you are, you will find *Him* in His Word through His Spirit! You will find Him when you search for Him with all your heart! Make your calling and election sure!

God is Holy. Men are not. Nothing can be in His presence that is not holy. Because He is Holy, He must punish all ungodliness and all unrighteousness. That means He must punish men. That means He must punish me, and He must punish you. The punishment for not being holy is death.

But because He doesn't want us to die (that is, to be separated from Him forever) He has made a way to save us from His wrath. I took that way. I realized that before God, I was filthy, I was a sinner, I was unrighteous and unholy even though I had always seen myself as a pretty nice person, a good person, even a righteous person.

I had grown up in a church and done all the "right things" and I thought I was safe. I thought I was a Christian, but I was wrong. I had never surrendered my life to Him. I was still running my life. I thought I was doing a pretty good job of it too, but as long as I was calling the shots in my life, He wasn't my God—I was my god.

I started studying the Bible, not just reading it, but really studying it, and I saw God for the first time. I got to know Him. I found out about Him. Yes, I saw that He was a God of "love," but I also saw that He was a God Who was *Holy!* He could not just overlook my unholiness.

Let me explain what holiness is. "Holy" means to be set apart unto something. God is *Holy* so God is set apart unto Himself. If things or people that were different from Him were to dwell with Him, He wouldn't be holy anymore.

God's character is Who He is. He is righteous, loving, faithful, long-suffering, wrathful, perfect, just, unchangeable, etc. Let me give you an illustration. Think of there being a big "bubble" around God. Inside the bubble there is nothing but God, Himself, with all His Own characteristics. He is Holy, set apart unto Himself. He wants man to be inside the bubble with Him, but man can't because man has characteristics that are not like God. Man is unrighteousness, unloving, unfaithful, not long-suffering, etc.

To solve the problem, there are two possibilities.
1) God could become unholy and be like man—leave His bubble.
2) Man could become holy and be like God—then enter God's bubble.

But there are problems with both possibilities:
1) God *can not* become unholy. He *can not* change! He won't ever leave His bubble. And I am so glad! I would not want a God Who was unholy or even capable of being unholy! I am glad God will never change, that He will always be *God!*
2) Man *can not* become holy. He is totally unable to make himself righteous before God. He is unholy and stuck with it! There is nothing man can do to enter God's bubble.

And remember, because God is Holy, He will necessarily have to punish man for being unholy! He will punish all ungodliness and all unrighteousness at the end of the age by sending it (us) to the lake of fire, an eternal death, an eternal separation from God. So man, you and I included, needs to be saved from that punishment!

Since God cannot make Himself unholy (it is impossible), and since man cannot make himself holy (it is impossible), God steps in and solves the problem for us. He gives us a way! He can't just excuse us and forget all about our unholiness because then He wouldn't be just, and it is impossible for Him *not* to be just because it is the essence of Who He is! All His judgments are righteous and true so He has to judge our sin! The penalty has to be paid—and the penalty is death!

Now think of God as being a Judge sitting behind the bench. You and I have been caught red-handed committing a crime. We are guilty, without a doubt. As a Righteous and True Judge, He would *have* to punish us! He couldn't just let us walk free! And yet that's exactly what He wants to do! As we watch, He motions for someone at the back door of the courtroom to come forward. This person walks up to the Judge's bench where God says, "I want you to take the punishment that these people deserve so that I can set them free." That someone answers God and says, "Let them go free. You may punish me instead of them."

As a Righteous Judge, He has designed a plan to let us walk out of that courtroom free instead of going to prison—and yet justice has been served. This other person is not free. He must pay for our crime. He does pay. He has paid. That someone is God's Son, Jesus. Our crime of unholiness demanded that we die. Jesus died instead of us. He paid the penalty that we deserved to pay.

Now it's up to us. We can agree that we are guilty as charged and let Jesus pay the penalty of death for us, or we can claim we are innocent or try to pay it ourselves. One way or the other, it will be paid! I chose to let Jesus pay my penalty for me. I am so grateful to Him. He saved me from having to pay for my unholiness with my own life. But the decision to let Him is costly. Salvation is a free gift because there is nothing you can do to earn it. And yet it costs everything, it costs your life! Let me explain what is involved in this decision.

- *First*, you must realize and accept that you are unholy. You are judged according to God's righteous standard and not the world's, or your own. When we look at the world or ourselves, we tend to think we are doing just fine, even pretty good sometimes! But we need to look instead at

God, Himself (through His Word and what He says about Himself). When we look at *Him*, and then look back at ourselves, we can see just how disgusting we truly are.

- *Secondly*, we must realize and accept that there is nothing, absolutely nothing, we can do about it! We can't make ourselves holy. We can't clean ourselves up. We can't become righteous at all!

- *Thirdly*, we must realize and accept that there is only one way that can save us...God's Way!

- *Fourthly*, we must understand what His way is. We must take the time to truly understand it so we can truly believe it.

His way is *not* just saying a prayer. His way is *not* making a decision to try living more righteously. His way is to depend *entirely* on His Son—for being saved from God's wrath *and* for living a new life that is holy before Him. You see, back to the courtroom illustration, God doesn't just let us walk out of there so we can go out and sin again! He takes care of our future by changing us so we don't *want* to sin again! He takes care of our future by putting the Spirit of His Own *Righteous* Son inside of us so that we now have the ability to be holy and to walk righteously from then on.

In order to depend *entirely* on Jesus, you must be willing to die to your old self, your old way of living. You must be willing to let Jesus control the rest of your life. You must lay down the reins of your life and be willing to let Jesus rule every moment of your life from now on!

- *Fifthly*, you must ask Him to do so. You must speak to Him, ask Him for the faith to believe Him, acknowledge His Holiness, acknowledge your unholiness, acknowledge His Son paid your penalty for you, and sincerely offer your entire life to Him. But most importantly, you must repent. You must declare your ways as evil and His as righteous, and ask for a new heart that is able to walk in His ways to be righteous. If your heart is true in this prayer, He will hear it and answer by forgiving you of your sin. You will *not* have to pay the penalty because you and God both have accepted Jesus' payment instead.

Then He will change you. He will make you into a brand new person. You will be born again. He will give you a new spirit that wants to obey Him, that loves Him dearly. And He will put His Holy Spirit, the Spirit of Jesus, inside of you to *cause* you to obey Him! He will write His ways on your heart and you will know right from wrong. You will have access to God, Himself, *all the time!!!*

You can go to Him and He will hear you and answer you, if you ask according to His will. And you will ask according to His will because He has written His will on your heart and you will want His will *more* than your own! You will have laid your own will down at the time of your salvation!

You will understand the Bible! You will read and study, and it won't be difficult anymore. It will make sense; you will understand it and you will believe it. You will have a hunger and a thirst for righteousness. You will study His Word because you want to know Him better and you want to be pleasing to Him. His Word will be more important to you than the very food you eat each day!

God has called you:

- To seek *Him*, rather than His plan for you.

- To walk in *His* footsteps, rather than your own.

- To bring Glory to *Him*, rather than to yourself.

You were born for one purpose → to bring Glory to God. Set your heart to show the world Who God is by walking in a manner worthy of the Kingdom of God.

P.S. I sat down one day and compared my life "now and then". I've copied it here. Which column do you fall under? My "then" testimony, over 30 years of trying to believe I was saved, did not give Glory to God. I was so blind! My "now" testimony, however, gives an accurate picture of Who He is and what He has done. Isn't He Wonderful!!!

NOW	THEN
See Him in His Holiness and Righteousness See what I truly was → filthy and unrighteous	Thought it was great of Jesus to die for the whole world but didn't think it was necessary on *my* behalf After all, I was a pretty nice person with no remarkable vices!
Understand Gospel	Had no clue *why* His death saved anybody I knew the facts, but didn't understand them
Understand Word	Couldn't understand the words I was reading Nothing really made sense I would read the same passages over and over and still draw a blank
Unsatisfiable hunger and Unquenchable thirst for His Word	Read and "studied" out of obligation
Indescribable Freedom, Joy, Peace	Always anxious, Tried to make sure everyone was pleased with me
Supernaturally remember Scripture and where it is in the Bible Can take people to verses in the Bible at any time!	Only remembered parts of verses (out of context) Couldn't remember where any verses were in the Bible
Consistent and supernatural answers to prayer	Didn't really know if He was answering my prayers
His Spirit bears witness with my spirit – *I am saved!*	Didn't feel an assurance that I was saved Always pleaded with Him to save me Questioned salvation constantly
Never ask Him to save me. *He already has!*	Asked Him to save me constantly
Have supernatural abilities such as teaching, giving, exhorting, understanding, discernment, and wisdom	Did not have any true spiritual abilities
Sin does not have control over me	Sin had control over me
He lives His life through me and accomplishes whatever He wills	Performed works to try and please God

Dear Heavenly Father, please use HISTORY to bring Glory to You and You alone.
Please conform those who are trained by YOUR WORD
into men, women, and children...
Whose hearts don't beat the same as the world's.
Whose lives are not entwined with those of Your enemies.
Who don't compare themselves to others, but to You.
Who have seen their own filthiness by catching a glimpse of Your purity.
Who don't use prayer as a means to make themselves feel better.
Who don't count material goods as rewards or blessings from God for their behavior.
Who don't count hard times as punishment,
but count every moment of them as what they are, the True blessings.
Who don't fast to get more out of You, but fast so that You can get more out of them.
Who don't offer to You that which was no longer good enough for them.
Who don't focus on their house more than on Your house.
Who would never dream of keeping track of what they have given to You.
Who know that their "stuff" is actually Your "stuff."
Who check with Your "daily planner" instead of their own.
Who understand that their responsibility to please You will never, ever end.
Whose mouths won't open, because You have closed them.
Whose mouths open only at Your command.
Who aren't still trying to hide their filthy clothing underneath Your robe of righteousness.
Who don't hang out with people they enjoy –
nearly as much as they do with people who need them.
Who are no longer running their lives, but running to You.
Who don't want to order their own steps, but beg You to keep them where You are.
Who are concerned about being comfortable, not in their zone, but in Your hand.
Who aren't afraid to keep practicing Holiness even though they have blundered in the past.
Who don't hold onto wounds that You have already healed.
Who don't shy away from confrontation as though it were a negative thing.
Who aren't afraid to be "sandpaper" in the body of Christ
and who don't resist being sanded.
Who aren't upset with sinners for fulfilling their job description so well,
but instead try to recruit them to a new position.
Who don't fear men or what men can do to them.
Who don't seek after signs or wonders, but who seek only the face of the God they point to.
Whose knees are ever imprinted with the pattern from their flooring.

Who don't ever forget that their next breath is entirely Your choice.
Who always, always, always, always, always remember
that You will never, never, never, never, never forsake them.
Who truly understand the Everlasting Covenant they have entered into with
the Everlasting God of the Universe.
Who fully comprehend that they don't have to sin anymore.
Whose hearts beat the same as Yours.
Whose hearts are broken with whatever breaks Yours.
Whose new hearts of flesh quiver at Your every touch.
Whose eyes are opened to see Your Awesomeness in all of Your Frightening Power.
Whose eyes are opened to see You in all of Your Holiness and Blazing Purity.
Whose eyes are opened to see Your Excellence in all of Your Majestic Righteousness.
Whose minds You have opened to understand the Scriptures.
Who diligently study, hear, and heed the Scriptures.
Who want to know Truth more than they want to be right.
Who want Your will and Your way to be their goal each and every day.
Who seek the way that You want them to go, not their own.
Who look to Your Word to find Your Will.
Who know You by Your Name, El Elyon, Sovereign God of the Universe.
Who trust in Your Sovereignty more than their might.
Who won't shrink back from delivering the entire Gospel
to those who haven't surrendered to the Savior of their souls.
Whose marriages are accurate pictures of Your Heavenly Family.
Who can't sleep at night until they are right with You and others.
Who are obedient to the point of death.
Whose eyes are burned by the grotesqueness of sin.
Who know what they believe and believe what they know.
Who know that the world does not rotate around man.
Who know they were created for one thing → to bring You pleasure by Glorifying You.
Who Glorify You by showing the world Who You really are,
not just through their talk, but through their obedient walk.
Who feed Your sheep with True Food.
Who are known as Faithful and True.
Who are not exhausted by footmen, but triumphantly compete with horses.
Who will one day stand before You, Without Regrets and Unashamed…
…In The Name of The Seed… Amen and Amen.

From the Authors:

"Oh, the depth of the riches both of the wisdom and knowledge of God! How unsearchable are His judgments and unfathomable His ways! For who has known the mind of the LORD, or who became His Counselor? Or who has first given to Him that it might be paid back to him again? For from Him and through Him and to Him are all things. To Him be the Glory forever. Amen." Romans 11:33-36

All thanks belong to God! All Glory belongs to God! He is the One Who sovereignly hands out our assignments and equips us to perform them. Wherever shortcomings or errors occur in this work, it is owed entirely to me and is no fault whatsoever of anyone else. I am quite willing, even eager, to correct such in any subsequent edition.

"Blessed be the Lord God, the God of Israel, Who alone works wonders. And blessed be His Glorious Name forever; and may the whole earth be filled with His Glory. Amen, and Amen. Psalm 72:18-19

His Grateful Child...
Sharon Jensen

"Great is the LORD and highly to be praised, and His greatness is unsearchable. One generation shall praise Your works to another, and shall declare Your mighty acts." Psalms 145:3-4

I praise God that He has given me the privilege to be a part of this project in a larger way than I had ever anticipated. It has been a wonderful opportunity to come alongside of my mother in this project and help bring it to completion.

I am excited and look forward to the plans that God has for HIStory with this small ministry He has established at WORD CENTER. And I know that whether in book or in song, in writing or in composing, in preaching or in singing I humbly accept whatever work He has allotted for me to do.

For His Glory...
Caleb Jensen

www.ingramcontent.com/pod-product-compliance
Lightning Source LLC
Chambersburg PA
CBHW081755300426
44116CB00014B/2130